QUESTIONS & ANSWERS ON DOG AGILITY TRAINING

MARY ANN NESTER

QUESTIONS & ANSWERS ON

DOG AGILITY TRAINING

TFH PUBLICATIONS

Published by
T.F.H. Publications, Inc.
One TFH Plaza
Third and Union Avenues
Neptune City, NJ 07753

© 2007 Interpet Publishing Ltd.
All rights reserved

ISBN 978-0-7938-0612-6

Library of Congress Cataloging-in-
    Publication Data
Nester, Mary Ann.
Questions and answers on dog agility
    training / Mary Ann Nester.
  p. cm.
Includes index.
ISBN 978-0-7938-0612-6 (alk. paper)
1. Dogs--Agility trials. 2. Dogs--
    Training. I. Title.
SF425.4.N47 2007
636.7'0888--dc22
                          2007010835

Printed and bound in China
07 08 09 10 11 1 3 5 7 9 8 6 4 2

The Author

Mary Ann Nester arrived in England from New York in the early 1970s and never went home. In 1977 she set up Aslan Dog Training, a dog training school named after her first agility dog, a Lurcher. She holds puppy parties and offers classes in obedience and agility in her home town of Northampton and conducts training days and workshops throughout Britain and abroad.

Her credentials are impressive. Mary Ann is a member of the Association of Pet Dog Trainers as well as an Agility Club Approved Instructor. As a licensed SAQ® trainer and accredited trainer in the DAQ® method, she is qualified to design functional training programs for agility handlers and their dogs.

Mary Ann's most successful agility dogs have been her Miniature Poodles, Brillo Pad and Daz. They have both been finalists at Olympia and Crufts and have competed at international level. Brillo represented Great Britain at the World Agility Championships in Portugal 2001 and Daz in Germany 2002 and France 2003. When not competing, Mary Ann accepts judging appointments throughout the year.

Committed to promoting agility to anyone who has a dog, Mary Ann has been a guest expert on BBC Radio Northampton answering listeners' canine queries and, for many years, has posed as the Agility Auntie for the internet magazine, Agilitynet. She has written for Britain's most popular agility magazines, *The Agility Voice* and *Agility Eye*, and served as a committee member for the British Agility Club as well as the Poodle Training Club. In addition, Mary Ann is an official measurer for the Kennel Club.

When not chasing her own dogs around the agility course or teaching other people how to catch theirs, Mary Ann works as a part-time receptionist at an out-of-hours veterinary emergency service.

Introducing The Sport   6

Starting Out   26

Solving Problems   60

Better Handling   104

Competition Craft   142

Fit for the Ring   164

Resources & Index   192

Let **MARY ANN NESTER** *be your guide...*

If you've already tried agility with your dog, you'll know that it's fast and furious fun. But also you'll know that it's not as easy as it may first appear. Problems can and do occur and many a promising round ends in frustration when a silly mistake undoes all the good work. But don't despair ... that's where this book comes in. I've suffered those disappointments just like you and I hope that the answers to the questions outlined in the following pages may help you to reach the promised land – a clear round!

Introducing the sport

I will never forget my first agility dog. She was a Lurcher named Aslan, a dog that had the elegance of a glamour model and the speed of a bullet. I can't help but compare all the dogs that have come after to Alsan. Do they have her willingness to try something new? Do they have her sense of humor? Why are they missing the contact on the A-frame? Aslan never did! In agility, handlers get a lot of things right through good training and practice. Aslan was born good and I was lucky to have her. I didn't know how lucky I was until I got my second agility dog and had to start problem-solving in earnest.

I loved Aslan with all my heart, but I won't mention her again. This book is not about dogs like her that have impeccable manners and perform perfect agility. It is about the mistakes, problems and goof-ups. Despite the best intentions to get things right, things can end up terribly wrong. Dogs miss weave entries, bark at judges' hats and run under jumps. No matter how well you prepare yourself and your dog for competition, you will encounter the unexpected. Your dog emerges from the tunnel backwards or the zipper on your pants breaks just as you reach the fourth obstacle on the course. What are you going to do?

# of AGILITY

Each time I open the gates to my agility field to welcome a new intake of beginner handlers I anticipate a number of familiar problems. I can guarantee that there will be one dog that barks at everything and one handler who hasn't brought any treats for his pet. But I'm bound to get a few surprises too. "What do I do with my false teeth when I'm running?" This is one unforgettable question that momentarily stopped me in my tracks.

And these are the questions that this book tries to answer. They have come from first-time pet owners or from handlers on their third or fourth agility dog. When I started writing, I thought I would be pushed to find 50 questions. When I reached the 70 mark, I thought I had exhausted the subject. Then I got my second wind and I couldn't stop. My task became one of limiting the number of questions that I would address in one book.

Sitting in front of my PC, a dog curled on each foot, has been bliss. Writing about agility is almost as satisfying as doing it. If any of the answers to these questions have helped a reader solve a training problem or understand their dog a little better, I can pat myself on the back for a job well done. My dogs have enjoyed the break, but they would rather jump fences than be foot warmers. Can you blame them?

LEARN TO SPEAK AGILITY

consists of two ramps hinged at the apex 5ft 6in (1.7m) to 6ft 3in (1.9m) from the ground. Each ramp is 4ft (1.2m) wide. At the bottom of each ramp is a contact area which is painted in a different color from the rest of the A-frame.

Note: Every agility organization uses different guidelines. The obstacle specifications are average approximations.

A

ABC An ABC (Anything But Collies) is any breed or type of dog except a collie or collie cross. Classes that limit entry to non-collies are called ABC classes.

Agility course An agility course will include contact obstacles in addition to jumps, weaves, tire and tunnel.

A-frame This obstacle is also known as the **A-ramp**. It

A-frame

B

Back chaining Training the last behavior in a chain of actions first.

Back cross See **rear cross**.

Back jumping Jumping a hurdle in the wrong direction.

Back weaving Performing the weave poles in the wrong direction.

Banking When a dog pushes off the top of an obstacle with his hind feet.

Baton The baton can be a stick of wood or pipe that is exchanged in pair or relay classes. Fun classes are renowned for imaginative batons such as balloons or spoons.

Blind cross The handler changes sides and crosses in front of his dog with his back to

Brush jump

him. The handler is running blind unless he turns his head to look over his shoulder to look at his dog.

Blocking When the handler stands in front of an obstacle, he is physically blocking it from his dog and prevents the dog attempting it.

Box Four jumps set out in the shape of a square box, one on each side.

Briefing The judge will hold his briefing immediately before starting his class. He will give the course time, scoring and answer any questions.

Brush jump A hurdle that is made with a base of twigs, with or without foliage. Brush jumps are not often seen in agility these days. The twigs and leaves tend to dry out or disintegrate and so need regular renewing to keep the hurdle looking attractive.

C

Call off A handler will call his dog off an incorrect obstacle. He will use a call-off if the obstacle is part of a trap in the judge's course or if his dog is taking his own line through the equipment.

Caller/Gate Steward The person who is responsible for booking in competitors and sending them to the start line in the approved running order.

Carousel An arrangement of jumps in a circle. The dog rotates around the handler in the middle as if he is a horse on a merry-go-round.

Channel weaves Channel weaves are a training aid consisting of two lines of poles that form a channel for the dog to run through. The two lines can be moved closer together or further apart. Guide wires running down the sides from one pole to the next keep the dog within the channel.

Clear round The dog and handler complete the course without faults and within the course time.

Clicker A clicker is a small hand-held device that makes a clicking noise when you press a button or tab. It is used as a training aid.

Collapsible tunnel The collapsible tunnel is also known as the **cloth, soft** or **chute tunnel**. The entrance is made from rigid material so that it stands upright and the chute is usually made from plastic, nylon or soft material.

Come This is the recall command used by handlers when they want their dog to come towards them.

Contact The contacts are the demarcated areas at the base of the seesaw, dog walk and A-frame. The dog must touch them when they mount or dismount these obstacles or incur faults. They are always painted in a contrasting color, most often yellow.

Course The course usually contains between ten and 20 obstacles, and is designed by the judge.

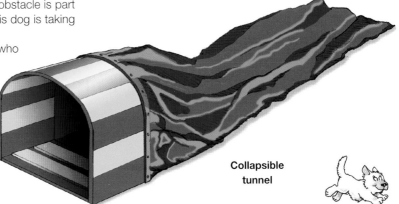

Collapsible tunnel

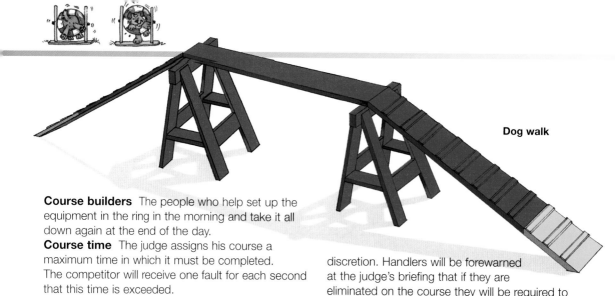

Dog walk

Course builders The people who help set up the equipment in the ring in the morning and take it all down again at the end of the day.

Course time The judge assigns his course a maximum time in which it must be completed. The competitor will receive one fault for each second that this time is exceeded.

D

Directional command A command given to the dog to turn or send him in a specific direction.

Dog walk The dog walk is composed of three planks that are at least 10ft (3m) long and 12in (305mm) wide. The middle plank is fixed approximately 4ft (1.22m) off the ground. The other two planks are ramps at each end. The bottom of each ramp is a contact area which is painted a different color from the rest of the obstacle.

Double handling This occurs when someone outside the ring attempts to help the handler and dog inside the ring. Double handling will be penalized by the judge.

E

E The abbreviation for **Elimination**. Some would argue that it also stands for entertaining, enthusiastic or energetic. Elimination is a result of the dog taking the wrong course or moving on to the next obstacle before completing the preceding one. A dog that is given three refusals will be eliminated as will the dog that is out of control or fouls in the ring.

Electronic timing The dog's time is recorded by electronic equipment when the dog breaks a beam at the start and finish of the course.

Elimination and out This is enforced at the judge's discretion. Handlers will be forewarned at the judge's briefing that if they are eliminated on the course they will be required to leave the ring immediately. This restriction is most likely to be imposed when time is running short.

F

Faults Penalties are awarded for both course and time faults. Course faults occur when a dogs fails to perform an obstacle correctly, for example knocks a pole, misses a contact, or refuses a jump. Time faults are awarded if the competitor's dog exceeds the course time. The dog that has run clear and under the course time will be placed ahead of the dog that is faster, but has accumulated course faults.

Fence See **hurdle**.

Flick flack See **snake**.

Front cross The handler changes sides and crosses in front of his dog while facing his dog.

G

Go on A directional command telling the dog to go straight ahead and away from the handler. Also known as a **send away**.

Hurdle or fence

H

Handler focus When the dog focuses on the handler rather than the obstacles.
Heel position
The dog's heel position is on the handler's left side.
Hoop See **tire**.
Hurdle Also known as **jumps** or **fences**. The height will vary. Large dogs jump between 20in (508mm) and 26in (660mm), medium dogs jump between 16in (406mm) and 20in (508mm) and small dogs jump between 8in (203mm) and 12in (305mm). The width of a jump should be a minimum of 4ft (1.219m). If the dog knocks the pole or bar, it should fall out easily.

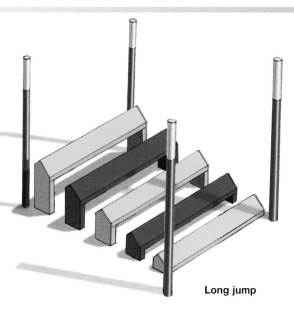

Long jump

I J

Judge This is the person who has designed the course and will judge each dog and handler at a competition. He will indicate faults to his scribe or scrimer.
Jump See **hurdle**.
Jumping course The course will include jumps, tunnels, tires and weaves but no contact equipment.

Long jump The long jump is made up of three to five units. The total length of the long jump will vary. Large dogs will jump 3 to 5 units. Medium dogs will jump 3 to 4 units. Small dogs will jump 2 to 3 units. In addition, poles should mark each corner independently of the units.

L

Large dogs Usually dogs that measure over 17in (430mm) at the withers are classified as large. Height classifications will vary depending on which organization licenses the show.
  Lead-out When the handler leaves his dog at the start line in a wait and walks out on to the course, positions himself and then calls his dog.
    Leash runner The person who collects the competitor's leash or lead from the start line and takes it to the finish for collection by the competitor after the run.

M

Manual timing When the time keeper records a dog's time on the course with a stop watch.
Medium dogs Usually dogs that measure over 13in (330mm) and measure about 17in (432mm) or under at the withers compete as medium dogs. Height classifications will vary depending which organization licenses the show.

N

NFC This stands for Not For Competition. Dogs can be entered at a show even if they are not going to compete.
Nonstandard class These are **special classes**; for example, veterans classes (dogs

over a certain age), or gamblers (in addition to accruing points on the course, competitors must perform a gamble, usually a specific sequence of obstacles in a short space of time). Any variation from standard marking will be explained at the judge's briefing.

O

Obstacle discrimination When a dog can tell the difference between one obstacle and another on the basis of the handler's verbal command or body signal.

Obstacle focus When the dog focuses on the obstacles rather than the handler.

Off-course When a dog deviates from the course set by the judge by taking the wrong obstacle, he is off-course.

Off side The dog's off-side position is on the handler's right side.

P Q

Pad runner This is the person who is responsible for making sure each competitor has the correct sheet from the score pad. The pad runner will give it to the scrimer and scribe to fill out and then give it to the score keeper.

Paddling This term refers to dogs that step on the units of the long jump. Instead of leaping the obstacle, they try to walk over it using each unit as a stepping stone.

Pivot When the handler turns on the spot. He can either pivot towards his dog or away from him.

Pole This is the horizontal bar on a hurdle that the dog has to jump.

Pole setter This is the person who sits at the edge of the ring during a competition. If a pole is knocked to the ground, it is his responsibility to replace it when it is safe to do so. He must not get in the way of the competitor, dog or judge. The pole setter keeps his eye on the course and may also straighten

the collapsible tunnel if it gets twisted or re-peg the weave poles if they become loose.

Pull-off This is the opposite of pushing the dog forward onto the obstacles. The handler pulls his dog away from the obstacle instead of towards it by verbal command or body signal. A pull-off may be intentional or accidental.

Pull-through This is a maneuver that takes place between two fences. The handler sends the dog over the first fence, calls him back through the gap between the wings of two hurdles and then turns the dog back and over the second fence.

R

Rear cross The handler changes sides and crosses behind his dog. This maneuver is sometimes

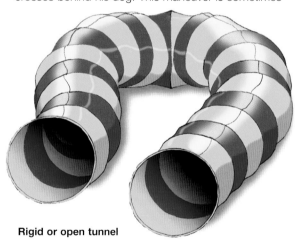

Rigid or open tunnel

called a **back cross**.

Refusal If a dog fails to attempt an obstacle, for example if he runs by a jump or goes underneath it, he will be marked with a refusal.

Rigid tunnel Sometimes called the open tunnel.

Ring This is the test area where competitors are judged. It should be a minimum of 35yd x 35yd (32m x 32m) at outdoor venues.

Ring party Everyone who helps the ring run smoothly. This includes scrimers, pole setters, callers, leash runners, show manager, pad runners and scorers.

Ring number Each competitor will have a ring number that identifies him and his dog.

Run This is the handler's competitive round on the course.

Run by This is a type of refusal. The dog runs past the obstacle rather than attempting to perform it.

Running order Dogs will receive a numerical running order randomly drawn for each class entered at a competition.

S

Schedule This is the printed notice of an agility show and will contain information such as host club, venue, entry fees, and so on.

Score keeper A show official responsible for posting, ranking and recording the performances of the agility competitors.

Scribe The person who records the dog's faults as signaled by the judge as well as the dog's time on the course.

Scrimer This word is a recent addition to agility vocabulary. The scrimer is the person who records faults as signalled by the judge as well as the times measured by electronic timing equipment. It is a combination or "scribe" and "time keeper."

Seesaw Also called the teeter, a 12in (305mm) wide plank is mounted on a central

bracket. At each end of the plank is a contact zone painted in a contrasting color from the rest of the seesaw.

Send away See **go on**.

Show manager The person who is responsible for organizing and running the show.

Small dogs Usually dogs that measure 12in (350mm) or under at the withers are classified as small. Height classifications will vary depending which organization licenses the show.

Snake Three or more jumps in a line that the handler must send his dog over in a back and forth

Spread

Seesaw

action. Also known as a **flick flack**.

Spread A spread is composed of two jumps placed next to one another. The maximum spread will vary according to the size of dog.

Standard classification Each organization will have a classification system. Entries to classes will either be based on previous wins or points gained.

Star This is an arrangement of fences that mimics a star, a fence at each point. A three-fenced star is also known as a **pinwheel**.

T

Table Also called a pause table. The table needs to be solid with a non-slip surface, its height will vary depending upon the size of the dog.

Table

Target Popular choices include plastic lids, mouse pads or squares of carpet. A target may be big enough for the dog to lie down on or so small that he can only touch it with his nose.

Threadle A threadle is a series of **pull-throughs** on a course.

Time keeper The person who holds the stopwatch and times each competitor's run.

Tire A jump resembling a tire suspended in a retangular frame. The height of the tire will vary depending on the size of the dog.

Trap Traps can occur anywhere on the course. To avoid them, handlers must have good directional control over their dog and confidence in their dog's obstacle discrimination.

U V

V-weaves Weave poles that are set in a base that allows them to pivot to different angles. They are used for training rather than competition.

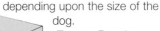

Tyre

W

Wall This obstacle is a hurdle but it is built to look like a wall and is often painted to look as if it is constructed of bricks.

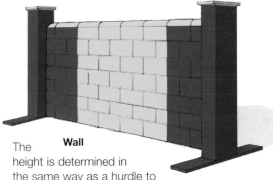

Wall

The height is determined in the same way as a hurdle to accommodate small, medium or large dogs. The wall has displaceable units on top. If one of these units is knocked off, the dog is faulted just as if he had knocked a pole off a hurdle. If one of the units is touched but doesn't fall to the ground, the dog is not marked.

Weave poles The dog has to wiggle in and out of the poles. There should be at least five poles but no more than 12. The poles should be set about 20in (508mm) apart. The poles themselves should be sturdy, between 0.75in (19mm) and 1.5in (38mm) in diameter, and with a minimum height of 2ft 6in (762mm).

Walking the course There will be time set aside before the class starts for competitors to walk the course. They must use the time to learn the sequence of the obstacles and plan their handling strategy.

Wings These are the bits on the hurdle that hold up the pole. They are usually

Above: *A dog must always enter the weave poles with the first pole on his left side. If he fails to do so, he will be marked by the judge with a refusal. And three refusals will result in an elimination.*

fashioned to look like a section of picket fence but they may be shaped like anything else, even a tin of dog food.

Wishing well Sometimes called

the lych gate, this obstacle has a little roof not less than 5ft (1.524m) from the ground and a displaceable top pole that the dog must jump over like a hurdle. The pole will be set at the height appropriate to the category of dog. The wishing well should be sturdy and of solid construction and have a minimum width of 2ft 8in (813mm). There's not really any water at the bottom!

X Y Z

Zoomies When a dog is disracted and the handler has lost control of him, he will zoom around the ring at a hundred miles an hour. The dog has the zoomies.

Wishing well

Below: *A dog with the zoomies doesn't always look where he is going and may run under or around the obstacles!*

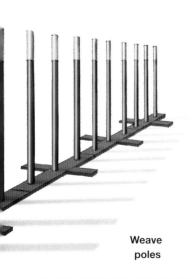
Weave poles

Chapter One

INTRODUCTORY QUESTIONS

You've seen a bit of dog agility on television and you've heard a little about it from a friend. But what exactly is agility training? Is it a form of canine callisthenics or is it more relaxing like yoga? And just how long have dogs been leaping over fences at agility competitions? Have you just not noticed or are these events a recent addition to the canine sporting calendar? There are so many activities for dogs these days, why should you choose to go to an agility class rather than something else? Your friend must be having a good time as nothing will make her miss a date with her dog and the agility equipment. Time to get some answers to your questions. Agility is not just about physical fitness or training techniques. It's not just about winning ribbons. It's about having fun with your dog. Find out for yourself!

The Agility Game

Q *What is dog agility? Please explain it to me in simple terms so that I can relay it to my grandmother who thinks that a good dog is one that earns his keep by eliminating the rat populations or working sheep. She lives on a farm and just can't understand why I love my "useless" King Charles Cavalier Spaniel, Tulip, so much and want to learn agility!*

A I don't think that you will be able to convince your grandmother that dog agility will add to the family coffers, but you might be able get her to admit that Tulip is much more than a lap dog!

The obstacles Agility is a canine assault course over obstacles. There are obstacles to jump like the hurdles, tire, long jump, walls or spreads. There are the rigid and collapsible tunnel to run in one end and out the other. These are my dogs' favorite pieces of equipment. There are also the weave poles to wiggle in between. The contact equipment includes the A-frame, dog walk and seesaw. Learning how to perform all the obstacles correctly is just the first step. The next is stringing them all together.

Sequencing When you can execute each obstacle competently, you will start learning how to put them together in a sequence, one after the other. For example, you might start with a line of hurdles and then progress to a box or a star of hurdles. Your instructor will want to familiarize you with the different patterns of obstacles that you will find on a course. When you and Tulip are stringing together more than ten obstacles at a time and consistently performing them faultlessly, you are ready to try an agility course.

The course The course is set by the judge and will consist of ten to 20 obstacles in a square test area. The jumps will be set at a height appropriate to your dog's height classification. Tulip will either be Small or Medium and will have to be measured before her first official show to determine in which category she will compete. The distance between the jump obstacles will vary. If it is an agility course, it will contain contact obstacles. If it is a jumping course, it won't. The challenge will be to perform the obstacles in the correct manner and in the correct order within the course time. Obstacle three must follow obstacle two.

The classes You must enter the lowest class for which you are eligible so start with elementary classes that have simple courses. You can qualify into more difficult and challenging classes as you gain more advanced handling skills and experience. Most shows will have a choice of types of class that people can enter.
• Jumping classes will include jumps, tunnels, and weaves but no contact equipment.
• In addition to jumps, weaves and tunnels, agility

Above: *There are more hurdles on an agility course than any other piece of equipment and dogs love jumping them.*

classes will include the contact obstacles, the A-frame, dog walk and seesaw. These obstacles have contact areas at each end painted in a contrasting color, usually yellow. Tulip must touch the contact area when she mounts or dismounts or else she will be faulted. A toenail will do! However, it is good practice to ensure that, in training at least, the dog performs a solid contact – either stopping on it or passing through it with four feet. Dogs that are allowed to jump over the yellow areas are risking injury.

- Special classes include pairs competitions, veterans classes (dogs over a certain age), knock-outs (two dogs compete against each other on the course) or gamblers (in addition to accruing points on the course, competitors must perform a gamble, usually a specific sequence of obstacles in a short space of time).

From start to finish Different clubs have different rules. The judge will mark you as you run from start to finish. Your aim will be to get around all the obstacles without getting eliminated or incurring course or time faults.

Elimination Tulip will be eliminated if she pees or poops in the ring, so make sure she has an opportunity to relieve herself before you join the line. She will be eliminated if she is out of control; for example, if she runs merrily around the judge snapping at his ankles or if she leaves the ring and won't come back. And Tulip will be eliminated if she makes up her own course. She must take the obstacles in the order decreed by the judge even if the tunnel is her favorite and she wants to do it first. Finally, if Tulip collects three refusals on the course, she will be eliminated.

Course faults Each obstacle on the course must be attempted. If Tulip runs by a jump, misses the mouth of the tunnel or fails to find the correct entry to the weaving poles, it counts as a refusal. And the obstacles must be performed correctly. So, if Tulip knocks a pole off a hurdle, leaps off the seesaw before it touches the ground or jumps over the contacts on the A-frame, she will be faulted. You will also incur faults if you touch Tulip while she is on the course or touch the equipment.

Time faults Hurrah! Tulip has made it around the course without a single mistake. You are clear, but are you in the course time? The judge will have set a maximum time on the course and time faults are awarded if the competitor's dog exceeds the course time. The dog that has run clear and under the course time will be placed ahead of the dog that is faster, but has course faults.

Take your grandmother to an agility show and let her see for herself dogs in action on a course. She will be impressed by the number of well-trained dogs with wagging tails And she can't fail to notice how delighted the handlers are with their agility accomplishments, no matter how large or how small. I'm sure your grandmother will be very proud of you and Tulip although she might not admit it at first!

Born Jumping

Q *Whenever I visit dog shows, I watch the agility contests. The dogs love it and so do the crowds. Whoever thought of putting a dog and his handler with some jumps in one ring was on to something! How old is agility?*

A Some of us are pre-programmed to find an animal that they can partner over an obstacle course. As a child, I guided my pet turtle over pencils laid on the floor. My next victim was an athletic hamster. No wheel for him, but rows of toilet rolls and matchboxes. Thank heavens I was eventually allowed to have a dog and go to training classes.

I'm sure that dog owners have been teaching their pets to leap over fallen logs in the woods for centuries, but agility as we know it was first seen at the Crufts Dog Show in England on February 10, 1978. There was a gap in the schedule between the Obedience Championship and the Group Judging in Breed and the organizers needed something

entertaining that would keep people in their seats. Show-jumping certainly wowed the horsey set, so why not a canine version? The Crufts crowd loved it!

And they couldn't wait to get home and try agility with their own pets. Dog training clubs started to set up obstacle courses and soon national clubs developed a scoring system and a set of rules and regulations to govern competitions. It didn't stop there. Good news spreads. Agility is fun! Countries like Brazil, Korea, and Canada have their own governing bodies for the sport and competition is now international with teams vying for the title "World Agility Champions."

Agility has come a long way since it first appeared at Crufts and it continues to grow in popularity. Turtle agility? It never would have caught on.

Below: *Weaving can be a challenge to teach but, once proficient, dogs find it fun right to the very last pole!*

What's The Buzz?

Q *My Staffie cross, Buzz, is very clever and I think he would like agility. I'm tempted to try but I live on a tight budget and have to count my pennies. How expensive is it to get started?*

A Agility is accessible to people from all walks of life no matter what their incomes or lifestyle may be. My star pupil came to his first class with his sheep dog tied to a piece of twine. He is a

farmer who never normally has his dog on a leash (lead) and I've never been able to convince him to buy one. The dog follows the tractor when he's ploughing and roads are few and far between in his neck of the woods, so who needs a lead?

The dog You already have the most expensive part of the agility package – the dog. Even if you rescued your dog and named him "Freebie," he won't be cheap. There is no such thing as a low-maintenance dog and even the most routine health care can be costly.

The clothes The track suit and sneakers you already have in your wardrobe are perfect, provided you don't mind them getting dirty. The important thing is to have clothing that is comfortable and washable. You don't want to feel cold and wet or hot and sticky. Shoes with soles that have plenty of grip are ideal. Falling over hurts and you don't want any more mud on your knees than necessary.

The classes It's worth shopping around to find an agility club that will suit your pocket as a night out with Buzz will be good value for money. There are a number of charging systems – pay as you go, pay for a course of six lessons or pay a single lump sum for the year. Some clubs ask you to pay a membership fee as well as class subscriptions. Remember, the most expensive classes will not necessarily be the best.

Put some money aside for mixing with your new friends after class in the bar. The talk will be all about dogs – Shelia's new puppy, what Molly the collie ate out on her afternoon walk or the handsome new vet at the local animal hospital. You don't need to dress in Armani or buy Buzz a diamond collar to do agility. But do please buy him a lead. Twine is so out this year! Go ahead. Look for some beginner classes and try your luck. You will not regret it.

Above: *Agility handlers come in all shapes and sizes. The attraction of agility is hard to resist whatever is in your closet. People from different social backgrounds are united by their love of dogs and enjoyment of agility training.*

Collies Rule OK?

Q *I have a beautiful nine month old Border Collie puppy. I know that Tara is a working dog that needs mental stimulation and I want to make sure she gets it. I visited a dog show last year and saw that collies were participating and excelling in every sport available to dogs. Why should I choose to train Tara in agility rather than obedience, flyball, or heelwork to music?*

Left: Having one blue eye and one brown eye won't affect this little merle pup's ability to learn quickly.
Right: Collie owners quickly find out that their pet's feet rarely touch the ground. They are ideal agility dogs.

A Because agility will be more fun! But I'm bound to say that because agility is my passion. Ask the same question to a flyball competitor and they will say flyball, an obedience competitor will say obedience and a heelwork to music competitor will say heelwork to music. Each will try to persuade you that their chosen discipline is superior to all others. There are two reasons why I love agility more than anything else.

It's just me and the dog When I compete in agility, I have to work out how to get the best out of my dog over the course set by the judge on the day and I love that challenge. It's like doing a crossword puzzle. I might get it right or I could mess it up, but I'm in command and the onus is on me. I don't have to worry about the performance of flyball team-mates. I don't have to listen to an obedience steward saying "forward, left turn and into slow pace." I don't have to follow the rhythm of a tune as I would in heelwork to music. The only person I listen to is me and hope my dog is doing likewise.

Speed is intoxicating I get a real buzz from running in partnership with my dog over a course. There is nothing more exhilarating than pushing yourself to the limits and biting the wind with your canine friend. Time is important in agility and "slow down" and "steady" are not in the vocabulary. The fastest dog clear takes home the trophy. Although speed is important in the other canine disciplines, handlers aren't expected to run with their dogs in competition. You won't see anyone sprinting with their dog to a flyball box or racing ahead of their pet to a send away marker. None of them will collapse over the finish line gasping for oxygen like I do.

But what is to stop you from trying more than one sport with Tara? There are many handlers who have trained their dogs in two or three disciplines and are successful competitors in each. The more you do with your dog, the more your relationship with her will be tested and enriched. Obedience, flyball and heelwork to music all have something of special value to offer, but I'm sure that agility will be your favorite. Not that I'm biased…

Left: Border Collies are commonly black and white although other color combinations are seen. Regardless of markings, all collies love to work and need mental stimulation.

Hooked On Agility

Q *I am going to my first agility lesson next week with my Standard Poodle, Bella. My friend who already does agility with her dog has been teasing me that it will change my whole life and I'll wonder what I did with myself before I took it up. She can't be serious?*

A I'm afraid she is. It has certainly changed mine. The number of dogs in my household has grown to five and there is an A-frame in the yard. I'm rarely at home. I never have time to do the dishes, wash the laundry or mow the lawn. I'd rather miss a party than an agility show. And that's because agility is more fun and it is very addictive.

You teach your dog to jump a line of hurdles. Wow! Look at that dog go! So you sign up for the next set of lessons. Your dog can do a course and he has great contacts. You enter a show and he goes clear in the time! You enter another show, then another. Soon you have a bulletin board full of ribbons. You look for another club so you can get an additional night's training. It's worth the extra work because you win your first trophy! If you don't get to the top with this dog, then you surely will with your new puppy! He will be easy to socialize because all your new friends are eager to meet him.

And your new friends will be many. You will meet people from all over the country and from all walks of life. And most

of them will believe that their dog is the best dog on the circuit – no matter how many times their pooch has been eliminated! You will meet large families with children, newly married couples and confirmed bachelors – all competing in agility with dogs that double as family pets. Agility people are very sociable and love to talk about their dogs or the meaning of life over a cup of coffee or a beer. I would rather train my dogs than watch TV and my best friends are my agility friends. I'm hooked. Agility has changed my life and for the better!

Below: *Don't be fooled by this Poodle's exquisite grooming. He is perfectly willing to mess his hair to get the contact on the A-frame.*

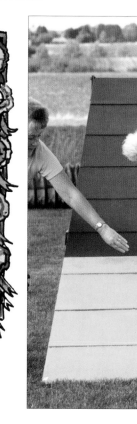

Olympic Gold

Q *Agility looks simple and lots of fun. The dogs are really eager to get started and run around the course. Can you call something that looks so easy a "sport"?*

A Yes, you can and I'm all for seeing dog agility at the Olympics! Of course it's a sport and here are three reasons why…

It is a physical activity Running around a field with your dog means wearing sneakers and getting out of breath.

It is a mental activity Handlers are challenged by the test set by the judge and must develop a strategy to steer their dog over the course in the shortest time.

It is governed by a set of rules Many people take up agility as a hobby, but handlers who enter shows are marked by a judge whose decision is final. If the judge's hand goes up, faults go down on the score sheet.

Done well, agility looks easy. Horseback riding looks easy once you know how, so how much greater is the accomplishment of directing your dog over jumps and walls without a saddle or reins? Intensive training ensures a dog is focused and responsive, not sitting in the middle of the ring scratching itself for fleas. If everything goes to plan, the handler should be a competition winner.

But often it doesn't work out that way, no matter how many hours are put in perfecting contacts or tightening turns. A run will last approximately 30 seconds and you can make a lot of mistakes in 30 seconds. If you shout a command a split-second too late, you risk losing your dog in the wrong end of the tunnel. Or worse, the dog is just having an off day and decides to head for the ice cream truck instead of the jumps. Herein lies much of agility's spectator appeal – you never know what is going to happen. Even the elite handlers can trip over their own feet.

Tennis? Football? Athletics? Those don't keep me on the edge of my seat. Give me the sport of dog agility any day. It's as fun to do as it is to watch.

Above: *Four feet are usually faster than two. But while speed is important, to cross the finish line first, you also need a course strategy.*

Chapter Two

STARTING OUT

Are you and your dog up to a bit of agility? Do you need to be a super fit to stay the course? Are black and white collies essential for success? The best thing about agility is that it is open to anyone and any dog – regardless of age or breeding. If you own a pair of sneakers and a dog with a leg on each corner, you can learn how to teach your pet to zoom through tunnels or wiggle between weave poles. However, there are important questions to be asked before you sign up for a class. Is your puppy too young to start jumping fences? Can you bring your dog's treats with you to training? To get the most from agility, you need to be prepared. Dogs who have learned the basics of obedience and who are good canine citizens have a head start, but anyone can catch up

Age For Agility

Q *What is the best age to start training my dog for agility? My Springer Spaniel, Tinker, is ten weeks old and I can't wait to start jumping.*

A Puppies are such a joy! It's so much fun rediscovering the world through their eyes. Tinker has a lot to learn before he gets down to the nitty-gritty of serious agility training. It will vary, but most agility clubs insist that new dogs should have finished growing before they start training. This usually occurs when a dog is about a year old, a little earlier for miniature dogs that tend to mature more quickly than the larger breeds.

While still a puppy, Tinker will naturally be pursuing his own fitness program just by the way he behaves. He will be busy climbing stairs, balancing on the furniture and turning somersaults chasing leaves in the yard. He doesn't need to visit the gym. In addition, Tinker will be exploring his surroundings. One minute he'll be startled by a daisy, the next he'll be sniffing it and then he'll decide to eat it! Little puppies don't have the stamina for an hour's class or the strength and co-ordination for jumping hurdles or climbing the A-frame. Save these exercises for later when Tinker is a big boy.

Time flies when you have a puppy but for now Tinker is just a baby and agility is beyond his capabilities. You wouldn't enter a toddler for a triathlon, would you? Don't compromise Tinker's future.

What if he fell off the dog walk, landed badly after a jump, or tumbled down the A-frame? Puppies don't bounce. Be patient.

There are, however, lots of things that you can teach Tinker while you wait for him to grow up.

Become your puppy's best friend and play mate.

Don't assume that just because you are putting food in his bowl that Tinker will love you. Have fun together – a game of fetch or tug. Develop a bond. If you have a good relationship with your dog, Tinker will enjoy working with you and want to please you.

Socialize your puppy Do you want a juvenile deliquent as your best friend? Make sure your spaniel is getting out and about and meeting new people and dogs. Go for a walk with him or visit the Post Office. Manners are important in agility. You don't want Tinker to jump up at people the moment you open the door to your house, so he will need training and socialization. Helping Tinker to mix socially now will pay dividends later on.

Have some basic obedience lessons Put your name down for a puppy party at your veterinary office or join a puppy class at your local obedience club. Learn the basics. A dog that will sit, go down and come on command is easy to control. These exercises are all fundamental to agility and have practical implications for everyday life.

Tinker will soon be old enough to join an agility class. At ten weeks old, make toilet training your immediate priority!

Left: Teaching your puppy to sit for a treat or toy is rewarding and fun.

Picking A Puppy

Q *I am finally in the position to have a puppy! In the past I have always adopted older dogs because I was working full-time, but now I have taken early retirement and I can indulge myself! What should I be looking for in a puppy?*

A Every puppy is a surprise package. As soon as you first get him through the front door, anything can happen and it often does. Health and temperament are important in agility and there are a number of things to consider when choosing a potentially suitable dog.

You can get a puppy from almost anywhere
They are advertised on the internet, in magazines and in the local paper. I like puppies from a reputable breeder because they are accustomed to the sound of the TV, the vacuum cleaner and pots and pans on the stove. They are more likely to meet lots of different types of people – the mail carrier, other family members and all the neighborhood kids. The puppy's education and socialization has started before you bring him home.

Make sure your puppy isn't sick. Does he look healthy? Ask the breeder when he was last wormed and if he has been treated for fleas. Pick the pup that looks to have the best chances of a disease-free life in the future. If you are choosing a pedigree dog, talk to your breeder about inheritable diseases and whether the sire and dam have been screened for these conditions. You don't want to spend any more time at the vet than you have to!

Ask to see the parents and as many of your intended puppy's relatives as possible You will get a good idea of what your puppy will look like when he grows up, as well as an indication of likely temperament. Will he have short legs like his aunt or be grumpy like his uncle?

Think of how your puppy will fit into your family

when making your choice If you still have other dogs, will they be more welcoming to a female or a male? Do you want a submissive character or someone to will rule the roost? If you already have small dogs, do you think it would be fair to get a large breed?

And, finally, what sort of trainer are you? Try to pick yourself a good match. Are you a little inhibited and find it difficult to motivate and excite your dogs? Don't pick the laid-back puppy in that case. When you stand up, do you exude authority? If not, you may be storing up a lifetime of trouble if you take home the puppy that wants to be the leader of the pack.

When you choose a puppy, all you can do is try to stack the cards in your favor. No-one will promise you a winner and good breeding will not guarantee you reliable contacts on the agility course. Despite the odds, a sickly pup may turn out to be an agility champion. In the end it's not so much which one you pick, but what

Breed Of Choice

Q *I would love to get a dog and do agility but whenever I have seen it on TV everyone has collies. Do other breeds of dog compete in agility? Would I have to get a collie if I wanted to do well?*

A Collies are the breed of choice for dog agility. They are agile athletes, independent workers and quick learners. All the ingredients are there to make an agility winner. Collies are great dogs, but there is no guarantee that they will be star performers—and could you live with one? Just consider the following factors.

Above: *This spaniel proves that small size and flyaway ears are no impediment to being a great agility dog.*

Physical exercise Collies are not the type of dog that likes to lounge around at home. They need daily exercise and love long walks or chasing balls. If you live in the city, you may find it difficult to provide enough of these activities.

Mental stimulation Collies like to flex their mental muscles. Out all day? Your bored collie might decide to entertain himself by ripping your sofa into little pieces and trying to put it back together again before you come home from work. A dog lacking mental stimulation can become a destructive presence in the home.

Keen learners Collies pick things up very quickly and they are easy to train. This means that they will learn the wrong things as fast as they will the right ones. You might anticipate a speedy ascent onto the winner's podium if you get a collie, but the reality can be elimination after elimination on the course.

Need a job Collies hate being unemployed. If you don't have sheep, a collie will happily herd and pen your children, perhaps even giving them a little nip for encouragement if they don't move fast enough!

Collies meet the job specification for agility dog, but they are not the only dogs competing in the sport of agility. Belgian Shepherd Dogs, Golden Retrievers and Cavalier King Charles Spaniels do well too. Large dogs, medium dogs and small dogs all enjoy flying over the jumps and racing through tunnels. Consider other types of dogs and their breed traits. Get a dog that you like and that fits in with your lifestyle. If you live in an apartment, think about a miniature breed like a Papillon. If you hate dog hair, consider a non-shedding type like the Poodle. If you like spots, put your name down for a Dalmatian

Above: *Jumping fences is just as much fun as chasing foxes. Beagles are one of the many small breeds that can excel at agility.*

Left: *Will this collie hit or miss the contact at the bottom of the dog walk? It's all in the training!*

puppy. Don't choose a breed just because of its popularity as an agility dog. Pick one you like through and through.

Other breeds might take a little longer to train to become proficient in agility, but they will get there in the end and many of them eventually turn out to beat the collies! Visit an agility show. You'll be surprised by the variety of dogs in the ring. Stay open minded. You may end up losing your heart to a bouncy Springer Spaniel!

Agility To The Rescue

Q *I have just re-homed a collie. I couldn't resist her big eyes and I've named her Shona. She is about eight to ten months old and loves everybody and everything. I've had her about four weeks and it's just like she has always lived here. She is such an active dog that I would like to take her agility training. Are rescue dogs accepted?*

A I'm so glad to hear that Shona has been given a second chance. There are so many waifs and strays out there. Working breeds, like collies or lurchers, often end up in rescue centers because they don't always settle down to family life. They want to round up and herd the children or chase the cat. Happily there are many successful rescue dogs in agility and they are a popular choice for many agility handlers because:

Agility handlers have big hearts Who could fail to feel good about themselves after adopting a dog? Rescue organizations work hard to keep their animals happy and to make them comfortable, but a kennel cannot compete with a loving home.

Agility handlers love training their dogs Most of the dogs offered for re-homing are past puppyhood. Those that are ten months plus and well balanced individuals are ready to start agility training as soon as they are settled into their new surroundings. For those handlers who can't wait, they are the perfect choice for a new dog.

Size and shape matters You know more or less what you are getting with a rescue dog. Don't fall into the trap experienced by the agility handler who

Above: *Give me a home and I'll be your agility dog – provided you give me lots of love, toys and treats too!*

bought a puppy believing it would compete in the Small height category. It grew and grew and kept on growing. It ended up competing as a Large dog. Re-homing an adult dog that has already reached maturity takes the guesswork out of the equation.

Agility handlers love a challenge A rescue dog may have a number of behavioral problems and gaps in his education. You will never know why he is up for adoption. Is it because his owners divorced or is it because he tried to bite the mother-in-law? Perhaps he simply barked too much? A rescue dog might understand the commands "Sit" and "Down" but may have missed the lesson on coming back when called. Bad habits like food bowl guarding won't be revealed until his first meal. These problems will have to be addressed before the rescue dog can begin agility training.

You are very lucky to have found Shona. She sounds the perfect companion and a real gem. And she has agility potential – the right age to start a little training and the right breed to excel at canine sports. Shona will keep you on your toes and you will have loads of fun with her. Have a look at the different agility clubs in your area and sign up for some classes. But beware … agility is very addictive!

One Of A Kind

Q My dog is a real cultural hodge-podge. She has a little German Shepherd, a dash of Japanese Spitz and more than her fair share of Italian Spinone. Who knows what else went into the making of Minkie. You will never see another dog that looks like her and she is a fine example of a mix. Can Minkie try agility or is it only for pedigree dogs?

A Agility is for all sizes and for all breeds of dogs and their crosses. If Minkie is in good health and at least a year old, there is no reason why she shouldn't try agility.

Above: *Sometimes it's easy to confuse a pedigree dog with a crossbreed. The owner of this championship-winning Pyrenean Sheepdog would be most upset if you mistook her pet for a mix!*

Not everyone wants a pedigree dog. You can be on a waiting list for a puppy for years and some blue-blooded dogs are exorbitantly expensive. Puppies from an accidental mating of your neighbor's pet can be had more quickly and are usually a cheaper option. You won't be able to anticipate what the pups will look like when they grow up, but you do know that they will be individuals that stand out in a crowd.

You will be surprised to learn that many agility folk actually choose a crossbreed over a pedigree dog. They see a combination dog working in the ring, admire the dog's style and set out to find a pup with a similar make-up. Border Collie crossed with German Shepherds, Poodles and Bearded Collies have all been popular mixes and sometimes are deliberately bred for obedience and agility handlers. In addition, some crosses have been planned with size in mind. Small dog handlers have tried to miniaturize Border Collies by mating them with Jack Russells. Sadly, just because a dog sports black and white markings doesn't mean he will have the trainability and work ethic of a collie! There is no guarantee that the best traits of both breeds will dominate in the pups of a cross-mating.

Any breed or mixed breed can participate in agility and sometimes you will see them beating the pedigree dogs! A number of organizations welcome crossbreeds and will have their own registration policies and rules and regulations governing competitions. Regulations may vary in other countries. For example, a type of dog may be recognized as a pedigree in one country, but not in another. In addition to a national kennel club, a country will probably host a number of alternative agility organizations and each will have their own registration policies regarding crossbreeds and competition events. Who knows what went into making Minkie, but she's sure to have a jumping gene somewhere!

Agility Ability

Q *I've had my dog now for about a month. Zipper is from a rescue organization and I believe he is about a year old. He's a medium-sized mix that will do anything for food. I have always been interested in agility and thought that if he showed some aptitude for it, we would try it. Well, his latest trick is to get up on the kitchen worktop to look out of the window! In view of his acrobatic leanings, do you think agility is a good idea or will it create more problems at home?*

A Zipper is the ideal candidate for agility training. He's handsome, quick to learn and athletic. He just has to learn that the items of furniture in your living room are not obstacles on an agility course.

Above: *No piece of furniture is too tall or too wide for this appealing rescue dog to jump or climb. He's*

Discrimination
Agility can provide a constructive channel for Zipper's energy and turn him into a discerning dog. He has probably already learned to discriminate between the things in the house that he must not touch, like your slippers, and what he can play with to his heart's delight, like his squeaky toy. Similarly, he will quickly catch on to what behavior is appropriate for an armchair at home and what is appropriate for an A-frame in agility.

Control Acrobatic ability is not the only prerequisite of agility. In addition to the obedience basics, dogs are trained to jump, climb or weave only when commanded to do so. If a dog takes his own line on an agility course because he prefers the blue jump to the red one, he will be eliminated. Zipper should only vault over the fence to visit his friends if you give him permission by saying, "Zipper jump!"

Agility rarely creates more problems than it cures. Find your nearest agility club and sign up for a course of lessons. You'll make new friends and Zipper will delight you with feats of athleticism that have nothing to do with the kitchen counter. At the very least, Zipper should be too tired after training to get into mischief, but if he does still have enough energy to wonder what's passing the kitchen window, buy a blind!

A Rough Start

Q *I would like to start agility training with my rescue dog, Benny. Benny did not have the best start in life. He is very hand-shy and I think he must have been beaten as a puppy. He is very loving to me, but suspicious of people, especially men. He's a very handsome dog that attracts notice and he once nipped someone who only wanted to pet him. Will agility help him overcome his fears?*

A Benny is very lucky to have found a home with an owner who understands his anxieties. Agility will certainly give Benny something different to think about, but it is not a cure. Care must be taken to make sure that your dog has professional help to overcome his problems and that they are not compounded by the stress or anxiety that Benny could experience on his encounters with agility. You need to be aware of the following factors.

The early stages of agility are hands-on There will be a number of occasions when your instructor will want to touch Benny. He might hold Benny for you while you call him over a fence or he might help you lift Benny into a position on a contact. If Benny looked unsteady on the dog walk, your instructor could reach out to steady him so that he didn't fall off. Do you think Benny would be frightened and protest at this kind of handling?

Right: *Two pairs of hands are better than one to keep this dog on the seesaw. They guide him up the trail of cheese and are ready to catch him if he decides to jump off too soon.*

It's hard to learn when you are thinking of something else Agility classes can be stressful. If Benny is worried because he can't keep track of all the new people he is meeting and is getting a headache from all the barking dogs around him, he won't be able to pay much attention to what you are trying to teach him. And you may well become worried about how Benny will react to the class environment which will compound his anxieties and make him even more nervous.

Agility is a very sociable sport Although Benny might relax and make friends with your trainer and the other students in his class, he will inevitably continue to meet new people as classes progress. What if one of your classmates brings her young children to a lesson during the summer, and they want to pet Benny?

It is never too late to socialize a dog to new people, different dogs and strange places, but an agility class is not the best place to start. Benny might have very good reasons to be distrustful of people, but he can learn that not everyone is bad. Begin by talking to a canine behaviorist who will be able to assess your dog and find practical solutions. Not all agility instructors are qualified to give advice on problem dogs, but they are usually happy to support and help implement recommendations from those that are. There are many dogs enjoying agility today that have had a rough start and overcome their fear of people. Benny has already taken the first step. He has found an owner who loves him and wants to help him enjoy life.

Many Happy Returns

Q *Sammy my Lurcher loves running. When I take him out he disappears over the horizon and I may not see him for ages. Often he brings back a rabbit. Then we go home and he sleeps. Would agility be a better way to exercise him and tire him out?*

are needed, both to give you some control and to help you become a team. And also for safety. When Sammy is off in the fields hunting, you don't know what he is doing. An out-of-sight dog is a dog courting trouble. Is he raiding a trashcan for scraps? Is he terrorizing someone's cat? Is he stopping to

A From the rabbit's point of view, agility is the choice option.

Lurchers are a type of crossbreed found mostly in Britain. It is said that they were developed in the Middle Ages by gypsies to be used for hunting and poaching. They are usually sighthounds crossed with a collie or terrier type – an attempt to combine speed and brains – and they can be exceptionally beautiful and athletic dogs. My first agility partner was a Lurcher and I have always had a soft spot for this type of dog.

Agility would be something that you and Sammy could do together – then you could both go home and have a snooze – but first I think a few lessons in basic obedience

Above: *Lurchers are speed demons. They make great agility dogs, provided they are pointed in the right direction – at the jumps and tunnels, not the rabbits.*

look both ways before he crosses the road? He may already have had a few lucky escapes. If Sammy does not come when you call him, he might decide to go hunting rather than jumping the first time you take his leash off in agility class.

Yes, agility will be great exercise for Sammy once he has a recall under his belt and he will still enjoy his walks with you. Every dog should have his training supplemented with time off to relax and do the things that dog do. Dogs love to smell where other dogs have been, roll on their backs with their legs in the air or play with their doggie pals. These are all acceptable behaviors in free time … as long as the dog comes back securely when he is called.

Agility Best Buys

Q *My husband has offered to take me out for the day shopping. He thinks he will be buying me a little black number for Saturday nights, but I will be looking for something sporty and practical for my first agility lesson with Penny our Cocker Spaniel next week. What would you suggest?*

A Oooh shopping! After agility, shopping is my favorite hobby and what a lucky lady you are to have a husband who wants to accompany you. Convince him that you can look just as good in rain gear as you can in silk!

Above: *Footwear is important in agility. You don't want to fall over and end up sitting on your bottom. Leave your galoshes and high heels at home and buy a good pair of running shoes.*

Shoes Your first port of call should be the shoe shop. You want something that you can run in comfortably and that will cushion your feet. Shoes that grip all types of surfaces in all types of weather are ideal. Many agility enthusiasts wear field hockey shoes with rubber studs. Avoid shoes with metal studs – you may accidentally step on your dog. Don't buy anything that may give you blisters.

Clothes Make sure that whatever you buy allows you to move around freely and protects you from the weather. You will need something to keep you warm and dry if you are training outdoors in winter. Don't forget hats and gloves. If it's summer and the sun is shining, look for shorts and T-shirts. I try to buy clothes with lots of pockets to accommodate my dog's treats and toys. I look out for things that wash well and dry quickly. I'm a big fan of sporting/ camping shops and practical casual wear outlets as their clothing is practical rather than fashionable. I also have a number of sweatshirts and fleeces embroidered with my club logo, agility slogans and favorite breeds.

Underwear Don't forget to visit the lingerie department. If you are a well-endowed lady, you should consider investing in a sports bra. It should be the dog that is doing all the bouncing around on the course, not you.

Accessories What else? If you have long hair, you will probably want something to tie it back so you can see where you are running. And something just for fun – how about a pair of paw print earrings?

Best buys The two things I can't do without are my silk long underwear and my waterproof socks. OK, they don't make me look sexy or improve my handling skills but I feel like a hundred bucks when I wear them.

Room To Maneuver

Q *You need lots of room to do agility, don't you? I'd like to have a go with my Cocker Spaniel Barclay, but how could I practice? I have a small yard – there is no room for a lot of jumps and an A-frame.*

A Few of us have the room to lay out a full agility course. Our yards are for flower beds and lounge chairs. But that is no excuse for not practicing. Basic obedience exercises and target training requires only a little space and can be perfected indoors. And you'll be surprised at what you can accomplish without "proper" agility equipment by using lots of imagination.

Contact position Is there a step out your back door into your yard? Make it a "contact" step. Teach Barclay a two foot on/two foot off position (back feet on the step and two front feet on the ground). If he holds it for a few seconds, praise and release him into the yard to play.

A-frame Your stairs are an A-frame. Whenever Barclay comes down the stairs ask him to wait on the "contact" step at the bottom. Praise and release him into the room. Not all staircases are ideal for this exercise; for example, spiral or open tread staircases are not

Below: *Walking along the top of a wall is just like walking along the top of the dog walk. The views over the lake may*

recommended. You will have to use some common sense assessing their safety and suitability.

Dog walk Walk a wall with Barclay. I lift my young dogs up onto a brick wall that divides one side of my local park from the other. They walk along while I hold their collar, just like on a dog walk. Choose a wall that is wide enough for Barclay and, again, think about safety. Avoid walls that are too tall or have crumbling brickwork. Check what's on the other side – a steep drop onto a busy lane of traffic or a rose bed would be hazardous.

Hurdles You will find loads of these in your local woods. Logs and branches that have fallen down are perfect hurdles. The best time to find them is after a storm. There are lots of jumping exercises you can practice over a few well placed logs, but remember that Barclay is supposed to jump them, not crawl over or dive under them.

Miniaturized equipment Not all agility equipment is huge or heavy. I have a mini A-frame that I use to practice contacts and I can lift it with one hand. I also have a mini-tunnel which is only a few feet long. Neither is as big as the real thing, but perfectly fine for giving my dog a taste of the sport. Both can be folded away in minutes and stored out of sight in the garage.

Above: *Is it a Poodle masquerading as a curly coated squirrel? No. It's an agility dog practicing his climbing technique during a walk in the woods.*

There are also lots of potential agility obstacles in children's play areas and fitness circuits in neighborhood parks. Remember, however, that these are for humans and resist the temptation of taking Barclay down the slide. Think about campaigning for a dog park in your community instead. I'm sure it would be popular.

Absolute Beginner

Q *I called my local agility club to find out the times and dates of classes for absolute beginners. I'm eager to do some training with my*

Patterdale Terrier, Zena. I thought I'd be the one asking the questions, but they wanted to know what kind of dog I had, how old she was and whether she had attended obedience classes. I thought I could do agility classes instead of obedience classes.

A I'm sorry if you felt you were being interrogated by your agility club. It's not only important for you to ask a lot of questions when you are looking for classes but for the club to find out as much as possible about you so that they can decide where you will fit in best. Otherwise you could end up the smallest dog in a class of Irish Wolfhounds!

Dogs that have attended obedience classes are usually under control and receptive to learning new things. They will have already covered some of the basics such as:

Heelwork It is important in agility that dogs are able to walk on or off lead by their handler's side. If Zena pulls you through doorways, she is likely to pull you through the tunnel.

Recall Everyone likes their dog to come back to them when they call. And right away, not after the dog has disappeared down a rabbit hole. If Zena ignores your call, you could end up spending the first ten minutes of every agility class trying to catch her.

Positions The "Sit" and the "Down" are the agility handler's favorite positions and are used in a variety of ways. A dog can be told to go "Down" on a contact or to go "Down" when waiting in the line for her turn. She can be told to "Sit" at the beginning of a new exercise or to "Sit" on the start line at a competition. Can Zena "Sit" and "Down" on command?

Wait or Stay The more eager an agility dog becomes the harder it is to "Wait" your turn! Agility handlers get a head start on the course by telling their dogs to "Wait" behind the first fence. Or they place their dog in a "Stay" while they return to a jump and pick up a pole that has been knocked down. Will Zena stay put?

Zena may have received no formal obedience training yet still be able to perform these exercises proficiently. Each exercise has practical implications for everyday life and a well mannered dog is easier to live with than a delinquent. And just because a dog receives an "A" grade at obedience class doesn't mean she will remember all her lessons when she gets onto the agility field – much to her owner's stupefaction!

Obedience basics are a prerequisite for agility. While some agility clubs will incorporate a number of control exercises into their beginners' courses, others leave teaching the basics to the obedience clubs.

Below: *Waiting for your turn can be the hardest lesson in agility.*

The Sky's The Limit

Q *I have a collie cross called Sky and I want to do obedience and agility with her. I've already taught her to "Sit," "Down," "Walk to heel" and "Come" on command. What are the training techniques used in agility and how are they different from those used in obedience?*

A Agility dogs are not only trained to jump fences, but to be good canine citizens with a degree of proficiency in most obedience exercises. The training methods used by a handler to teach his dog the basic obedience exercises will usually be the same ones used to teach more specialized agility activities. If you take up agility with Sky, you will have an advantage because you are already familiar and practiced with some of these training methods.

Take the A-frame contact as an example. The A-frame has a contact area at the end of its ramp measuring about 3ft 6in (106.7cm) up from the bottom and the dog must touch this or be faulted by the judge. How the handler chooses to teach his dog to hit the contact area demonstrates a choice of training techniques. You may have already used one of these techniques to teach Sky to lie "Down" in obedience.

Hands-on shaping When training the A-frame contact, the agility handler physically places the dog in the position he wants the dog to adopt on the contact. While she is in this position, she is rewarded with praise and a treat. Did you teach Sky to lie down by starting in the Sit, then lifting and lowering her front legs to the ground and finally rewarding her with praise and a treat when her tummy was flat on the floor? That is an example of hands-on shaping

Barrier shaping The agility handler places a hoop at the bottom of the A-frame that the dog must run under as she exits the contact. He hopes that enough repetitions of this action will embed it in the dog's muscle memory. Perhaps you got Sky to crawl under a table so that similarly she had to lie down?

Luring Armed with his dog's favorite treat or toy,

Above: *Dogs will follow a treat anywhere and luring a dog into the contact area can be a successful training method.*

the agility handler lures the dog to the very bottom of the contact. Dogs will follow a treat anywhere! Did you hold a treat just above Sky's nose and then slowly lower it to the floor so that she was lured down into the flat position?

Click and treat The agility handler clicker-trains his dog to nose-touch a target. He places the target at the bottom of the A-frame and asks his dog to touch it. You may have used a clicker to teach Sky to lie down. Click means the same thing in any discipline – a treat is coming.

Training techniques often cross divides. Some are better suited for specific actions than others. Choose one that works for you and your dog to get the results you want.

Pre-Agility Classes

Q *I have a lively and exceptionally clever six-month-old Border Terrier, Nellie, that I believe would be great at agility. I have never done agility before but understand that although she is too young to do it properly, some clubs run pre-agility classes for youngsters. Have you heard of these classes? What should I expect?*

A There are a number of clubs that run pre-agility classes, sometimes called "foundation classes" or "fundamentals for agility." They are ideal for youngsters that are too young to jump high hurdles but are old enough to master some basics. The classes concentrate on the agility essentials like motivation, control and attitude. Graduate dogs are receptive to further agility training and progress quickly. A good pre-agility class will cover some of the following:

Motivation You will learn how to use a toy or food as motivational aids. Nellie may like to chase a tennis ball but will she bring it back to you? She may love to shake a tug toy, but will she let go of it on command? A high play drive can make teaching your dog new things in agility a lot of fun.

Distractions If your dog is going to do agility, she must learn to ignore distractions such as other people, dogs or food – no matter how tempting. Will Nellie walk by your side or wander off to hunt squirrels? When you call her, will she come straight back to you or will she make a detour to the food container?

Socialization Some dogs are nervous in mixed company. They can be overwhelmed by new environments. Pre-agility classes can help Nellie relax and take things in her stride. Dogs find it easier to learn when they are not stressed or anxious.

Tricks In addition to some of the obedience basics, Nellie may be taught a few tricks like walking backwards, waving a paw or taking a bow. Tricks will amaze your friends, but more importantly, they will engage Nellie's brain, improve her flexibility and give her confidence in you. Just what you need for agility.

Flat work There are many agility exercises that can be done without the equipment like directional commands, target training or teaching Nellie to run on both your left and right side. And, Nellie can learn to run between the hurdle wings – on the left and right, as a recall and as a send away. This is a good preparation for jumping later on.

Partnership The aim will be to make sure that you and Nellie are having a good time. Doing things together will strengthen the rapport you have with your dog.

I would like to see more agility clubs offer classes like these, but until there is a sufficient demand, pre-agility classes won't appear on your club's schedule and they will rely on local obedience schools to teach traditional exercises like "Sit," "Down" or "Stay." I hope you will be able to find a pre-agility class near you.

Left *Puppies too young to start*

Getting A Head Start

 I have a ten-month-old collie spaniel mix named Charlie. I have competed in obedience with my other dogs, but would like to try agility. We live on a remote hill farm and my nearest training club is 60 miles away. Their "Introduction to Agility" class doesn't start for another 12 weeks and I may have to miss some of these if we get snowed in. Is there anything I can teach Charlie now so that we can make a good impression on our trainer? We don't have any agility equipment.

You can introduce Charlie to a great deal in agility without him touching a piece of proper equipment. Keep your training at ground level so that Charlie will avoid accidents and continue growing into a confident, bold adult.

The plank Put a 6-8ft (two-meter) plank of wood on two bricks on the ground and teach Charlie to walk along it. Gymnasts practice new moves and routines on a balance beam laid on the floor before they move to a competition-height beam. Charlie will become a confident performer on his plank and be better prepared for balancing on a real dog walk. Make sure there are no nails or splinters sticking out of the plank before you begin any exercises.

The wobble board Put a small log under a flat square of wood so that one side rests on the ground and the other is raised about 6in (15cm). Voilà, a miniature seesaw! Charlie will have to get accustomed to the ground moving under his feet and keeping his balance while you lead him from one side to the other.

The ladder
Lay six poles (broom handles or PVC tubing cut into lengths) on the ground about 3 to 4ft (1 to 1.2m)

apart like a ladder and walk Charlie up through the middle. Charlie's co-ordination will improve and he will learn to pick his feet up to avoid the ladder's rungs – just as he will have to pick up his feet to avoid knocking a pole when he is old enough to start jumping.

Running through the wings Put a pole on the ground between two chairs that act as hurdle wings. You can teach Charlie to run over the pole with you positioned on either his left or on his right. You can recall him over the pole or you can send him away to fetch a toy. Charlie will be learning to run between the wings of a hurdle rather than running around them.

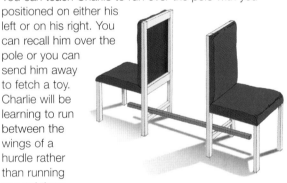

Left or right You can start teaching Charlie directional commands. If he has been clicker-trained, you can click and treat when he looks right or left and give these actions directional commands. Or teach Charlie to spin to the right or twist to the left, luring him with a toy.

Build his confidence. You want each exercise not only to be fun and successful, but to lay solid foundations for subsequent agility training in a few months time.

Top Dog

Q *I'm not ashamed to admit that I'm very competitive. Whether at work or at play, I take the time to make sure I come out on top. What are the characteristics of a great agility dog? What should I be looking for if I want to end up on the podium in a few years time?*

A A truly great agility dog will be the one that the judge has been waiting for all day. As the dog steps onto the start line a hush will descend over the crowds. Everyone will hold their breath while the dog takes center stage. His handler will be rallying every ounce of grit and determination in order to do the dog justice. This dog is likely to cross the finish line with either the fastest clear run of the day or the biggest elimination points tally. The characteristics of a great agility dog are:

Peak physical condition The dog will be in his prime; fit and healthy. He is a superb canine specimen with a sparkle in his eye.

Above: *If your dog doesn't skip the last pole, a tight turn exiting the weaves can cut seconds off your course time.*

Bold and fearless If this dog falls off the dog walk, he dusts himself off and gets back on again. He is prepared to take risks as he flies around the course

– getting contacts by a toenail or tightening a turn so much he almost knocks a pole. He is not afraid to take the initiative if his handler is too slow.

Drive Acceleration is not a problem, slowing down often is. A great agility dog will have drive and work in top gear even if his handler has a hangover.

The "I want" factor A top class agility dog is always hungry for the jumps and contact equipment. The minute he sees the training venue or show ground, he begins to pull on the leash.

As a judge, this is the kind of dog that I like to see step into my ring. Whether the handler loses control or goes on to win the class is irrelevant. I can appreciate not just the fine agility dog in front of me but the work that has gone into making him so formidable. I know appearances are deceptive. Who expected that the "jump everything in sight" Sheltie would be brought under control with no loss of enthusiasm? Who would have put money on the Papillon ever breaking out of a trot? And who would believe that a few months ago that terrier was badly spooked by an umbrella? Their handlers have succeeded in motivating their dogs and teaching them not just competency over the equipment, but a joy and love of agility.

Few top agility dogs are born ready made and even fewer land in the laps of experienced handlers. More often top agility dogs are the result of hard work, good training and a few embarrassing moments in the ring from which they happily learn.

Short In The Leg

Q *I've seen dog agility on TV. Everyone looks like they are having fun and I would like to have a go with Freya, my Bichon Frise. She's big on personality, but is she too small for agility?*

A No. She's probably the perfect size for a Bichon! Agility is for all shapes and sizes of dogs. Dogs are measured before they enter their first show and compete in three different height categories (heights may vary depending on organization):

- **Small** – open to dogs measuring 12in (350mm) or under at the withers.
- **Medium** – open to dogs measuring over 12in (350mm) but under 17in (430mm) at the withers.
- **Large** – open to dogs measuring over 17in (430mm) at the withers.

And no one would expect your little Bichon to jump big fences. The approximate jump heights are:

- **Small dogs** – jump obstacles will be 9.8-13.75in (250-350mm).
- **Medium dogs** – jump obstacles will be 13.75-17.7in (350-450mm).
- **Large dogs** – jump obstacles will be 21.6-25.6in (550-650mm).

Small dogs are as passionate about agility as the big dogs. A dog is a dog, regardless of size – they all jump, weave and miss contacts. They all have a trigger button that turns on their motors. Small dogs can do everything that the larger Border Collies can do. It's just sometimes a little harder because of their size, but their training will take their size into account.

Short legs Shorter legs mean that small dogs will have to take three to four times as many strides to cover the same ground as big dogs with longer legs. Consequently they can run out of steam quickly.

Small mouths A tennis ball can be too big to fit comfortably between their jaws so they aren't always

Above: *Good things come in small packages. Many miniature breeds enjoy competing in Small dog agility classes.*

eager to retrieve. Tug games need care. Pull a toy out of a small dog's mouth with too much gusto and you could extract a few teeth too! And many little dogs are fussy eaters turning their noses up at gourmet morsels. As a consequence, play and treat training can be hard work.

Small dog breed traits Dogs that were miniaturized to fit in your lap can be difficult to motivate and switch on. They worry about breaking their nails if you ask them to do some work. On the other hand, small terrier-type dogs that have been bred to go down rabbit holes or kill vermin never stop. Offer this type of mini-dog a job and he will sign on the dotted line.

There are a number of small dogs on the agility circuit that should be given speeding tickets. They achieve course times faster than many of the large dogs. Find an agility class near you. Agility is lots of fun and you won't be the only one with a small dog. Freya may be little, but inside there's a big dog waiting to be let loose on the jumps.

Big Is Beautiful

Q *I have a Great Dane called Pernod and I would love to do agility with her but have been told that my breed of dog is too big and heavy. Is this true? I just want to have some fun.*

A It doesn't matter how large or how small your dog is to have fun. However, Pernod is a big girl and you need to make sure that she has fun safely. You will both stop smiling if Pernod hurts herself and you end up with a big, big vet's bill to match your big, big dog. There are three areas that give me concern.

Tunnels Pernod would have to get down on her knees to fit in and crawl through the tunnel. Such a tight squeeze would not be very comfortable for her.

Weave poles These could be a problem, too. Most poles are a minimum height of 2ft 6in (76cm). The distance between the poles is usually a minimum of 18in (46cm) to a maximum of 2ft (61cm). If Pernod is taller than the poles

she risks being poked in her tummy. And bending one way with her front end while her back end is bending another way would not be easy.

Dog walk and seesaw I think these two pieces of agility equipment could be very challenging for Pernod. The plank for both has a width of between 10 to 12in (25 to 30cm) – probably considerably less than Pernod's shoulder width. For her, placing one foot in front of the other will be like tightrope walking. Moreover, I am not aware of any regulations regarding the weight-bearing capacity of the equipment. If the dog walk and seesaw are left outside in all weathers or are very old, they won't be particularly sturdy and could collapse under the weight of a big dog.

But don't let this stop you. I suggest the following:

Talk to an agility instructor You would be taking Pernod to classes purely for her pleasure and entertainment. Why not ask if you could participate in class activities but abstain from those that would be uncomfortable or risky for Pernod?

Find a "big" dog agility club These clubs cater for the larger breeds like yours and train over purpose-built equipment to withstand the size and weight of Great Danes, Irish Wolfhounds, Bernese Mountain Dogs and others. They realize that big dogs are capable canines who love to run and jump as much as their smaller cousins.

Start your own "big" dog club Large breeds can do agility. Make your own reinforced, super-sized equipment and have some fun. Pernod could be your club's mascot! You will be setting a new trend in your area. Size is important and does pose some particular problems, but it shouldn't stop you from having fun with your dog.

Below: *Samoyeds are built for pulling sleds in the Arctic, but are also valued as pets. If your dog is missing the snow, introduce him to agility. He'll soon dream of nothing else!*

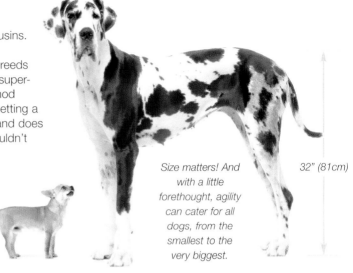

Size matters! And with a little forethought, agility can cater for all dogs, from the smallest to the very biggest.

6" (15cm)

32" (81cm)

How To Be A Champion

Q Sometimes I look at my dog and feel sorry for him. I make so many mistakes and let him down. Turbo is a superb boy who always does his best for me. If he was someone else's dog, he would be an Agility Champion by now. What makes a good agility trainer?

There are three types of agility trainer who stand on the podium holding ribbons and trophies.

The born good trainer A few people are born good trainers. The born good trainer has been blessed with perfect timing, great co-ordination and tons of patience. His intuition is always right and he appears to be able to communicate with his pets telepathically.

The trainer with a born good dog This trainer has a once-in-a-lifetime dog. God's gift. His dog learns despite the trainer's mistakes. The dog always gets his handler out of trouble on the course and people say that he must have been an agility dog in a previous life. God's gift would be on the podium no matter who owned and handled him.

The trainer who works hard Most of us have to work our socks off to be a good trainer. It's not easy and a good trainer can be years in the making. As time goes by, he will accrue a vast knowledge of canines and develop the skills to communicate clearly with his dogs. He will understand how to make learning fun and how to guide his dogs to make the right choices. And he will have spent hours practicing agility to perfect his handling moves. If you want to follow in his footsteps, here are a few tips:

- **Be consistent** Consistency makes learning easy. Don't say "Over" one day and "Jump" the next.
- **Be patient** A good trainer knows how to be patient and will master the basic moves before trying advanced ones. Take it easy and don't try to run courses before you can do all the obstacles.

- **Stay up to date** A good trainer will arm himself with a sound knowledge of current training methods and learning theories. Curl up in your armchair with a good dog training book.

- **Perfect timing** A good trainer knows the importance of a few seconds. Make sure your commands and praise are precise. Tell your dog he is a "Good boy" for sitting, not scratching his ear after his bottom hit the ground.
- **Learn from mistakes** Even the best dog trainers make them. Never blame the dog for your errors but adjust your training program to make sure the same thing won't happen again.
- **Practice** A good dog trainer will make practice count. Spend time practicing what you need to improve but stop before your dog reaches saturation point. There is just so much a dog can learn in one day.

Don't feel sorry for Turbo. He is lucky to have you. You don't love him any less for not being an Agility Champion and Turbo loves you despite your mistakes.

What's In A Name?

Q *I will be bringing home my first puppy in a few weeks time. He is going to be a star agility dog, but has so much to learn. What is the most important thing that I can teach him?*

A The most important thing that you will ever teach your dog is his name. He should be listening for his name even in his sleep. When he hears it, your dog should snap to attention in anticipation of some fun. His name will precede every command you give him. Listen to some of the top agility handlers when they are in action. Often the dog's name is the only thing they say when they run their dogs, so choose your dog's name carefully.

Keep it short Your dog may already have a fancy pedigree name like "Torrington's Mad Hatter Over Tabasco." What a mouthful! By the time you spit that out your dog could have taken the wrong turn on an agility course and been eliminated. Choose a pet name that is easy to say and rolls off the tongue.

Avoid people's names If you are standing in the middle of the park yelling for "Brian" and a good-looking young man approaches and asks how he can help you, how are you going to explain the mix-up?

Feel comfortable with your choice The kids might think that "Twit" or "Dummy" is a cute name for your pup, but how happy will you be registering him at the vet or introducing him to your friends?

Think of everyone in the family when making your decision I have a friend who named her dog "Vodka." A few years later she got married and had babies. Her neighbors now believe the children have a drinking problem because someone in the household is always shouting for Vodka.

Name and command Make sure that the name you choose does not sound like an agility command. If your jump command is "over," you don't really want to call your dog "Clover."

It's easy to teach your puppy his name. Put some cubed cheese or diced chicken in your pocket and when your puppy is looking away from you, say his name in a happy voice. If he looks at you, praise him and give him a treat. Practice in all the rooms in your house and out in the yard. When he is investigating under the sofa or sniffing daffodils in

Above: *Don't call your dog by his name unless you want him. If you shout your dog's name while he is weaving, he may leave the poles uncompleted to return to you.*

the back yard, call his name and offer a titbit as soon as he turns to you. Responding to his name gets the reward – not the names of your husband, children or other dogs. He will start listening for his name and giving you his attention when he hears it. And let's face it. Before you can teach your dog anything, you have to be able to get his attention!

Packing Your Bag For Class

Q *I am going to my first agility lesson next week with my dog, Tansy. I'm so excited! I don't know if I'll be able to get to sleep the night before because I'm already dreaming about it. What do I need to take with me to class?*

A I am so glad that you and Tansy are looking forward to your first class with such enthusiasm and, like a good boy scout, you want to be prepared. Here is a list of things that you should take with you.

Collar and lead Choose a flat leather or webbing collar (not a choke chain). Some organizations allow dogs to wear collars in competition provided there are no tags hanging from the D-ring but some don't, so check the rules. You will also need a lead to keep your dog under control and introduce him to the agility equipment. Avoid flexi or extra long leads. You don't want your dog to tie himself up or trip over.

Treats Take a selection of treats with you – diced cheese, sliced sausage, or biscuits. Used wisely, treats help a dog to make correct choices and encourage him to give his best performance. Make sure your treats are in a dog-proof container. Determined dogs will try to open or chew through treat jars to get to the yummies inside.

Toys Don't forget your dog's favorite toys. Does your dog like to tug on a piece of rope or fetch a ball? Use that instinct to your advantage. Dogs that love to play, love agility and toys will become an intrinsic part of their training.

Clicker and target If you have already trained your dog with a clicker, you will be ahead of the game. Clickers have many applications in agility and there are many different ways that a target can be used to teach new skills.

Diary Buy a training diary. Record your progress, triumphs and disasters. A training diary is not essential, but it will make good reading later on when you are a superstar or get a second dog.

Poop bags Never go out without these. Your dog may want to go to the toilet before class starts so be prepared to pick up the feces and deposit it in the trash can provided.

Training bag Buy a bag for all your training gear. If you keep all your training paraphernalia in one place, you won't end up hunting through your pockets for a toy that you left in your car. Be selective and don't overload Tansy's training bag. You want to be able to carry it easily to and from agility.

Sense of humor Never leave this at home. It is the most important thing to bring to an agility class. Laugh and enjoy yourself.

Left: *Walk into any pet store and you'll see that the shelves are filled with all shapes, sizes and colors of tempting toys.*

Picking A Toy

Q *I have been told by my agility instructor to bring a toy to agility class. I looked through my Troy's treasure chest and most of his toys are half chewed or filthy. I would be too embarrassed to be seen in public with any of them. I'm going to the pet store today to buy him something new. What should I be looking for?*

Above: *These collies can't take their eyes off the tennis balls on a rope.*

A Manufacturers really know how to make adorable toys for dogs these days. I have a collection of little toy animals I bought at a pet store. They live on my bedspread, match my wall paper and are forbidden territory. I wouldn't consider giving such sweet things to my dogs – they would cover them in slobber! When you shop for Troy, consider some of the following:

What does your dog like? Would Troy like a ball or a toy in the shape of a hoop or a bone? Does he have a passion for vinyl or rubber? Does he love soft plush toys? There are toys that squeak, jingle or make mooing noises. There are toys with pockets in which to stuff treats. Tug ropes come in different colors, widths and lengths. Despite this wealth of choice, Troy still may simply prefer a pair of old socks.

How big is your dog? What will fit comfortably into the mouth of a German Shepherd Dog will not fit into the mouth of a Papillon. The Pap will need something smaller and lighter. And never buy a toy that is so small that your dog might swallow it accidentally or choke on it.

What games can you play? Choose interactive toys. Some toys are easy to throw and great for games of fetch. Other toys are ideal for tug games. Small toys are great for hide and seek. The only limit on the number of games you can play is your imagination.

Is your toy easy to hold? If your dog's favorite toy is a big soccer ball, you'll have trouble holding it while you run an agility course. And it will be a difficult toy to fade from training because it's too big to tuck in your pocket. I like toys that fit in my hand or up my sleeve. My dogs never know for sure whether I have a toy on me so they work really hard, just in case I do. Sometimes it is so well hidden, I don't find it till I change for bed.

Wash and play Will the toy you choose go in the washing machine? Tennis balls bounce around a bit but come out looking brand new. It won't matter how many times Troy drops his toy in a puddle if it can be easily cleaned.

Can you make a toy valuable? You are halfway there if Troy has already fallen in love with his toy. Make him love it even more by making it an "agility only" toy. Restrict his access to his toys in the house. Don't leave them lying around for him to chew on in idle moments. My dogs would give their eye teeth for a toy animal off my bed. One day perhaps…

Tasty Treats

Q *I don't know what kind of treats to use at agility class with Tinsel, my Yorkshire Terrier. She is a fussy eater and I'm sure that some treats are better for her than others. What would you suggest?*

A Treats can be used in agility in a number of ways and are especially important for dogs that don't like to tug or fetch a toy. You can use a treat as a lure, a reward or an incentive. Something tasty will motivate a dog not only to learn something new but to perform existing behaviors faster. Treats are versatile. You can give your dog a lick of her favorite titbit or you can jackpot her with a handful if she has done something really spectacular. It's worth while finding something that Tinsel likes.

Yummy The perfect treat will be delicious – the greasier and smellier, the more attractive to your dog. Cubes of cheese and slices of hot dog are popular choices with many dog trainers or you can buy readymade treats from the supermarket or pet store. Experiment with different food types to see what makes Tinsel's eyes light up. How about diced carrot or chunks of cooked chicken? But do remember NOT to use human chocolate as a treat; this is harmful to dogs and even quite small quantities can be toxic.

Easy to eat Choose a treat that is quick and easy to eat. You don't want Tinsel to spend ages gnawing on a hard biscuit. She'll forget why you gave it to her. The rest of the class won't wait for her to finish eating and think of all the crumbs she'll be leaving behind that may distract the other dogs.

Small Little dogs have little mouths and stomachs. Don't use a whole chicken leg as a treat – a sliver will be enough! Remember that you will be treating Tinsel frequently in class and you want her to be able to run without feeling full or bloated.

Special A treat must be special. If you feed Tinsel dried biscuit everyday, she is unlikely to get excited when you try and tempt her over a jump with the same biscuit. How boring! Choose something different.

Bon appetit Is Tinsel's food bowl always full? She won't have much interest in food if it's on tap all day. Stick to regular meal times so that in between she will have a good appetite and appreciate a treat.

Sensitive stomachs Some dogs have sensitive digestive tracts and introducing a new food type can upset their stomachs. Other dogs are prescribed special diets due to medical conditions or allergies that should be fed exclusively – not even one day off for good behavior! If Tinsel has a touchy tum, try setting aside a portion of her daily food ration to use as training titbits. Her tummy won't be upset by it and you'll be able to monitor her weight.

Stress Appetite is not just a good measure of a dog's physical condition but of a dog's mental state. If Tinsel refuses treats at training, it might be that she is worried or stressed. Try and help her to relax. Give her time to acclimatize to her surroundings.

Keep trying. It's only a matter of time before you find something that Tinsel likes.

Play Training

Q *As instructed by my agility trainer, I have bought my collie Zak a toy. I took Zak with me to the pet store and he picked it out himself. It's a pink ball on a rope. Then he picked another toy, then another. This is going to cost me a fortune. Why do I need a toy for agility?*

A I must congratulate Zak on his first choice of toy. A pink toy is very visible and will be hard to lose in the green grass. It's multi-purpose, doubling either as a fetch toy or as a tug toy. And another bonus is that you will be able to throw your pink ball even further because it's on a rope. But do practice your aim. If you sling the ball too high up in the air near a tree, it may get tangled in the branches and you will have to plan another shopping expedition to replace it! You ask why toys are needed –

Playing with toys will arouse and stimulate your dog Toys make practice fun and exciting. They are the key to mental ignition. When dogs are playing, everything is turned on. You need that kind of excitement in competitive agility to obtain a tip-top course performance from your dog.

Toys are filters There are many things that can catch a dog's eye in agility – strange people, new dogs, strange scents. Having an exciting game with Zak's tug toy can filter out many of these distractions and focus his attention on you. He'll be too engrossed trying to win the toy from you to worry about the lady wearing a funny hat selling ice cream.

Toys can create distance between you and your dog Whenever you want Zak to accelerate away from you, throw a toy for him to chase. Zak will drive down a line of fences in order to catch a ball. It will be traveling much faster than you will ever be able to run. Just try and beat him to it!

Above: *Soft toys can be too delicate for tug games but they are ideal mouth fillers. A dog can't bark when he is holding one in his mouth or he'll drop it!*

Toys can bring your dog back to you If you want a sharp turn after the tunnel, call Zak to you and have a tug game with his toy. If you want to pull Zak through the gap between two fences, he will return to you more quickly if he gets a game of tug as a reward. If your dog wants to get his teeth into his favorite toy, he has to be within arm's reach. And don't let go of your end.

You will have as much fun playing with a toy as your dog That is the best reason for buying Zak a toy. Play is something you do together and a good way to learn about your dog. Toys are not for solitary individuals. Become Zak's favorite playmate. And remember, a toy can last forever. A titbit disappears in seconds.

Left: *Throw a toy for your dog to chase and hope that he will bring back to you to throw again! Games keep a dog motivated.*

He Won't Touch The Toys

Q *My beagle, Horace, has no interest in toys. I have filled a drawer in my kitchen with balls, rubber hedgehogs, plush mice, tug ropes and old slippers (he loved chewing them when he was teething). All of them, except for the slippers, are in pristine condition. He would rather have a worming tablet than a toy in his mouth. My agility instructor keeps telling me to get Horace interested in a toy. How?*

A Handlers who have dogs "born" with a tug toy in their mouths never really understand the difficulties of coaching a dog to play with a toy. If you want Horace to beg you to open your kitchen drawer, you'll have to work hard to make his toys interesting.

Keep the toy moving There is nothing more boring than a static ball. Drag it along the floor like it is a small dying bird. Throw it across the ground. Make the toy's actions mimic an injured prey animal. Praise him for looking at it and Horace might be inclined to show even more interest next time and stretch out a paw to touch it.

Right: *Where is that squeaking noise coming from? If I squeeze it between my jaws, will it squeak even louder?*

Squeak your toy If your toy makes a noise, it will attract Horace's attention. At the very least he will wander over to investigate. If you are lucky, he will think it is a small animal about to expire and dive in to put it out of its misery. You can join in as well by praising him.

Hide food in your toy Some toys have little pockets that you can stuff with titbits. If Horace likes food, he'll be keen to get inside. Give him a treat from the toy if he sniffs it. Cheer him on if he starts to disembowel it!

You play with the toy You might feel foolish throwing a rubber hedgehog up in the air, catching it and chuckling with glee, but don't stop. If you are convincing, Horace will want to join in the fun. It's like watching someone eat chocolates, you wish they would share them with you.

Left: *Stuffing a rubber food toy with treats will keep a dog occupied for hours. And when it's empty, he will bring it to you to fill up again!*

You become a toy Does Horace like to wrestle with you? Push him away from you. Does he bounce back? If you run in the yard, does he chase you? Have a toy in your hand ready to add into the game.

The right toy The most unlikely objects might elicit a response from Horace. Be prepared to praise him even if he's playing with the toilet brush.

There are many reasons why a dog will not play. Sometimes they are inadvertently taught to stay away from toys. A possessive older dog will teach a puppy "All toys are mine. Touch one at your peril."

Above: *Take a favorite toy to the beach, on a walk in the woods or out into the yard. You can have an energetic game with your dog anywhere and anytime and when you get home, spoil yourselves with a treat and a cuddle.*

A puppy may be scolded for chewing a dishcloth and he will never tug again. Or a puppy is teased with a toy but never given the chance to get hold of it so gives up trying.

Toys are an important tool in agility, but they are not the only ones. If Horace likes worming tablets, he's bound to like treats, so that may the answer.

You're Never Too Old

Q *I'm no spring chicken. I'm a little fatter and a little slower than I was 20 years ago, but otherwise I'm a very fit senior citizen. My Boxer, Barney, is in his prime and would love agility. Would my attempt to run around a field embarrass him and would I have to wear Lycra?*

A Don't let your age prevent you from joining an agility club. Start slowly if you are afraid of tripping over your shoe laces. After a few lessons, running will start to feel more natural and you'll be more confident in your own abilities. Everyone feels a little self-conscious at first running a dog, but this soon passes especially when you see how willing other people are to act silly to keep their dog's attention. It's people who get embarrassed, not their pets. Barney will love you no matter what. Speak to him in a funny voice or jump up and down on the spot if this is what he likes. He won't be able to take his eyes off you.

It's Barney that has to do all the running and jumping, not you. He's the one that your instructor and class will be watching. Especially if you teach him to work independently of you on the course. He'll be able to cover the distance to leave you far behind but you will be able to take all the short cuts so as to catch him up.

Running fast is not so important for the handler in agility, but knowing the course is. You must know that the weaves follow the A-frame or that there is a left turn after the tunnel. If you teach Barney to follow your directions, your speed won't matter. The clock stops when Barney, not you, crosses the line!

Above: *There is no age limit for agility. Strut your stuff with pride and show those youngsters how it's done. Your dog will love you all the more for taking him to agility classes. It's so much more fun than sitting on your lap watching TV.*

You don't have to wear Lycra if it makes you feel uncomfortable. Anything that allows you to move freely and keeps out the cold will do the job. As far as Barney is concerned, anything you wear with treats in the pocket is fashionable. I have seen many 20-year-olds that should have left their Lycra in the closet, and I have been beaten by many retirees who tell me that when I get to their age, I'll finally lose all my inhibitions and be a great handler! Let agility liberate you!

Agility's Juniors

Q *My 14-year-old year old daughter Judy has a pet Cocker Spaniel called Kylie and they are best friends. Judy would like to take Kylie to agility classes but I am worried that she may not be old enough to train a dog. Are there classes that cater for children?*

A If Judy is old enough to look after a puppy, she is old to join an agility club. It is committed children like Judy who become the agility handlers of the future. Young dog lovers need to be encouraged to get involved in an activity with their pet that will not only be fun but teach them something about the care and training of dogs. Agility has much to offer.

Above: *If you get a puppy, you will always have a best friend while you are growing up.*

Classes Judy will start with an introductory or beginner's course of agility lessons and once she has learned all the obstacles and is proficient at course work, she will be able to progress through the classes. Her classmates are likely to be other adults of all ages and backgrounds. Not all agility clubs run classes especially for youngsters, but more and more do, operating as weekend or afterschool activities. It depends on what is available in your area.

Sportsmanship Part of growing up is learning about winning and losing and entering an agility competition is a great way to start. Children have a choice of classes. They can compete in standard classes against adults (often beating them) as well as special classes whose entry is limited; for example, "handlers must be under 18 years of age." There are a number of tournaments, finals and league tables run just for young people.

New friends Agility is a great way to meet new people and share a passion for dogs. Many of the agility magazines have a section written for and by junior handlers. Here Judy will find all the information she needs – what shows are scheduled, what classes to enter, as well as special events for young people like weekend training camps. Judy will have plenty to do with her new buddies instead of homework.

Agility parents are keen that their kids should get involved and learn to run the family dog. But beware – agility kids often want their parents to take hold of the leash. Till Judy gets her driver's licence, you will probably be chauffeuring Judy to training and shows.

Left: *Learning to care and train a dog can teach young people important life skills.*

His Highness and Her Majesty

Q My husband and I have two Border Collies, one for him and one for me. Bliss is a dear sweet girl and my dog. Bonus is about two years younger. He's a bit of a delinquent but dotes on my husband. We are looking for a hobby to share and thought about taking the dogs to agility class. Is this a good idea?

A It's a great idea! Agility will keep you both fit and give you lots to talk about over dinner. There are a number of successful husband-and-wife teams competing in agility. Here are some tips to make sure that you become the King and Queen of agility.

Below: When husband and wife agree, can there be any doubt in a dog's mind that "Stay" means "Stay"?

One handler, one dog It's hard for a dog to learn new things and it's even harder if more than one person is telling her what to do. Bliss is your baby so you stick with her and let your husband work with Bonus. Don't treat or fuss over each other's dogs in class. It will confuse them if the commands are coming from one direction and the rewards appear from another.

Instructors instruct If the instructor is talking to your husband, don't interrupt. Let your husband offer his own excuses for not doing his homework. Never say, "Do it like this" or "This always works for me." It is the instructor's job to make corrections and suggestions. Your husband will be more receptive to criticism from the instructor than his wife which he is more likely to take personally.

Agility class is fun If you have been arguing all week about who left the top off the toothpaste, don't continue the fight at agility class. Your dogs will pick up on the discord and get stressed. Agility is not the place for arguments, so leave your troubles at home. It is also rather embarrassing for your classmates if you indulge in a shouting match.

Lend a hand Help each other. Take turns toileting the dogs, chopping up treats for training or filling

Right: *A dog's loyalty may lie with the agility equipment rather than the handler. This collie would work as happily for his mistress as he would for his master as long as he can beat them to the finishing line.*

in entry forms. Be supportive and sensitive. Dog training will always be plagued with highs and lows. Sometimes a run goes really well and at other times disaster strikes. If your husband is having difficulty teaching his dog a new obstacle, don't brag about how Bliss found it really easy. It won't help.

Wait your turn It is hard not to be a little jealous if your husband brings home trophy after trophy while your dog's only consistent quality is

getting eliminated. Friendly rivalry is one thing. Hiding his running shoes and the car keys is another. Your turn on the podium will come.

As you become more experienced agility competitors you might divide tasks even further. Perhaps one of you is better at training youngsters while the other has nerves of steel, a good competitor. Whatever happens, remember that you've taken up agility to enrich your marriage – not to end it with divorce!

Left: *Don't be tempted to shift the blame for a fault to your dog. Your wife told you the pole would drop if you continued to push for speed on the corner.*

Chapter Three

SOLVING PROBLEMS

Agility training is not always smooth sailing. Some problems are common and the result of youth and inexperience. With luck, they disappear with maturity. Other problems are unique and rare. You'll see them all if you attend an agility class and you'll start asking questions to learn about your pet. Why does your dog pee on the tunnel? Why does he try and limbo dance under the fences? At home, your dog is a quiet member of the household, but at agility club he won't stop barking. And you need an explanation for other odd quirks of canine personality. He is the only dog in the class that perches on the A-frame and won't come down and what's this obsession with hats? By trying to understand your dog's behavior and find solutions to your problems, you will also find out about yourself...

Barking Mad

Q *I have just started agility with my very eager Labrador Spice who barks incessantly! In the beginning I didn't want to yell at him for barking because I was afraid it would dampen his enthusiasm. But now it is a real problem and any tips would be greatly appreciated.*

A Take out your ear plugs. What is Spice telling you? The barking can mean various things.

"I'm so excited to be here!" I think this type of bark is permissible in agility. It expresses joy in life and anticipation of good things to come. I don't object to this kind of barking in class. You hear it at every agility show, so get used to it. However, as an instructor, I would not compete with it during lessons. No woofs when I'm talking or my pearls of wisdom will go unheard. Teach Spice to speak and to be quiet on command, divert his attention with a toy or simply remove him temporarily from the training area which is triggering his excited barks.

"I'm so excited I could eat you!" This type of bark verges on the hysterical. Take it as a warning that Spice has wound himself up and could explode. He may even try to nip you. He won't mean to hurt you, but he just won't be able to help himself. Put Spice in a Down stay until he has gained control of himself.

"You are SO frustrating!" If you hear this bark, it is because you have slowed down on the course or lost your way. Make sure you know where you are going and what you are doing. Plan each run in advance and execute it confidently and positively. Your commands should be clear and your timing immaculate. Spice won't be baffled and he'll have to work to keep up with you.

"Come on, come on, COME ON!" Spice is pressuring you to get a move on. He is even more frustrated and about to burst because you are hesitating again. There is a hint of desperation and his body posture might be a tad confrontational. If you don't hurry up and decide which fence to send him over, he'll decide for you. As your handling improves, these situations should reduce in number. In the meantime, turn your back on Spice. Go to the end of the line till he has regained his composure. Leave the building if you have to. You don't do agility with dogs that try to handle you over the course. That is your job. When Spice is quiet, take up where you left off, on your terms. Teach him that silence is the starter whistle for agility.

For some dogs, barking is as natural as breathing. It can be as addictive as gambling, alcohol or drugs. A spray of water might help break the barking habit. But if Spice is making noise because he is frustrated or confused on the agility course, you need to concentrate on sharpening your handling skills to help Spice become a quieter dog.

Below: *Given the choice would you rather bark or play ball? Encourage your dog to think with his mind, not his mouth.*

Snipping The Nipping

Q *I have a very fast and excitable collie, Smudge. Recently, he has started to nip me if I slow down or hesitate on the agility course. At the moment I grit my teeth and keep going. The biggest nip is saved for the end of the round when he's actually come close to removing items of my clothing. If this keeps up, I'm going to have to give up agility. Please help.*

A I see many dogs at shows nipping their handlers. Some people learn to live with it. They have mastered the art of crossing their arms to protect the more sensitive parts of their body as they surge over the finish line.

Herding sheep
Nipping is in a collie's job description. Giving a particularly slow member of the flock a nip is all part of a day's work. When you slow down or hesitate in agility, Smudge is nipping you to get you to move faster or change direction. He is herding you round the course and, unlike sheep, we humans haven't any wool to protect our flesh. We puncture! Make sure that you are doing the shepherding. Don't give Smudge a reason to harass you.

Know where you are going Plan your run in advance. You won't have time to think on the course. Smudge is quick and impatient for instructions. If you get lost or hesitate, he will start pressing you with his teeth to make a decision. Smudge doesn't have the map. You do.

Tell Smudge what to do Smudge is not a mind reader. Fail to direct him with a command or body signal and he will start nipping to remind you that he needs orders. The better you are at steering, the less Smudge will nip.

Don't stop if you make a mistake If you halt, Smudge will have a reason to start complaining with his teeth. Finish and then, if necessary, re-start the sequence from the beginning.

Speed up your handling
Nipping often starts because the dog has become confident on the agility field more quickly than the handler. Don't try to slow Smudge down. Learn to drive your canine missile while he is in top gear. You won't have time to look in your rear-view mirror.

Don't anticipate a nip If you worry that Smudge is going to nip you, you will be less focused on the course and you'll slow down. You'll be thinking about your personal comfort rather than mapping the course. Smudge will know your mind is elsewhere and bring you back to the agility ring with a nip.

Still nipping? If Smudge forgets himself in the heat of the moment and nips, down him and stand still until he has regained his composure. You don't play agility with a dog that nips.

I am sure that with preparation and practice you will be able to improve your handling skills and Smudge will lose the urge to nip. Good luck nipping his bad habits in the bud!

Little Nipper

Q *I hope you can help me and my dog, Gunner. Gunner bites the end of the seesaw as he dismounts. He bites the last weave pole as he exits. He also bites the hurdle poles but not as often as when he started agility training. Gunner is a rescue dog and has always been difficult, but at least he has stopped biting my hands and feet. He loves agility.*

A If Gunner loves agility, he must stop sinking his teeth into the equipment. Take him out of the ring before he chips a tooth. Which of the following dog types is Gunner?

Below: *The dog knows where he wants to go but do you? Take the lead!*

Dog number one Dog number one starts well, but half way through the course picks a pole off the jump wings and proceeds to parade it round the ring in his mouth. No need for a ribbon. He already has his trophy. The spectators love it. There is laughter and applause as the dog plays the clown and his handler begs him to drop it. I suspect that this dog has inadvertently learned that pole-picking is a good way to get attention. What might have started as a way to relieve stress has turned into a great act that has everyone laughing.

Do you see similarities between Gunner and this dog? If Gunner picks up a pole, leave the ring and go sit in the parking lot. Don't join in the game. In contrast, if Gunner negotiates the obstacles as the designers intended, be delighted. Fuss and praise him. Gunner will soon learn the new rules and will want to stay a player. Also address the problem of stress. Improve your handling skills and make sure you are always making the best of your communication channels.

Dog number two The dog drags his handler to the start, takes his own line on the course and attacks obstacles in his path, especially the ones that slow him down. He vents his frustration at his handler's inability to keep up directly onto the agility equipment. When the handler crosses the finish line and attempts to collect his dog to attach the lead, the dog snaps at him but misses. The handler is oblivious. I would guess that this dog is very sensitive to movement and has bitten his owner in the past. His bite has never really been inhibited, simply displaced onto the agility equipment.

Does this sound like Gunner? Gunner knows he can snap at the seesaw before you can stop him. Correction only fuels his desire to do it again. He loves agility but you frustrate him because you allow him to go his own way one minute and the next you are reprimanding him for something that happened earlier on the course. I think you have pushed ahead in agility too quickly and missed out many dog training fundamentals. Also, I wonder if your problems in the agility arena aren't tied up with more general problems at home. Consider consulting a canine behaviorist and shelving agility for a little while.

Left: *So many poles and so little time to collect them. Don't let your dog clown around. Poles are for jumping, not retrieving.*

Heel!

Q *Flynn, my big Border Collie, is doing well this season, but I have one problem. He attaches himself to my foot with his teeth at the end of each round. He never does it in training, but always at shows. I'm only five foot tall and weigh 112 pounds (51.2kg). You can imagine how difficult this makes it to leave the ring with any dignity! Should I yell at him in front of the judge? If I praise him for doing a nice round, he might think I'm praising him for grabbing my foot.*

A Puppies love to chew old sneakers and chase dangling laces. No wonder they grow up with a foot fetish and take it with them to the agility ring. Flynn gets excited at training, but he can contain himself. The buzz of competition tips the balance. He is not nipping your trunk or arms, but grabbing your feet. It's not as daring, but it's still challenging. And, once Flynn has caught a foot, I bet the spectators chuckle at your predicament. So, not only has Flynn been allowed to chomp your sneakers, he has been rewarded for it with laughter.

react if you praised him in the middle of the course at obstacle sixteen, thanked the judge for his time and left the ring (with your foot intact)?

Fake ring Set up a "competition" ring and have a friend wait at the finish with a water pistol to give Flynn a soaking if he dives at your shoes. However, Flynn may be so determined that he won't mind getting wet.

Stand still Flynn will not have a moving target to chase. His attacks on your feet may continue for a while, but if they fail to get a response from you they should eventually cease.

Target a toy Encourage Flynn to have something in his mouth besides your foot. Offer him a toy at the end of his rounds in training and at shows.

Down After each round, whether in training or at a show, put Flynn in the Down. Wait a few seconds for him to collect his wits. Praise him and then release him onto a toy or give him a treat.

Try the unexpected I wonder how Flynn would

A nasty taste Spray your sneakers with something unpalatable, like mustard or bitter apple spray. It may not stop the more aroused foot-fetish dogs, but it's worth a try.

Bare feet Run in bare feet. It will strengthen your resolve to find a solution to the problem.

Ignore it The more you try and push Flynn off your feet, the more firmly he will try to attach himself. Arguing with you is a rewarding game played at the end of an agility round that breaks all the rules of good behavior. If you stop playing, it won't be fun anymore. But it will take time for the message to sink in.

What A Drag!

Q *I do agility and obedience with my young working sheep dog, Quasar. She's a good girl until we get to training. She's so excited to get to agility that she lunges and pulls on the lead. I'm afraid she is going to drag me into the ring. After about 15 minutes, she calms down a bit and starts working. What should I do?*

Ignore her Quasar gets excited in anticipation of having lots of fun in agility. If she is pulling on her lead at the start of your class, don't yank it or yell at her. You will only make matters worse. She'll be more determined to leap around and it will take longer for her to settle the next time you go to class. Loop her lead over a fence post and turn your back on her.

A I'm glad to hear that Quasar is enthusiastic, but her pulling must be checked or you could end up with one arm longer than the other!

Turning your back on your dog is the worst punishment you can inflict on your pet. You have withdrawn your attention and worse, he won't be able to see your face.

When she quits lunging and is quiet, return to her and give her a treat. She'll soon get the message – loose leads are good. A dog that walks in a controlled way to the start line gets to run the course.

Work mode Like most collies, Quasar is keen to work. Help her put on her thinking cap earlier by asking her to perform some tricks or basic obedience exercises before you start your agility class. Do some heelwork in the parking lot and continue working her through the door into your training venue. Teach Quasar to watch you on command. This is something that you can do quietly and calmly. It will encourage her to focus on you and give you a reason to reward her when she gives you eye contact.

Head collar/halter There are a number of different types of head halters on the market; for example, the Halti or Gentle Leader. Not only do head halters prevent your dog from pulling you into traffic, but they seem to have a calming effect on the dog. Many dogs wear a head halters at agility shows on their way to the exercise area or while they are lining up to enter the ring. Their handlers can concentrate on the course rather than trying to stop their dogs lunging on the lead. Buy one for Quasar.

I think your dog will settle down as she matures.

She sounds eager to please and still has four feet on the ground. Some dogs arrive at agility class excited and become increasingly demented. They throw themselves into orbit trailing their owners behind them. Quasar is dragging you to the launch pad. Teach her that a loose lead means that she will be first in the line for the jumps and tunnels.

3 *When the handler halts, the dog sits but is ready to move off again as soon as the handler steps forward.*

2 *The dog takes his cue from his handler and maintains his position by the leg, neither pulling ahead or to the side.*

1 *Dogs that learn to walk on a loose lead are a pleasure to own. Heelwork is a basic obedience exercise that teaches the dog to walk on the handler's left hand side.*

Above: *All dressed up and ready to go for a walk to the park or training class. A head halter is the must-have accessory for every fashion-conscious dog that pulls on the lead. And they can be bought in a variety of colors for special occasions.*

Learning To Line Up

Q My problem is not with agility, but lining up. My rescue dog Felix turns into a demented monster and no one will stand next to me near the ring. I don't blame them. Can you help?

A Lining up is an important part of agility. Dogs should be able to wait patiently and quietly for their turn whether they be at their local training club or at an agility show. It's not always easy. The sight of another dog working is very exciting and dogs that are sensitive to movement can be aroused to fever-pitch, expressing their frustration through barking.

A groom Ask a friend to hold Felix away from the ring while you line up. If he is a Momma's boy, he will be looking for you rather than watching other dogs run. But remember that as soon as you have hold of the lead, Felix will turn his attention back to what's happening in the ring.

A head halter A head halter will give you more control in the line. It will help you battle the more severe symptoms of Felix's fidgeting, while you work on attention exercises at home.

Attention exercises Teach Felix to pay attention and watch you, not the other dogs. Start in your living room where there are few distractions. Each time Felix looks at you, click and offer a treat. Use a high value food reward like diced cheese. A few seconds attention will do and training sessions should be short and intense. Once Felix gets the idea, he won't be able to take his eyes off you. Progress slowly. Will Felix look at you when he is sitting on your left, on your right and in front of you? Eventually you will be able to perform these attention exercises in a noisy line at an agility show. They don't take up much room and won't be disruptive. They will allow you to enter the ring with Felix by your side, relaxed and under control.

Sights and sounds Be aware that it is not only in the line that Felix can hear and see agility. If he can watch round after round from the back of your car, he'll be truly frantic before you even attach his lead. He's lost it and so have you. Cover the windows of your car or park somewhere else out of view.

The experienced handler will practice lining up with their young dogs as part of their agility program. Although their dogs may be too young to compete, they will walk their youngsters around the showground and practice a few obedience basics. They know that the earlier they train their dogs to pay attention and ignore exciting distractions in their environment, the easier it will be for them later. Felix already knows that hurdles mean agility and he demands to be let loose on them, so your task will be harder.

Help Felix relax in the line and you will have a dog that listens for your commands and watches for your body signals. A clear round will be much closer.

Below: *Good manners in the line ensures that everyone has a good time both at agility training and at shows.*

Crazy Collies

Q *My two-year-old collie, Blue, is crazy. He gets more and more wound up as he travels around the course and ends up a slobbering wreck. It's worse at shows. He gets hyper and so do I. Blue knocks poles and he flies his contacts. The more excited he becomes, the less interested he is in me. How can I keep him calm? Is there something I can give him to help him relax?*

A Ah, those mad, crazy collies! Blue is discharging his pent-up adrenalin in an exciting environment in the only way he knows how – by launching himself into orbit.

Herbal remedies Many handlers swear that herbal remedies such as skullcap or valerian help their dogs calm down. But before you give Blue any pills or potions, it's a good idea to have a chat with your vet first. He is familiar with your dog and the best person to advise you on different kinds of medication. And remember that although herbal remedies might help Blue relax, he still may be unable to contain himself in a highly charged, stimulating environment like agility.

Keep cool and calm Dogs are very quick to pick up and act on a handler's excitement. Don't let adrenalin turn you into a nervous wreck who paces the floor muttering to yourself. Sit down and shut up. Blue will follow suit.

Slow motion Don't aggravate Blue's excitement by trying to win the class. Forget your time. Don't hurry. Take giant steps instead of little busy ones. You will feel like you are running in slow motion, but you will be well within the course time. When you try to do things as fast as possible, your adrenalin levels rise. Keep them lowered by thinking "slow."

No reward For many agility-loving dogs, the next obstacle on the course rewards the previous. If Blue makes an error, mark it with a word or phrase like "Shame" or "Oh dear." Then leave the ring taking your dog with you. Blue will quickly come down to Earth. And use your marker phrase accurately. It's no good saying it because Blue has missed contact when he has already jumped the next set of hurdles. Moreover, make sure that the mistake is his and not yours. Did the dog go the wrong way because he was over-excited or because your command was late and you were out of position on the course?

Praise Take the time to praise your dog calmly if he gets it right. You do this in class; don't forget to do it in the ring. Blue needs some kind words to reinforce the correct behavior when he is under a judge. Don't take something like good contacts for granted. You won't get eliminated if you smile and call Blue a "clever boy." If you have already been eliminated somewhere else on the course, why not take the opportunity to stroke him on the head too?

I think you are as much a victim of the excitement of a show as Blue is. You feed off each other. A little nervous buzz is good for you – too much and you and your dog end up out of control.

Ballistic Missiles

Q *My young collie, Pippin, loves agility. Too much! She knows which night we go to training and as soon as we set off in the car, she goes ballistic. We can hardly get through the door, she is so excited to have arrived. I spent a lot of time working on the lead over the A-frame, dog walk and seesaw, but off-lead she misses all her contacts. She is so fast – what can I do?*

A Count your blessings. You are lucky to have a dog with so much enthusiasm and energy. But don't let Pippin's excitement turn her into a raving lunatic.

Start out calm Before you leave home, make sure that Pippin is still on planet Earth and you are in control. Tell her to sit before you attach the lead or open the car door. Don't allow her to race or pull you into class – try a head halter. Don't let her run around the field or arena while the equipment is being set out for the lesson.

Class size Dogs that are susceptible to excitement can benefit from smaller classes or private lessons. The mere sight of other dogs having a good time can tip the balance and transform a well-behaved pet into a whirling dervish. When Pippin's feet are firmly on the ground and there are fewer distractions, you can learn more and gain confidence in your ability to train and handle your dog. This confidence eventually enables you to cope in any situation, with any number of exciting things going on in the background.

Short and simple Running long courses before Pippin has built up some mental stamina can blow her mind. It's similar to serving a feast to a famine victim – impossible to eat it all, but you try anyway.

Far better to praise and reward Pippin after she has successfully completed a short sequence than to start pulling your hair out when she has gone crazy over twenty obstacles and made five errors.

Bridge the gap There is a big jump between doing contacts on the lead and doing them without it. Bridge the gap. Can Pippin perform contacts without the lead in a short sequence? Think about what you will do if she jumps off. Doing course work too early encourages many handlers to ignore mistakes and carry on to the last obstacle. It's such a relief just to finish! But it can lead to bad habits and undo all the good work you have done in training.

Pippin is still young and has the most important ingredient for an agility dog – she loves it. Take your time and make sure that all her basic skills are sound so that you will have a firm foundation to build new ones. There is still lots for you both to learn. In the meantime, you and Pippin can still have lots of fun together.

Above: *Don't push too hard or fast with a young dog. Paying only lip service to the basics can create problems later on.*

Hot Pursuit

Q *How can I stop Trim, my Belgian Shepherd, acting aggressively when she sees other dogs running? She looks desperate to chase them, especially if it is a really fast, noisy dog. I have to hold on tight to the lead and it would be so embarrassing if she pulled out of my hands. She's normally such a sweetie, but I don't know what she would do if she got loose.*

A This is an embarrassing but common problem with dogs that are easily stimulated by agility. They see a fast dog whizzing his way around the course and they can't take their eyes off it. Who knows what would happen if the lead snapped. Would the dogs climb the A-frame together as a double act? Or would there be a big fight and bloodshed? Your problem is not just ruining your own enjoyment of agility, but it could potentially jeopardize the safety of dogs on the course.

Attention exercises If Trim is looking at you, she will be missing the visual stimulation of watching agility dogs that triggers her unruly behavior in the line. The "Watch" exercise is a good place to start and she should be rewarded generously with her favorite treats for looking up at your face. Whenever and wherever Trim hears the "Watch" command, she should fix her eyes on her owner. Is she watching you?

Above: *A Belgian Shepherd gaining speed with every jump. It's a race to the finish, not another ring!*

Turn away. Has she moved around so that she can watch you? Yeah! Give her a treat as a reward. Drop a ball on the floor. Did she look at her toy or did she continue to look up at you? Reward if it's you.

Concentration exercises You can't teach a dog anything unless you have its attention. If you have practiced the attention exercises in different environments and gradually increased the number of distractions, Trim should be ready for action at agility training. Before starting a sequence of jumps, ask Trim to pay attention. If you get it, proceed. Concentration will be improved and you will find that Trim is eager to please you. She will learn new things more quickly and remember them for longer.

Movement and speed exercises Trim is aroused by the movement and speed of other dogs running agility courses. Make that work to your advantage by moving the focus from other dogs to you and the agility equipment. Make Trim chase you for her favorite toy. Are your legs faster than hers? Race her to the end of a line of jumps. Can you beat her to the other side of the dog walk? Give yourself a head start so she has to pull out all the stops to catch you. Don't let Trim waste energy chasing other dogs when she could be chasing you.

I am sure if won't take long to redirect Trim's focus. You are probably much faster and prettier than any of the dogs Trim has been watching at agility!

Herding Instinct

Q *I have just started to train Marvel, my Border Collie. He is a year old and works beautifully and I think he could be really good at agility. However, if there is another dog running on the course, he wants to herd it. I can't keep his attention focused on me. If he is not on the lead, he will rush over and try to round it up. What can I do?*

A Agility enthusiasts love Border Collies because of their herding instinct. It enables them to work independently and use their initiative on an agility course. But it can also land them in hot water if

Above: *Collies need an occupation and their favorite games are chasing and herding – sheep, children or toys!*

they decide to round up the children. Start thinking like a shepherd if you have a sheep dog. You want to be able to work your dog over fences with the same skill and control that a shepherd uses to direct his dog to box and pen a few lambs.

Shepherd's crook You don't need a shepherd's crook – just a good collar and lead. Keep Marvel on the lead when you are in class. You don't want him to interfere with other dogs and it's not his turn yet! When you are confident that he is waiting for your cue to start work, let him off his lead to perform an exercise.

Shepherd's hut Train at home where there are no distractions. Marvel is young and bound to be stimulated and excited by other dogs running around. Cultivate control, increase his attention span and teach him concentration through basic obedience exercises or trick training. As Marvel becomes more mature, educated and well-mannered, he will become less interested in distractions and more willing to focus on you and his agility. That's how he scores brownie points. Herding other dogs is a real non-starter.

The sheep In lieu of sheep, buy some tennis balls. Collies are often obsessed with toys and you can use a ball to keep his attention on you and not the other dogs in class. Play with the ball at home and use it as a reward for completing an exercise in class. The more agility you do, the more your dog will love not only the tennis ball but all the equipment, especially tunnels. Try treating him with his favorite obstacle instead of a ball at the end of a difficult jump sequence. Many collies are so equipment-orientated that they are oblivious to everything else going on around them.

Above: *Two collies work as a team to keep the sheep in a bunch and eagerly await the shepherd's next command.*

Above: *Agility is a good substitute for sheep. Some collies become so obstacle-driven that they think of little else.*
Right: *Toys are a great way to take your collie's mind off sheep and redirect his attention towards you.*

Honest shepherd Any honest shepherd will admit to having a few problems training his dog. So don't get disheartened. Marvel is bound to make mistakes and misbehave. Give him time to learn what is the right place to aim his energy and enthusiasm. Make sure you dish out big rewards when he is offering you his best behavior and really trying to get it right on the agility course.

Be patient and keep training. Make your collie's herding instinct work for you rather than against you.

Shutting Down

Q *I have been training my terrier in agility for about 18 months. Millie is a good girl. However, sometimes she shuts down at shows. She sits in front of a fence and refuses to move. It can also happen at the start of training or if we are learning something new. Why is she doing this?*

A Millie is sitting on the start line and you give the signal to commence. Nothing happens. Has she gone deaf? Why is your eager and competent dog rooted to the spot? If Millie starts shutting down on a regular basis, your confidence in the ring will be shattered making matters ten times worse. Shut down happens for a number of reasons.

Stage fright Competitions are always a bit daunting for a young dog. You are expecting Millie to jump as well as keep an eye on what's going on around her – a hustling crowd, strange dogs and the food truck. She's not yet ready to multi-task in this way.

Perfectionist If this type of dog does anything at all, she wants to make sure she gets it right. Unfortunately, the learning process is fraught with pitfalls – especially in agility. Every course is different with so many variations based on 20 obstacles. Millie has to take risks and have the courage to make mistakes. The dog that is a perfectionist can shut down if there is the possibility of making an error.

Confidence The more confident Millie is in her own ability to execute the obstacles and in your skill at directing her over a course, the less likely she will be to shut down. Confidence comes with time, but it can also be fostered by training simple exercises which will give you an excuse to give her lots of praise. Repetition is another tool that you can use. If Millie performs an exercise hesitantly, do it again and then one more time for luck. She will know where she is going and get faster and surer-footed each time.

Motivation Once your dog has shut down, the lights are out. There is nothing on Earth that is going to switch them back on. It is too late to dangle a tug toy in her face or wave a treat under her nose. Treats and toys are positive training tools that should not become negatively associated with times of stress or confusion.

Bonding The more Millie trusts you, the better your working relationship will be. Spend quality time with her. Learn how she ticks and she will reciprocate by working out how to do her best for you. Instead of thinking "I can't do this. I'll get it all wrong," Millie will think "I'll try because you'll be there to help get it right."

Many handlers become frustrated and impatient when their dog shuts down. You are to be congratulated for not thinking that your dog is merely being naughty. Bravo for trying to understand why it happens before looking for remedies.

Above: *Refuse a jump? No, never! Switch your dog on to the joys of jumping with patience and understanding.*

Under Pressure

Q *Ollie, my Belgian Shepherd, and I have been doing agility for two years now and lately he seems to hate being in the ring. When we started competing, Ollie was so excited that I had trouble keeping up with him. I've got him back under control, but now he enters the ring looking stressed and pressured. His head hangs down and his tail is tucked under. I've always been nervous which doesn't help and now I'm getting frustrated by Ollie's behavior.*

A Dogs take their cue from their owners. I fall asleep and snore in front of the TV, so do my dogs. I stress and my dogs stress. We tend to forget how sensitive our pets are to our state of mind, our body language, the tone of our voice. The sweat on your palms tells your dog that you are nervous just like his tail tucked under his belly tells you that he's stressed. You aren't helping each other!

Have Ollie checked by a vet Whether the onset of Ollie's reluctance to jump was sudden or not, it is possible that there is a medical problem at the root of his behavior. Have him checked before you start any retraining.

Learn to relax So easy to say, but so hard to do! But you need to take the lead. Learn to be cool, calm and relaxed and Ollie will follow suit. Recite a mantra, meditate or hold a lucky charm. Whatever will help you to be in control of you nerves.

Practice competing under show conditions
Enter a simulated show, sign up for a training day or

Above: *Agility competition is about being a performer. Make it look fun and your dog will take his cue from you.*

join a new club. All of these will get you and Ollie accustomed to performing in front of strangers on different equipment in strange venues. You'll have to learn to cope with a little bit of pressure and this is a good way to start.

Have fun Ignore Ollie's mistakes. Don't expect him to be precise. Encourage him to take risks and praise him for independent actions. If you want to have a game in the middle of a round – do it. Let him jump up on you or chase you round the seesaw. You'll both have a giggle and loosen up.

Start rewarding attitude in training If you want a dog with a wagging tail, give him a treat when he wags it. If you want a dog with enthusiasm, let your control slip. So what if Ollie misses a weave entry. Do you want a dog that zooms through the poles or one that reluctantly bends in and out? Reward enthusiasm and speed.

As Ollie's attitude becomes more positive, you will have less reason to feel nervous and you will both look forward to stepping up to the start line with renewed confidence.

21st Century Schizoid Dog

Q *I have a problem with my hound, Rowan. We start our run and all goes well. She is really good. A superstar. Then, she goes hyper. She fools around and runs around in circles at a hundred miles an hour. If I plead with her to come back and hold out a treat, she runs straight past me. Does Rowan have a split personality?*

A Rowan sounds a delightful challenge. A hound going loopy in the ring is funny at first, less so the next loop and eventually plain infuriating. I think Rowan is more misunderstood than naughty.

Above: *She's on track to finish the course but if the pressure is too much she could start playing loop the loop.*

When? At what point does your superstar lose her grip on the course?
- Does Rowan start fooling around when you've made a mistake? If she has disappointed you, she'll provide you with a few crazy moments to lighten the mood.
- Does Rowan play loop the loop towards the end of class? If she has been an angel for the first half of training, it may be that she just doesn't have the mental reserves to be good for a minute longer.
- Does Rowan go hyper when confronted by something new? It could be her way of letting you know that she is confused and puzzled. She doesn't understand what you want her to do.

Mistakes If Rowan runs past a jump in class, it's not the end of the world. Don't stop and shrug your shoulders in despair. The minute you do, Rowan will start orbiting the equipment. Instead of calling her back to redo the jump she has missed, keep going and finish the sequence. Go to the end of the line, take a few deep breaths and ask your instructor how to get it right next time.

Concentration Build up Rowan's mental reserves. Concentration is hard work. If Rowan's had enough and is tired, she'll start fooling around and acting like a clown. Keep her focused with frequent rewards. Break up exercises with play so she can recharge her brain batteries for more learning. Shorten her agility sessions. Quit when she is still wanting more. If 18 obstacles blow her mind, train over ten or less. Add one more obstacle, then another until Rowan can complete a full course.

Confusion Rowan will stop acting like a lunatic when she is confident that she knows what you want her to do. Believe it or not, dogs try to please. Does it take you five attempts to get your weave entry on a course? Frustrated and confused, Rowan does a few laps of honor round the ring instead of making a sixth attempt. She's not being naughty. She doesn't understand what to do in the poles. Practice weave entries as a static exercise and she will reward you by getting it right on the course.

Relax Rowan doesn't have split personality. Running round the ring is her way of coping with stress. Relax and enjoy each other. Try and match her enthusiasm and I'm sure you will be bringing home a ribbon soon.

Sniffy Dog

Q *My Jack Russell cross, Susie, is driving me crazy! We've just started to compete and I never know what she will do in the ring. She measures only ten inches, so her nose is very close to the ground, which results in her finding interesting smells. She often ignores me and follows them. All she wants to do is sniff. What can be so interesting on the ground?*

A Sniffing is a big and important part of being a dog. Susie is not being naughty – just doing what comes naturally. She's not consciously trying to get you mad by tracking a mouse instead of climbing the A-frame. Try to figure out why she is sniffing.

If agility is boring… Susie will find something else that is interesting to do, like sniffing. Too many repetitions and too few rewards can make exercises tedious and dull. Make agility fun. Give Susie a reason to hold her nose in the air and reason to believe that there is nothing else she would rather be doing.

If you are boring… You will lose Susie's attention and she will start searching the ground for smells. Be an exciting companion and playmate rather than a stern disciplinarian. If you fall down in the mud and Susie jumps up and down on your tummy, try to see the funny side. Laugh with your dog.

If Susie is stressed… She will try and find some way to relax. Sniffing is a natural and comforting activity that, like most dogs, she does well. Confronted with an obstacle course at a strange venue with the whole world watching, young Susie may feel out of her depth. She sniffs to stress bust.

If you are stressed… Susie will pick up on your discomfort. She'll sniff in sympathy. You, like Susie, will find agility shows a bit daunting at first. But you will soon get used to it. Relax with your new agility friends. Sometimes talking about pre-competition nerves with someone else in the same boat makes them go away.

Dogs that think with their nose rather than their brain, can be a liability in agility. I've no doubt that the more agility you do, the more comfortable you will both feel and the less Susie will sniff. In the meantime,

- Train at a venue that is relatively smell-free. Do you train after the puppy class (more treats end up on the floor than in their mouths)?
- Teach Susie a "Watch" command so that she will look up at you and not at the ground.
- Add the "Leave" command to your tool box. Susie should withdraw her nose from whatever smell she is investigating when she hears it.
- And keep practicing your recall. When Susie takes off on an olfactory trail, she will return to you before she reaches its end.

Be patient. Your dog will soon be demonstrating her true potential in the ring.

Below: *No sniffing! On the seesaw a dog must concentrate on balancing while putting one paw in front of the other.*

Party Animal

Q *I have an 18-month-old Labrador called Charlie. He started agility a couple of months ago and was excellent, but lately he has turned into a social butterfly. He ducks and dives in front of me and then sprints out of the ring in great excitement looking for four-legged friends to play chase with him. As soon as he gets a little distance from me he runs off to party. What should I do?*

A Charlie is still a baby. He doesn't have years of agility behind him and the world out there still holds surprises and temptations.

Make agility fun Don't take it personally when Charlie accepts an invitation to boogie with a friend off course. Continue to teach Charlie that the best place to party is with you in the ring. Make training irresistible fun and call a halt to training sessions while Charlie still wants more – not when he's exhausted and has lost interest.

Distraction training The temptations at agility shows are many – squeaky toys, dropped titbits, new people and barking dogs. Start distraction training by inviting some friends to watch you in class. If Charlie leaves the ring to visit them,

call him back and give him a treat for returning to you quickly. When you are in the ring, reward him for being there with lots of play and treats. He will soon learn to keep his attention on you.

Stressed or confused If a dog is stressed or confused, distractions can be very hard to resist. If Charlie doesn't fully understand the rules of the agility game, he'll opt to play something easier that comes naturally, like rough and tumble with his canine buddies. Remember, he's confused not naughty. Running out of the ring may be Charlie's way of telling you that your instructions have not been clear or that the task you have set him is too difficult.

Great expectations Charlie may feel pressured. Are you expecting too much of him? Just because he can do all the equipment doesn't mean he can run a course. Working the space between the fences is not as easy as it often looks. Perhaps Charlie is happy doing five obstacles in a row, but not ten? When you ask more of him than he is able to give, he takes off. Stick with shorter sequences. If Charlie looks uncertain, rebuild your basics and return to exercises that he finds fun and easy. Increase his confidence and yours will get a boost too.

Charlie sounds a very lovable Labrador. You will soon become not only his best friend but his favorite playmate. As soon as he understand all the rules of the agility game, he won't want to play anything else.

Below: When you call your dog, make returning to you worthwhile. He will probably come back to you more quickly for a piece of liver than he would for a stale, dry biscuit. And he will come even faster if he hears a happy, rather than a scolding, voice.

Running Out

Q *I have been training my crossbreed, Abbey, in agility for about a year and I'm having trouble keeping her in the ring with me. She runs out to my husband and friends. She runs out to my handbag. She runs out to the score tent. She loves everyone and everything! Do you think she is just very smart and gets bored quickly in the ring? Any suggestions to help my runaway dog?*

A Oh dear! Abbey is a well-socialized individual with loads of geniality. So many people to meet and things to do. Abbey wants to share her successes with everyone. All you want her to do is concentrate on the task in hand so that she really has something to brag about. A span of 30 to 40 seconds in the agility ring is nothing to us, but for a dog it can be an eternity, especially if she is as happy chasing leaves as she is jumping hurdles. If you think that Abbey is bored in the ring, make it challenging and exciting to be there.

Center of the universe That should be you. Become more attractive, interesting and exciting to be with than the distractions outside the ring. All the action should begin and end with you. Enhance your appeal with a toy or treats. Does your dog rely on you for the good things in life like food and exercise? Make sure you are the one putting food in her bowl and clipping on her leash.

Distractions Become a slob at training. Leave a sweater on the ground here and a fanny pack over there. You will know where the distractions are in advance and you can work a little harder to get Abbey to run past them. Start with a few distractions of low interest and increase the number and level of their appeal as your dog gets better at ignoring them and concentrating on you.

Practical exercises Teach Abbey a "Leave" command. If she moves towards someone's treat bag, tell her to leave. Teach Abbey to "Watch" so that you can direct her gaze to you and away from distractions. Improve Abbey's recall. She should be so eager to get to you that she runs past the dropped treat.

Give it time As Abbey matures, you will get that 30 seconds of concentration in the ring. As her confidence in you as a handler and her own abilities grows, Abbey will become eager to work the obstacles instead of running to friends. She will remain a gregarious girl but she will want to share her love a little less often.

And, wouldn't you rather have a dog that loves everybody and everything than a dog that hates the world?

The Green Grass Of Agility

Q *I don't know what to do. My little crossbreed Cilla insists on grazing between the jumps. The minute we start doing agility she turns into a goat, snatching mouthfuls of grass and chomping her way around the course. It's driving me mad. How do I stop her being a lawn mower?*

A I don't know why dogs eat grass (and I don't know why we eat spinach), but it is a normal and harmless activity for dogs. Young tender shoots are a real delicacy in the Spring and dogs that gorge themselves on too much grass usually vomit it right back again. One explanation is that dogs eat grass to make themselves vomit unwanted or irritating substances from their stomachs. If Cilla is a real "grassaholic," keep her away from grass treated with chemicals or exotic plants that may be toxic.

Left: *OK – put your nose in the grass and smell the scents of daisies and buttercups. But don't eat them!*

Cilla's taste for grass on the agility field is a surefire way of getting your attention. Do you spend more time trying to stop her from grabbing a mouthful of the green stuff than you do teaching her how to jump? Also, eating grass is a great stress-busting activity. It's comforting and reassuring – a bit like chewing gum. If Cilla is confused in her learning environment, she stops and eats a few blades of it.

Don't train outdoors There won't be any grass for Cilla to munch at an indoor riding school or sports arena. Try to be positive and do everything you can to boost Cilla's confidence on the agility course. Concentrate on getting the basics right before your progress to more difficult exercises. When you both forget that eating grass was once a problem, it will be time to move back outdoors.

Distract with tasty treats Would Cilla rather have a slice of hot dog or a blade or grass? No contest. But you have to keep the tasty treats coming. Teach her to look up at you or a hand touch. She'll be too busy to have time to look at what's growing out of the ground at her feet.

Don't stop No time to eat and run. Don't stop when Cilla stops to have a snack of grass. She might think you are approving of her choice of snack. Keep going. Hurry to the finish line where there are better things to eat in your bait bag.

Keep moving Cilla should get praise and attention for running and chasing you. Play a catch-up game at home and in training. At first, Cilla shouldn't have to run too hard or too far to reach you and get her prize. When she gets the idea, go for it!

Try a toy Does Cilla have a favorite toy that she carries everywhere? She will find it impossible to hold it and eat grass at the same time so let her run over the course with it in her mouth.

Be patient. Cilla will become more sure of herself and what you want her to do. She will be less of a goat and more of an agility dog.

Keeping It In The Family

Q *I am 15 years old and my Dad drives me and my Golden Retriever Tyler to agility shows. Dad likes to watch me run and this causes problems. Tyler loves my Dad and he runs out to him in the middle of the round as if to say "Wasn't I great over there!" What should I do?*

A This is a tricky one! Your Dad provides your transportation to shows which is great, so you want to keep in his good graces. And I can understand him wanting to watch you. He believes that he is being a good parent by being there to support you. Unfortunately, his presence next to the ring is too much of a distraction for your Goldie. Every time Tyler runs out you risk elimination.

Hiding Your Dad can hide behind the nearest tree or score tent and watch you covertly. Out of sight can be out of mind. This ploy doesn't always work. Sometimes it just makes it more fun for the dog – agility plus a game of hide and seek for Dad. And sometimes the dog can become unsettled and worried if one of his family members suddenly disappears.

Ignoring Take your Dad to training. When Tyler runs out to him, tell him not to engage your dog. Tell him to turn his back on Tyler and ignore him. Call Tyler back to you and give him lots of praise and treats for returning. If Tyler wants attention, he gets it in the ring. This is where everything exciting happens. It will take Tyler a little while to catch on but he will start to lose interest in your Dad and will seek fun and approval from you.

Growling and shooing When Tyler runs out to your Dad, he could try growling at Tyler to show he is displeased and shoo him back into the ring. But Tyler may still see this as attention, even if it is negative. He'll continue to pay Dad a visit on his way around the course. Or your Dad could throw some noisy training discs (or a can full of pebbles) on the ground next to Tyler to startle him. But remember that Tyler loves your Dad too, and these actions may jeopardize their relationship.

Above: *Unless your dog passes his driving test, he'll never be able to take you to training class and shows. Keep in your Dad's good books!*

Keep practicing Your Dad is not the only distraction, but probably heads a long list – the food truck, barking dogs, and people picnicking by the ring. Work through it. Make agility so fun-packed, fast-paced and engrossing that Tyler doesn't have time to wonder what is going on elsewhere.

Your father wants to see you succeed in your chosen canine sport. I'm sure he will help you overcome this problem by ignoring Tyler's visits. And I know he will continue to be very proud of all your accomplishments.

Right: *Sorry! No attention or treats from me while you are doing your stuff at agility. But that doesn't mean that I don't love you …*

Tough Enough?

Q I'm thinking of signing up my whippet Fleur for agility classes, but she is such a sensitive flower. She doesn't like to get her feet wet or walk across pebbles. She always has to sit on a cushion instead of the floor. If I slam a door, she disappears under the sofa. Is she too much of a wimp for agility?

Left: *Whippets appear to be delicate creatures. Don't be fooled! They make excellent ratters and can become accomplished agility dogs.*

A We can all be a bit sensitive about certain things, but it shouldn't stop us from trying something new that we might enjoy. Fleur's introduction to the equipment should take into account her sensitivities – you don't want a sensitivity to be traumatized so it turns into a phobia. Watch out for:

The seesaw Sensitive dogs loathe the seesaw. Not only does it move up and down but it hits the ground with a loud bang. Fleur might think the world is coming to an end. Don't try to teach Fleur how to perform this obstacle until she is comfortable with its noise. Introduce her to it gradually, starting with a dull thump and slowly working up to a crash. Build a pleasant association, by giving Fleur a titbit every time the seesaw hits the ground.

The collapsible tunnel It's dark inside and the chute material is heavy – so claustrophobic. Prepare Fleur for this sensation. Get an old blanket and play tents with your dog. Get down on your hands and knees and invite her to chase you in and out. Hide toys and treats in the folds and make Fleur hunt for them. If she is having fun, she won't object to the weight of the blanket on her back.

Weaving poles Fleur might look at the weaving poles and think that the metal base has been expressly designed to stub toes and hurt dogs. Get Fleur accustomed to the feel of the poles on her body by using one to massage her ribs gently while you whisper sweet nothings or give her a treat to munch. Teach her on channel weaves. The two lines of poles can be kept wide open and gradually narrowed as Fleur gets used to them.

Jump poles Contrary to what many sensitive dogs think, jump poles do not leap out of the cups and

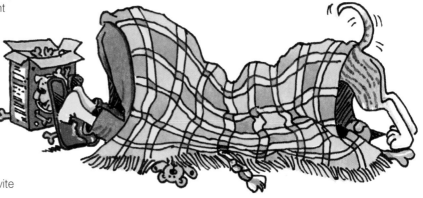

Above: *Whippets are simply miniaturized Greyhounds. They can turn on the speed and possess the same elegance and grace over the ground.*
Right: *A fearless Italian Greyhound shows that jumping is just as much fun as running if you do it really fast.*

bite dogs on the knees. Knocking a pole probably hurts, but not that much. If Fleur hits a pole, check that she is all right but don't make a big fuss of her. You don't want to encourage her belief that poles are vicious. Get her back in the agility saddle. Have a game with her toy, do a piece of agility equipment she likes or try a different jump. Praise her for being brave. She will forget about her knee if you distract her with fun somewhere else.

Don't push Fleur beyond what she can comfortably tolerate. She'll soon learn that jump poles don't bite. When she relaxes and starts enjoying herself, you'll forget that she was a wimp!

Sore Tootsies

Q *I hope you can help my rescue collie, Ricky. When I got Ricky he was about five months old and his nails kept splitting on his front feet. This problem has now been resolved with the help of a diet supplement, but it has left him with very sensitive toes. The weaves are difficult to train because Ricky is very wary of the cross supports and metal base. I've never actually seen him stub his toes, but he always pops out as if he has and always at the cross supports. Any bright ideas?*

A Dogs can suffer from sore and tender feet for all sorts of other reasons. Ask your vet to have a look at Ricky's nails just to make sure that all is well and as it should be. If it is, think about the following:

It's time for a manicure Dogs walk on their toes, so if their nails get too long, even a few steps can be painful. Plenty of exercise and road walking will help keep them short and a vet or groomer will show you how to clip Ricky's nails or do it for you.

Go back to the beginning and re-teach the weaves You probably don't want to do this, but it would pay dividends. Use a different command and a different training method. Ricky should think he is learning a new exercise, not re-hashing an old one.

Hide the base of the weave poles Cover the base and cross supports with soil or sand. Slowly reintroduce the base by scraping away the soil over the next few weeks until it is again plainly visible. If Ricky starts popping out, replace some earth.

Consider training with channel weaves The poles and base are gradually moved closer together to make a

Above: *A dog that is worried about where he is putting his feet will inevitably slow down in the weave poles.*

straight line which should allow Ricky time to get accustomed to touching or stepping on the base. If he balks, just take a step back and widen them again.

Teach the base as a separate exercise It might be that keeping his eye on the poles as well as watching his feet on the base is too much for Ricky to worry about all at once. Take all the poles out, put Ricky on his lead and walk with him across the base. Praise or click and treat him for stepping over the metal base in a relaxed manner. As he becomes more confident, you can try criss-crossing it back and forth. When Ricky shows no fear or anxiety, you increase your pace to a trot and then a run.

It will take time and effort to turn around Ricky's thinking on the weave poles. He may have stubbed his toe when you weren't looking and it's not easy to erase painful associations. They do fade in time and they can be supplanted with pleasant, positive ones given love and patience.

It's So Spooky!

Q *I'm 13 years old and have a two-year-old Golden Retriever, Prince. He was really good at agility until a few weeks ago. Prince knocked a jump and then got spooked at training when it started to thunder and rain. Now Prince won't go into the equestrian center where we train and he won't go over the equipment on the lead. Should I give up and do something else?*

A Just when everything is going so well, something like this happens. Your dog's confidence has been knocked and so has yours. One single negative experience can jeopardize all your positive training. Try and rise above it. If you have laid good agility foundations, you and Prince will recover ground quickly and be back to winning ribbons and trophies soon.

Vet check Prince may be refusing to jump because something hurts. Have him checked by your vet. He may have bruised his toe or pulled a muscle when he knocked the hurdle. The only way he can tell you that something is wrong is by changing from a dog that excels at agility to one that is reluctant to even try to go over the jumps.

Take a break The association between jumping and the thunderstorm is fresh in his mind. Rather than training Prince every day, let him have a vacation. Give it time and the memory will fade. Do some obedience or heelwork to music so he has something different to think about. And you'll forget his fears too.

Don't force the issue The more you try to drag Prince over the jumps, the more he may resist. You could make matters worse. The equipment will become obstacles of confrontation rather than fun. Encourage, but don't coerce. Praise and reward Prince for what he offers you voluntarily.

Baby steps Don't expect Prince to take giant steps back to being a fully functional agility dog. He has had a frightening experience. Prince will make a speedier recovery if he takes baby steps, although he will have to take many more of them. If he looks at a hurdle, reward him lavishly with treats. Next time, he will take a small step towards it, next time two steps and so on until he is leaping over it.

Start at the very beginning Take Prince right back to the beginning. Lay poles on the ground, lower the A-frame, and shorten the tunnel. You won't be starting from scratch, but retraining the basics. It will be an opportunity for you to make each step a positive experience for Prince. Your confidence and trust in each other on the equipment will resurface.

I believe that you and Prince will be back on the agility field very soon. You obviously love Prince very much and I know that will give you the patience and understanding to help him overcome his fears.

At The Drop Of A Hat

Q *My German Shepherd Dog Dilly is a sweet girl, but she has this thing about hats. The one time we competed, she started barking at the judge who was wearing a baseball cap. She has never done it before. What can I do?*

A I agree with Dilly. People who wear hats look different. They look funny, frightening or surreal. And she's not sure how to react.

Aliens Dogs are freaked by people with hats because they look like aliens. However, as soon as the "alien" speaks, they recognize the voice as human. This adds to their confusion. Take the hat off, and the dog realizes that it's not someone from another planet. It's the man from next door who passes treats over the fence. So embarrassing!

Dressing up I'm sure that your instructor or a class mate will help you with this problem by wearing a hat at agility lessons. Let Dilly sniff it before anyone wears it. And make sure that Dilly is comfortable with your helper before he puts a hat on his head. If she has been introduced to both, she should remain relaxed. Hats do not jump off people's heads and menace passers-by.

Out and about We can't dictate a dress code to judges but the more people Dilly sees wearing a hat, the more acceptable and mundane it will become. Take Dilly into town on a rainy or sunny day. Lots of people will be wearing something on their heads. These people will be going about their business, not staring at Dilly to see if she misses a contact. Dilly will soon understand that they are not interested in her and she will lose interest in them.

Above: *If you wear a hat that stays on your head while you are running, you can turn it into a toy at the last fence. Take it off for your dog to tug or throw it for him to chase.*

Introductions Once Dilly has started barking at someone with a hat, there is not much that you can do. She may be too frightened to be distracted by a treat or toy. And if you try to force the issue, she may become hysterical. Try laughing. Tell her she is a silly girl. The person wearing the hat has no fashion sense. They think they look glamorous? Ha! Laugh till your belly hurts and Dilly will take her cue from you. Yes, the hat is terrifying – terrifyingly funny.

One-off Perhaps you have developed a thing about hats and are misinterpreting Dilly's actions. It only happened once in competition and Dilly may have been objecting to the judge's choice of socks, not headgear. Worry about your course, not what the judge is wearing. The more experience Dilly gets in the ring, the more focused she will become on agility, and the less notice she will take of what is on the judge's head.

Toilet Trouble

Q *Please help me. My King Charles Spaniel Tina won't go to the toilet at agility shows. I've tried training her to relieve herself on command. I've tried jogging her up and down in the exercise area. Tina is a dynamo at training, but a snail at shows – I'm sure she would be able to run faster in the ring if she had been to the toilet first. As soon as she gets home, she runs into the yard to do her business.*

A Like Tina, I believe the toilets at shows are something to be avoided if possible – the facilities at home are much sweeter. However, nerves get the better of me and I spend as much time lining up at the bathroom as I do lining up to go into the ring.

If Tina is always fussy about where she squats, visit your vet for a check-up Her reluctance may be a sign of a medical problem and you need to rule this out.

If Tina is feeling vulnerable, she will not want to go to the toilet Many dogs don't want to go to relieve themselves in unfamiliar places. They like a bit of privacy and can't find it in the exercise area where there is a lot going on – dogs approaching and sniffing each other in greeting and lots of running around and barking. Help Tina by walking her somewhere that is quiet. Let her choose the pace. Give her time to get accustomed to the hustle and bustle of a show. When she feels comfortable in her surroundings and is relaxed, she will do her business.

If Tina feels pressured, she will hold on Don't spend all day at an agility show trying to make Tina go to the toilet. That's not what you are there for. Give Tina an opportunity to do her business. If she

doesn't go after 15 minutes or so, take her to the ring and forget about toileting. She has had her chance. Concentrate on your run. Tina will be in the ring for about 40 seconds and should be able to wait until her next visit to the exercise area later.

If Tina is stressed, she won't run as fast as she does in training I don't think that Tina's reluctance to relieve herself is the cause of her change in

Above: *When a dog is mentally and physically comfortable in her surroundings, her true agility colors will show.*

performance on the agility course. Yes, it is hard to run on a full bladder, but I think it is more likely that Tina is unnerved by show conditions. There is so much to keep your eye on. Peeing and jumping are the last things on Tina's mind.

If you are relaxed, Tina will follow your lead You will both start to enjoy yourself. In time, Tina will relieve herself when you take her to the exercise area instead of holding on until you get home. She will gain confidence and you will see her start to work in the ring like she does at training.

Measuring Up

Q *I am currently competing with my small collie cross Morgan over different jump heights. It all depends on who is running the show that I've entered. At one show, he is classified as a medium dog and jumps over 20 inches (51cm) and at another he is considered a mini dog and jumps over 15 inches (38cm). Morgan doesn't seem to have any trouble adjusting from one to the other and back again, but he does knock a few poles now and again. Should I stick to just one jump height?*

A **Five inches can make a big difference to some dogs** If you have a dog that can make the transition from 15 to 20 inches and back again without a problem, you are very lucky. Five inches can make a lot of difference to some dogs. Morgan must check the height of the pole, adjust his take off to sail over the top and nail his landing. The taller the jumps, the more rounded and less flat he will be going over the poles. Morgan is either a natural jumper or you have trained him well.

And the extra five inches can make a lot of difference to some handlers! Morgan may be faster over lower jumps and it may be more difficult to keep up with him. You have to be quicker to get in position and you need to give your commands a little sooner. Over the higher jumps, you need to

reset your timing once again. There is a little more time to get where you want to be on the course. So often it is the handler who has the most trouble adjusting between jump heights and will favor one over the other. You do not seem to have a preference and can compete happily at either height.

Take a few practice jumps with you to the show Set them to the height at which you will be competing and do a few jumping exercises with Morgan. This will not only allow Morgan to set his

Above left and right: *Can a big sheltie compete against a small collie? The answer is yes. It all depends on the height classification for dogs at the show. Both dogs' handlers must adjust their handling to the size of the jumps in order to run the course in a good time without faults.*

sights on the height he will be working over, but it will give you the chance to brush up on your timing.

Sticking to one jump height would certainly make things easier for both you and Morgan, but if you enjoy going to different shows and have no problem

competing over different jump heights, why stop? There are many other reasons for a pole dropping. If it happens only occasionally, I suspect that Morgan is knocking a pole because of one of these rather than being affected by different jump heights in his classes. When he becomes an old dog, Morgan may find the extra five inches more difficult. Then it will be time to reassess his jumping style and think about sticking to one type of class, but while he is fit and healthy I see no reason why you can't have fun doing both heights.

Limbo Dancer

Q *I started agility with my Staffordshire Terrier Tevo a few months ago. Did you know a Staffie could limbo dance? Tevo will run under the jumps no matter how low they are set. Sometimes this is really difficult and he has to duck to get underneath and crawl on his belly, but under he goes! My classmates think it's really funny. What should I do?*

A Your dog is so clever and so creative! Tevo is still new to agility and he is experimenting with the jumps. He thinks, "Hey! There's more than one way to get to the other side of a hurdle!" And Tevo gets a round of laughter for his antics if he goes under rather than over the pole. Which way would you choose?

When a dog is introduced to the hurdles, he has to learn that the object of the exercise is to jump between the wings and over the pole. It sounds as if Tevo is indeed targeting the pole and assessing its height, but failing to decide to jump it. It could be that the poles were raised too soon – before Tevo learned the right way to do it was up and over. Running underneath poles is a common fault in young or inexperienced dogs and many show real determination in picking this route.

Above: *Power and strength make Staffies awesome agility dogs. But their determination to do things their own way can cause problems for handlers.*

Put the poles on the ground Unless Tevo sticks his nose under the pole and lifts it over his back, he'll have to go over. It's the easier option, especially if there are a number of poles laid in a line.

Fill the gap underneath the pole Use a double poled, but low, jump. This might do the trick, but Tevo may try to jump between the two poles or try to crawl under the bottom one. Another method is to block the space under the pole with a board. Tevo will have no alternative but to take the high road. Praise him.

On your way up and over When Tevo has started to give up limbo dancing for jumping, he still might go under a pole every now and again. Put the pole on the ground and work your way back up again. Don't be tempted to lower it just a little. If Tevo stoops and scoots underneath, you will have to lower it again. Far better to start from ground level where mistakes are really hard to make and work up.

Do you have a jump command? You want Tevo to be checking the jump's height, so ensure that you point with your hand above the pole and not below it. Give Tevo space to take-off and land. Many inexperienced dogs often go under poles on turns because they arrive at the hurdle before they can gather themselves up and jump.

Jumps are always a problem. Dogs either refuse them outright, go around them, or go under them. When Tevo has turned into a speedo over the jumps, you might find that your next challenge is to stop him knocking them out of their cups.

Ducking The Issue

Q *My working sheepdog Diva is nearly two years old. I started training Diva when she was ten months and gradually brought the jumps up from the ground to full height. All was well until we started competing. She would rather do a piece of contact equipment than jump hurdles. She loves doing contacts and runs under most of the fences to get there. Should I train with the double poles? She doesn't have a problem with the lower height jumps so I can't see that there's much to gain from bringing the height down again.*

A When a dog starts competing, she starts making mistakes and exposes all the holes in a training program. Your contact training must have been thorough, but lots of fun. Diva loves the contacts and she can't wait to get there. Did you invest as much time and thought into your jumping exercises? I'm not surprised she runs under the poles to get to an A-frame on the other side.

Don't let going under poles become a habit
If your dog insists on running underneath, make it difficult for her to do so by using extra poles on each jump. Diva will start looking up to see how high she should jump and you can slowly fade the extra poles.

Use a jump command Back up your body signals with a verbal command. You should not only be facing the jump but giving the verbal command "Jump." You want Diva to check the jump's height, so point with your hand above the pole – not below it. When Diva gets the idea, body language may be all you need.

Reward Diva for going over If Diva goes under a fence, don't let her proceed to the next piece of equipment on the course. Recall her, set her up at the fence and re-command. For a dog that is struggling with agility, starting over again may be demotivating, but if your dog is running by fences with gusto you won't dampen her enthusiasm. Reward her for getting it right with lots of verbal praise and allowing her to go onto the next obstacle.

A-frame reward Set up a loop of fences that carries your dog past the A-frame. Start with them at mini height, as you know she can do this, and reward her for completing the sequence with a free trip up the A-frame. Raise the fences a few inches and do the same again. If she is sailing over the top of the fences, she wins another trip over the A-frame. Raise the fences till they are at full height. If at anytime Diva goes under, mark the refusal to jump with a "wrong" or "shame on you" and try again. No jump. No A-frame.

Teach Diva that hurdles are fun and rewarding too! Running under poles is a common fault with inexperienced agility dogs. Balance contacts in your training program with jumping exercises and I'm sure it won't be long till Diva is going clear on the course.

Above: *You can certainly get where you want to go much faster if you duck under the poles, but it won't make your handler very happy!*

Demolition Dog

Twister, the demolition dog, really makes the pole setters work. They see my screaming collie on the start line and roll their eyes. I don't know how to teach her to stop knocking the poles. She is a young and inexperienced dog, but we can't go on like this. Please help me to help her.

Dogs knock poles for a variety of reasons and the first thing you must do is to look carefully at your dog and yourself. A video recording of Twister on the course would help you evaluate the problem. Is Twister knocking poles because she is so excited? Is she taking off too far away from the jump to clear it cleanly? Is it the spacing of the obstacles that causes the problems? Or does she drop a hind leg on the turns and catch the bar?

From your description of Twister on the start line, I guess that she is a green collie and eager to go as fast as she can on the course. I hope these tips will help you to help Twister keep the fences up.

It's not a race Let Twister work ahead. She is anxious to stay out in front so you pull the strings from behind. Keep up, but remember that she, not you, has to cross the finish line.

Don't dip and flap Keep your body upright. If you point to a fence, don't bend your knees or drop your outstretched arm. If you do, Twister will mimic your dip and the fence will come down. Keep all your body movements to the minimum. You'll look neater and Twister won't be distracted by a lot of extraneous and meaningless signals.

Keep quiet You don't need to tell Twister to jump the fence in front of her. She has already worked that out. If you have been commanding her when to jump, you risk making her take off too early and knock a pole.

Jumping chute Set up a line of fences and give Twister the chance to establish clean jumping habits. Start with low hurdles and practice sendaways and recalls. And this is an opportunity for you to practice running from behind without flapping.

Respect for the poles Some trainers believe that dogs need to be taught to respect the poles. Poles are raised so that the dog has to jump higher than necessary or they are filled with sand to make them heavier and harder to dislodge. Other trainers attach cans to the poles so they rattle when they fall to the ground. And some trainers stretch elastic above the pole and between the wings to trip the dog that drops a leg. A few trainers even tell handlers to pick up dropped pole and threaten the dog with it. I disagree with this approach – I don't believe that lack of respect is the issue. These "solutions" could aggravate the problem and may be injurious to the dog.

Dogs knock poles on the course either because they don't know how to jump correctly or because they are handled badly.

The Last Hurdle

Q *This is my first season competing with my collie, Taggie. I've been told he has lots of potential and will go far if only he would jump the last fence. Instead of going over it, he turns back to me. Whatever I do, he won't take the last fence. It's the only thing stopping me from getting a clear round. Do you have any advice?*

A How very frustrating for you!
Why the last fence?

- Associations are made in a split second. Taggie may have knocked his toe on landing after the last fence – ouch! He hay have seen a helper throw a leash as he took off and assumed it was aimed at him – ouch! Is it a surprise that Taggie is suspicious of the last fence?
- All those dogs ringside are in a frenzy to get at the equipment. Taggie questions the wisdom of

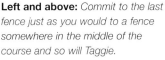

Left and above: *Commit to the last fence just as you would to a fence somewhere in the middle of the course and so will Taggie.*

jumping the last fence and landing in the middle of them.
• It is possible that Taggie is anticipating the praise he receives at the end of a round and is pre-

empting you. He turns back to his handler too early for congratulations on a job well done (but not finished).

Mental imagery You and Taggie are both apprehensive about the last fence and reinforce each other's anxiety. Picture another fence after the last one and continue to work Taggie over it. Pretend the finish line is not where the judge has set it. This should help you avoid tensing up as you approach the final hurdle.

All fences are the same By becoming last-fence-obsessed, you may be unwittingly rubber-stamping Taggie's behavior. Act at the last fence just like you do at fences number one, two and three. It's possible that your dog believes that all the extra attention he gets at the last fence is his reward for refusing it.

Lower the fence Make it as easy as possible for Taggie to jump the last fence so that you can praise him for his performance. Start with the fence at mini height. As the fence is raised, and your dog continues to jump it, both of you will relax and cease to think of the last hurdle as your biggest obstacle.

Go on Teach your dog the "Go on" command. Teach him to go over a fence to a target or toy. The reward and praise is delivered after the fence, not before it. And the spectators who cheer Tag to the end of his run will be shouting "Go on" too! Your command to send Tag down the home stretch will be reinforced by the crowd.

Have a break It's amazing. Some problems disappear as suddenly as they appear for no discernible reason. Have a week or two off and see what happens. You may be pleasantly surprised.

Don't let this problem dominate your dog's agility training. The last fence is only 1/20th of the course. Keep practicing other agility exercises. If you get a hang-up about the last fence, so will your dog.

Double Trouble

Q *I have two terriers called Saffron and Waldo, sister and brother. They do everything together – hunting squirrels, ripping up their toys or re-making their bed. And they both compete in agility. My problem is that they are in separate classes on different nights of the week and I seem to spend all my time driving back and forth from training. Should I try to run them both in the same class?*

A We would all like to have more time at home to catch up on chores, but the more dogs we have, the more time we spend at agility classes. Although working Saffron and Waldo in the same class will be economical, there are a number of minuses.

Above: *They look alike but the similarity ends there. Treat them as individuals when you take them agility training.*

Catching your breath Running two dogs in one class is tiring. As soon as you finish with Saffron, you will have to get Waldo ready for his turn. If class is a social occasion for you, you'll miss the chitchat with your friends but you will certainly get fit!

Two handling strategies Your dogs are both terriers, but they may be very different agility dogs. Perhaps Saffron is really motivated but Waldo is easily distracted. You will have to have two handling strategies at the ready and switching from one to the other may result in a few mistakes. How many times will you call Saffron when you want Waldo?

Separation If your dogs are accustomed to doing things in tandem, how will Saffron feel watching Waldo zip round the course with you? Will sibling love turn to rivalry? A little jealousy can fire up a dog, but it could also dampen his enthusiasm. "Let me try, I could do that!" may turn into "You do agility so well, I give up!"

Hitching post You have to decide what to do with the dog left out. Will you tie him up to a hitching post, get a friend to hold him, or rest him in a crate? Will you be bold and leave him in a sit stay?

Distracting Giving 100 per cent attention to the dog you are working while the other sits on the sideline is not easy. Will you be telling Saffron to stop barking when you should be telling Waldo to hit the contact? And what will you do if Waldo leaves the ring to join Saffron by her crate? Perhaps he prefers her company?

Homework It's a good idea to see how your dogs react to working in one another's company in advance. Put Waldo in his crate and have a game of tug with Saffron. What happens? If there is a

problem, solve it at home. Don't bring it with you to training.

If you are short of time, you may decide that the advantages of working two dogs in one class more than outweigh the disadvantages. But, whether Saffron and Waldo are in the same class or not, you should certainly still try to reserve a portion of the day for spending quality time with each of them individually.

Playing With Matches

Q *Sally goes like the wind around the agility course. But only if my retired agility dog, Nellie, is ringside with her. If I leave Nellie at home, Sally walks around as if she has all the time in the world and is about to get out her knitting. How can I light Sally's fire without Nellie being the spark?*

A It's nice that your two dogs get along. They are probably good company for each other and have formed a special bond. Sally is taking her cue from Nellie, not you. Is it a question of security or jealousy and what are you going to do about it?

Security Sally feels secure when Nellie is around and so is able to give a top performance on the agility field. She is taking her lead from the older dog who is relaxed. Nellie has been to many venues and training fields. She knows there is nothing to worry about and her confidence transmits itself to Sally.

Above: *The magic of agility is that it is just you and your dog on the course working together as a team.*

Jealousy Sally is a whiz kid on the agility field because she is having to work to earn your attention. She could be the one left on the sidelines instead of Nell. Jealousy can be a great motivator. When Nell is left at home, Sally doesn't have to make an effort. She has you all to herself.

Ignition Initially there is nothing wrong with using Nellie to light Sally's fire. In dog training, use whatever comes your way and works. If your dog likes playing with a cushion off the couch, bring it to class. But remember that these stimuli are only aids for ignition. Eventually, you must be the person that ignites Sally's flames and keeps the fire burning.

Independence Help Sally learn to stand up on her own four feet. Exercise and walk the two dogs separately. It will be extra work, but worth it. If you go to the supermarket, take Sal for the ride and leave Nellie at home. Sally will learn how to cope with new adventures in the outside world – and not just at agility shows – without Nell's back-up. What if Nellie had to spend the night at the vet's? Sally would have to go it alone.

Dependence Without Nell, Sally will look to you for guidance. Make sure you give it. She has to want brownie points from you, so earning them must be fun whether at home or at training. Reward effort, not just completed actions. Teach her the way to your heart and develop a partnership with Sally through doing things together.

Give it time You and Sally can't rely on Nellie all the time. The more agility you do together, the closer you will become and the harder Sally will work to please you.

Teaching By Example

Q *I wonder if you can tell me if it is normal for an agility instructor to work his own dog in the class that he is teaching? My instructor runs his dog at the end of every exercise. At first, I thought that it was going to be a one time thing, but the same thing happens every week. Sometimes he takes more time trying to get the exercise right than attending to us paying pupils.*

A This is a tricky one. Many instructors are unpaid volunteers who help at their local training club, on the proviso that they may work their own dog in the class that they are teaching. Like most things, there are different ways of looking at it. Here are some scenarios:

Demo dog The instructor's dog can show and tell. "What do weaves look like?" ask the beginners. The instructor's dog can not only demonstrate the building blocks, but the finished product. Can't he? How embarrassing if the dog misses the entry or pops out half way through the poles. Demo dogs can do things the wrong way just as easily as the right way!

Words fail Not all instructors are blessed with the ability to explain things clearly. When the class is still puzzled by the term "blind cross" after a ten-minute verbal description, it can be easier for the instructor simply to show the maneuver with his own dog. All will become clear if the instructor is successful. If not, the class will be even more confused and muddled!

Making up the numbers Football is on and there's an outbreak of flu. The class is reduced to two. The instructor may decide to work his dog in order to give his students a rest so they may catch their breath between turns.

Role model If the instructor is one of the elite, his performance in front of his students will be breathtaking. The class will either imitate and aspire to be just like him or they will become disillusioned, give up hope and go home.

Focus If your instructor can give his class his full attention with his dog beside him in the ring, that's great. But if his dog is menacing the line of students and takes ages to get the exercises right, you might start to question his agenda. The purpose of your class is not for your instructor to train his dog, but your dogs. You have reason to feel resentful and cause to complain.

If you do decide to voice your grievance to your club's committee, do so tactfully. They may be unaware of what is going on and you don't want anyone's feelings to be hurt. Worse, they may have no other instructors. It might be worth looking for another agility club and first observe other classes to see how things are run.

Above: *Agility classes are for you and your dog, so make sure that they are being run for your benefit and not for that of the instructor who should know better!*

Taking The Lead

Q *My dog Fergus is obsessed with his lead. He either tugs it noisily or chews it silently. Last week, he chewed straight through it without me realizing what he was doing. My mind was on the course and when I reached down to take his lead off for his run, Fergus had half of it in his mouth and I had the other half in my hand!*

A You are very lucky that Fergus did not realize that he was unattached. He could have wandered off and got up to all kinds of mischief!

Dogs love their leads Pick up a dog's lead and it's the signal for a walk in the woods or a ride in the car to agility training. Many agility handlers make their dog's lead seem more desirable and powerful by treating it as if it were a toy. They play tug with their lead to wind and warm up their dog. They send their dog to a lead at the end of a run. Or they tie it in a knot and throw it for their dog to fetch. Don't treat Fergus's lead as if it is a toy; then he won't try to play with it.

A new toy If you don't allow Fergus to play with his lead, you must buy him a new toy. Something similar but different

Right: *It's my lead! NO! It's my lead! Who will win this test of strength?*

– perhaps a knotted or plaited rope. Choose something inexpensive and easily replaceable. Dangle it in front of him and give him a game of tug. Encourage him to transfer his passion to chew on to his toy and discourage him from chewing his lead.

Unchewable You could buy Fergus a metal chain lead. These aren't so nice to chew – Fergus would blunt his teeth on one of those. He will prefer gnawing his new tug toy.

Be vigilant When you are standing in the line, keep your eye on Fergus. If he is resisting the temptation to chew his lead, praise him and give him a titbit. If he looks as if he is thinking about mouthing his lead, let him know that he has made the wrong choice. When you need to concentrate on the course, put Fergus in a down stay. Do your thinking. Return to Fergus and release him onto a toy and have a game. You could make this part of your warm-up routine.

Yanking, pulling and tugging If you try and get Fergus to let go of his lead by yanking, pulling or tugging, he will yank, pull and tug right back at you. It's so exciting and he will think you are having a game. Teach Fergus to "Leave" or "Drop," so that he will let go of his lead on command. If you exert all your strength to rip it out, you may end up damaging his teeth.

Of course, you could just let Fergus chew away. Chewing his lead isn't such a bad habit. But it could cost you a fortune in replacements!

Quick-Release Collar

Q *My biggest problem at a show is getting the collar and lead off my Sheltie, Taz. I get hold of her, but she is so eager to get into the ring she won't stay still. All the wiggling and straining to get started makes it impossible to find the buckle. She gets all snared up and her long coat doesn't help matters. I'm afraid the judge is going to fault me for delaying tactics.*

A I can picture you and Taz twisting together on the start line. Finding the collar is a common problem for handlers with long-haired dogs and by the time you have parted the fur and located it, the dog is agitated and restless. And then you lose it again! There are a number of options to help solve the problem.

Above: *Reward your dog for letting you touch her collar with a treat or, if you can fit a few fingers underneath it, massage her neck muscles until she turns to jelly.*

Clip the dog This is a drastic solution and Taz wouldn't be able to face herself in the mirror.

Collar shopping Go shopping and test-drive a few collars. Look for one without a buckle. Try some quick-release collars. If you can't get the collar to open when the dog isn't wearing it, you don't stand a chance when it is around Taz's neck. Think about the width. Thin collars tend to embed themselves deeply in the fur. Something thicker might be easier to locate in Taz's coat. Consider slip leads. Would one of these be any easier for you to take off?

Touch my collar exercise Start this at home. Part Taz's coat so that her collar is exposed and sit her in front of you. Find her collar and gently slip a finger underneath. Praise and give her a treat. She gets the treat, not for sitting, but for letting you touch her collar. After a few repetitions, Taz will be begging you to put your hand on her collar. Keep your hand there a little longer. If Taz has been clicker-trained, she will learn this exercise very quickly. Touch her collar and click. When she is proficient, add a command like "Undress" or "Lead off." With practice, you should be able to transfer this exercise from your living room to an agility show.

Game of statues Staying still is very hard for wiggly worm puppies and even harder for excited agility dogs. Teach your dog to freeze with a game of statues. Get Taz to play with her tug toy or chase a treat. Interject a "Sit" command into the game. She must remain motionless until you release her. At first, release her quickly onto her toy. When she thoroughly understands the games rules, wait a little bit longer. Build up slowly. Later still, introduce a distraction that she must sit through – clap your hands or take off her collar. She must sit still to get her reward. It might not help you to get Taz to stop squirming while you disrobe her at agility shows, but you will have had some fun together!

Eye On The Ball

Q *I have a little collie cross, Tetley. She's great at agility provided I have a ball in my hand. If I leave the ball at the side of the ring, or hide it in my pocket, she slows down or tries to find where I've hidden it. With her ball, she goes like greased lightning. Without it, she goes on strike. What can I do?*

A Tetley is a very, very good trainer. She has taught you to carry her beloved ball whenever the pair of you do any agility. No ball? No agility. Tetley needs to learn that her ball must be earned.

Small beginnings Start with one fence. Command Tetley to jump. After she jumps the hurdle, not before, she gets her reward. When she can do that, you can build up to two, three or four fences. She will start thinking "What do I have to do to get my ball?"

Battle of wills The first few times will be difficult. Tetley may rather have her hair dyed pink than lose sight of her ball. She may have a tantrum. Be patient and work through it. Tetley may pout and be unenthusiastic to start with but when she realizes that she will be rewarded with her ball she will start making an effort. In the beginning, keep Tetley interested by rewarding her frequently. Later, you can adjust your expectations. She will have to do more work to justify getting her ball.

Keep guessing Continue to use Tetley's ball in training, but keep her guessing. Is it in your hand? Is it in your pocket? Is it under the A-frame? Does someone else have it? Tetley will really be surprised when you retrieve her ball from the top of the car. Sometimes Tetley can have a game with it after a few jumps, sometimes in the middle of your run, sometimes at the end. You decide where and when.

Other motivators Experiment with other motivators. Does Tetley like treats, tug toys, a Frisbee? The advantage of having a range of rewards to choose from lies in their differing value to the dog. So if Tetley was stunningly excellent, she gets her cherished ball. If she was simply good, she gets a treat.

Out of sight Tetley will be learning that although she can't see her ball, it will be coming. All she has to do is be eager. The faster she goes, the sooner she gets her ball…from somewhere.

Your ball Think about your feelings and Tetley's ball. How do you feel running without it in your hand? Is it a bit of a crutch for you? Do you feel naked and useless without it? Change your attitude to yourself to something more positive.

Stick with it and you will have a dog that is as motivated in the ring as she is in training. She will know that a reward is on its way and will be on her best behavior to hurry it along.

Above: *Dogs can fall in love with a Frisbee as easily as a tennis ball. Take care not to substitute one obsession for another.*

Leaving His Mark

Q *It is so embarrassing. I have just started agility with Jake and he keeps cocking his leg. Although I've taught him to go on command, Jake doesn't care who or what he pees on. He has cocked his leg on other handlers in the class and the agility equipment. His favorite is the tunnel. How can I stop him from anointing everything in sight at class?*

Left: *Would you let your dog do this in your house? I doubt it.*

Castration Testosterone stimulates undesirable male behavior like scent marking so it is possible that castration may help control the problem. This is something you may like to discuss in more detail with your vet.

A It is important to recognize that Jake is scent-marking as opposed to urinating. Dominant dogs will repeatedly mark their territory with small amounts of urine deposited in strategically chosen places to let other dogs know that they are around. In addition, insecure dogs will mark in order to surround themselves with their own smell. It reassures them and boosts their confidence.

I ask new agility students to think of the agility obstacles as they think of the furniture in their living room. They don't allow their dogs to cock their legs on the corner of the couch so they must not allow them to do so on the tunnel. I explain further that if one dog pees on a jump wing, all the boys in the class will want to lift their leg in the same spot. Male

dogs like to cover another dog's urine scent with their own. They will be so busy peeing that they won't have anytime to learn agility. And some dogs, like Jake, are very determined.

Watch your dog Be vigilant. Don't stand near anything vertical that Jake might find tempting. And that includes people. Look out for warning signals. Jake will probably sniff the area he wants to mark before he lifts his leg. This is your cue to move away.

Keep moving It is hard to pee while moving. As Jake becomes more proficient at the obstacles and starts stringing them together, he will have to run. He won't have the opportunities or time to mark.

Correction You can interrupt a dog that is cocking his legs by shouting "No" or clapping your hands; however, any harsh corrections may make an insecure dog worse. Jake will simply mark quickly when you are not looking.

Time If Jake is marking because he feels threatened or insecure, it will pass as he becomes more confident over the agility equipment and more comfortable with his classmates. Give it time.

Pee post I have put two "pee posts" at opposite ends of the exercise field at my agility venue. Any competitive scent-marking is done here rather than on the equipment. There may be a tree or gatepost in your exercise area where all the boys leave their calling cards and this is where Jake should be allowed to lift his leg before coming into the training area.

Caught On Film

Q *I have been competing for about a year with my dog Gabby. She is doing well and I am turning into an agility addict. I've received a nice bonus from work this month and want to use it to indulge my addiction. I'm thinking of buying a video camera, but they are so expensive. Do you think it would be a good purchase?*

A Videos are an invaluable tool in agility training. Punch the playback button and you can see over and over again your best moves as well as your worst. The video never lies and you can learn a lot about yourself and Gabby. Consider a few of these hypothetical examples.

Posture You are fed up with hearing your instructor tell you to stop bending over your dog and stand up. You are standing up. But look at the video. See. There you are running around as if you are a camel with a hump on your back.

Timing How good is it? You may think that you're perfect, but you are not. You've been recorded giving your contact command after your dog has jumped off the A-frame.

Spooky Why did your dog spook in that corner? She really lost it. Look closely at the video and perhaps you will see a cigarette packet blowing across the ground by the jump. That's the evidence you need.

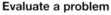

Explanation Your dog finishes the course but is limping. What happened? Watch the video and you will see that she stubbed her toe going into the weaves.

Voice Do you sound as authoritative and commanding as you think? No. On the video you sound desperate and are pleading with your dog to enter the weaves.

Body signals Stop wondering why your dog went into the tunnel when you wanted her to turn onto the A-frame. There you are facing the tunnel. No wonder your dog was sucked in.

Training v. competition Your dog always gets her weave entries in training, but never in competition. What are you doing differently? The video will give you a clue.

Evaluate a problem Your dog is knocking poles. Is it because of over-excitement, taking off too early, or a poorly timed command? Analyze the dog's jumping style with a video recording.

Video recorders provide irrefutable feedback and allow you to stand back and look at yourself in the ring. The video is the friend who will always tell you the truth. You should have bought shorts in the next size up and you should have called your dog sooner. Your instructor can tell you, your friends can tell you and even your dog can try and tell you what you are doing wrong on the course, but you won't necessarily believe them. If it's on video, you can't deny it. If you want to invest in your agility, buy one!

Above: *Seeing is believing. If you are wondering how your dog uses his fluffy tail to balance through the weaves, look no further than what's on the screen.*

Vertigo

Q My two-year-old female Apple has a problem on the A-frame. I think she is scared of heights because once she gets to the top, she stops dead and won't come down. When Apple does descend, she does so very slowly. Is it possible for dogs to have vertigo?

A Dogs are rarely afraid of heights. They have no problem jumping off the kitchen table when caught cleaning the dinner plates. Reluctance to descend the A-frame happens for a number of reasons.

The view from the top From this vantage point Apple can see everything that is going on and can scan the horizon for treats. She is savoring the view.

Elevated position Apple relishes looking down on all the people trying to entice her off the A-frame. The harder they try, the more determined she is to remain aloof.

Toenails Apple's nails may be catching in the A-frame's slats. Descent is slow and painful. Trim them.

Cooing encouragement Try to tempt Apple down with sweet words and she may think you are praising her for staying on her perch. Don't pursue this option.

Two feet on/two feet off This position is fine for dogs with drive, but demotivating for those that lack confidence. Apple looks down and sees you standing at the bottom of the A-frame. She elects to stay on top rather than face any argument when she hits the ground. It's safer for her to stick up top.

Retrain the A-frame

1 Lower the A-frame as far as it will go so it's easy to cross.

2 Give Apple a reason to get from one end to the other – a bowl of treats or a toy. Put it at the bottom of the A-frame.

3 With Apple on the lead, guide her over the A-frame to her prize. Let her clean up the bowl or give her a game with the toy.

4 When Apple knows the route to her goodies, try a recall. Ask someone to hold her, rev her up or tease her with toy and call her. She'll be eager to get to the other side.

5 If Apple is zooming over the A-frame as fast as she can to find her bowl or tug toy, it's time to try running along the right and left side. Leave Apple in a wait and, on your signal, make it a race between you to see who gets there first. If Apple lacks confidence or is a bit insecure, try letting her win by getting there first.

6 When you have the speed and drive that you want, it will be time to raise the A-frame gradually to its full height. Do this slowly over a period of time. If at any stage your dog loses her enthusiasm, lower the A-frame again.

7 Vary rewards. Sometimes instead of a treat, let Apple do her favorite piece of equipment or, if it's hot, enjoy an ice cream or a swim in the stream!

With a little patience, Apple will quickly overcome her fear of heights.

Left: *From the top of the A-frame it looks a long way down, doesn't it? But remember that your dog has no trouble racing you down the stairs at home to greet the mail carrier. Try putting a few old letters at the bottom of the A-frame and see if you get the same result. Use whatever motivates your dog!*

Above: *Get your dog accustomed to your forward movement by running on both the left and right side of the A-frame. Who will get to the other side first?*

Chapter Four

BETTER HANDLING

You have taught your dog to do all the agility obstacles. He is no longer a couch potato but an action dog. He can climb the A-frame and wiggle between the weave poles. Your dog does everything you tell him to do. Well, almost. Well, when he's in the mood. Sometimes he misses the first weave pole and sometimes he misses the last one. Sometimes he breaks his wait on the start line. Occasionally he goes right instead of left or he flies the seesaw. If only he hadn't jumped the contact on the A-frame you would have won the class. Your dog is good but, if you want him to be even better, you need to look at your handling skills on the course. There's room for improvement. Iron out all the little wrinkles in your training. What you do makes a difference to what your dog does as he runs over the obstacles.

I'm Lost!

Q *I get lost on the course. No matter how many times I walk it, I take a wrong turn somewhere. I've been blessed with Tilly because she does exactly what I tell her. It's me that gets her eliminated for sending her the wrong way. Are there any memory tricks that would help me?*

A It doesn't matter how many times you walk the course if you don't learn it as you go around. Concentrate! Are you looking for the bathroom or are you looking for fence number three? Focus! Don't stop to chat with a friend who wants to tell you about her new puppy. Think! It's not enough to spot a trap on the course. Figure out what you are going to do when you get there.

By ear Talk yourself through the course. Practice your commands as you move from one obstacle to the next. You may want to say some louder than others. Does Tilly need encouragement at that corner? Remember to say "Touch" at the contacts, if that is what you say in training. Recite them in the correct order until you are word perfect. Listen to yourself on mental feedback. It will help you remember the course.

By eye Shut your eyes after you have walked the course. Visualize it. How many weave poles are there? What comes after the tunnel? What color is the third jump? Can you see it all? Now add yourself and your dog. Imagine a perfect run. You will not only remember the course, but you will go clear!

By feet As you go walk around the course, rehearse your movements. Point, pull and pirouette. Refine your body language. Now run the course (but try not to crash into anyone) as if your dog is with you.

You can learn the course by just one of these methods or by a

Above: *Where the finger points, the nose will go. Practice pointing in the tunnel so your dog runs into it, rather than running around or jumping on top of it.*

combination of them. Whatever works for you. I usually walk the course at least three times. Once to get a feel for it. Again to learn it. And finally to test myself. Beware of over-walking a course. This is worse than not walking if at all. It's like staring at a page, seeing all the words but not reading it.

More than one course? If you have more than one course to walk at a show, walk the one you are going to run first, last. That way it will be freshest in your memory when the time comes to step up to the start line. You can always watch your second course from the sidelines later. You are human and it's not easy to remember everything! We are all sometimes guilty of going the wrong way or getting lost. Watching your dog, giving commands and trying not to bump into the judge is just multitasking. And the good news is that the more courses you run, the easier it will be. Just keep flexing your memory cells.

Turning Right And Left

Q *Do I have to teach my Staffordshire Terrier Riva verbal directional commands? I usually shout "Left" and point to the right. No wonder the poor dog is confused. I tried painting "R" and "L" on Riva's paws but that didn't work!*

A Did you try painting "R" and "L" on your running shoes? You have to teach Riva directional commands, but it is up to you to decide if you will use them. One day you will walk a course and think to yourself how much easier a maneuver would be if Riva understood the commands "Right" and "Left." Keep your options open by teaching Riva what they mean. If you make training fun, you'll learn your rights from your lefts too.

Circles Start with Riva in a stand and use a treat to start to lure her in a circle to her right. As soon as she starts to twist to the right, click and let her have the treat. Ask her to twist a little further each time until she has completed a circle. With practice she will be circling

Below: *Teaching your dog to twist to the right and the left is fun. She'll be doing a jive or boogie-woogie next!*

to the right without a lure and you can put a command to the action, your command to turn her to the right. Repeat these steps to teach Riva to turn to the left.

Maypole Pretend you are a Maypole and teach Riva to dance around you to the right and then to the left. You can use a treat as a lure to start her off and click her as soon as she starts to go. Give her treat. Riva will soon get the idea and will circle you in both directions and on command. And this is something you can do in the line at agility shows to remind your dog of the difference between left and right.

Apple tree I practice this around a little old apple tree in my yard, but a pole, flower pot, or even your mother-in-law will do. Start close to the tree with Riva on your left-hand side. Send her away from you with your left hand towards the tree. As she goes behind it, lure her with your right hand around it and back to you. Click as she starts to turn right and give the titbit to her. When she becomes proficient, you can add your directional command and start standing further away from the tree. Send her away and command her to turn right around the tree and call her back to you. Do the same thing on the other side, starting with Riva on your right, but turning her left to circle the tree.

Ambidextrous Not all dogs or people are ambidextrous or comfortable on both the left and right side. Make sure you practice turning exercises in both directions. You and Riva will both benefit and your brains will become a little more elastic. You'll be happy to perform maneuvers on either side.

Just make sure that you are saying "Right" when you want to turn right, not left!

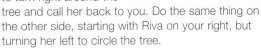

Agility Vocabulary

Q) *My instructor insisted that when Tigre, my terrier, and I started agility we had a different command for each piece of agility equipment. But she never explained why and I hardly ever use them now when I am competing. Why did I bother to teach them to Tigre?*

A) Your instructor wanted to make sure that you had as good a foundation in agility as possible. There are many good reasons to teach your dog the names of the different obstacles.

Above: *Help your dog to anticipate the different layout of the obstacles by using a separate command for each.*

Learning Names for the obstacles will make it easier for your dog to learn. If you say "over" for the long jump and "up" for a hurdle, Tigre will learn to jump low and long for one and high and short for the other. They need different actions and a verbal cue warns Tigre of what to expect.

Obstacle recognition When you say the name of an obstacle, Tigre should look for it and perform it. I bet that Tigre knows the word "tunnel" and you can send her into one from a distance. By saying "tunnel." Tigre goes into the tunnel while you take a short cut across the

course to position yourself ready for the next obstacle. Because she knows what a tunnel is, you can save seconds on the course time.

Obstacle discrimination Those nasty judges will place obstacles so close to each other. The A-frame is often placed over the tunnel and both are very tempting! If Tigre knows the names of the obstacles, she has a better chance of making the correct choice and she won't be eliminated for going in the tunnel when she should climb the A-frame.

Obstacle ambiguity A spread is easy to mistake for a hurdle in certain lights. Your dog is not able to walk the course and study the layout in advance like you. If you have a distinct command for the spread, Tigre will jump a little longer and the poles will stay up. If she mistook it for a hurdle, she could knock it and earn you five faults.

Not a shred of doubt Has this ever happened to you? You are running towards the seesaw. You run by it, assuming Tigre has done it. But no. She did not. Why should she? You didn't command her to do so. Maybe a "seesaw" would have helped her decide to walk up it rather than chase after you.

You might not use the names of the obstacles, but it does add another tool to your toolbox. You may rely on your body language to direct Tigre, but one day you might walk a course and find a trap where a verbal obstacle command will get you out of trouble. And if you do, then thank your instructor for teaching them to you!

Getting It Wrong

Q *How should I correct my Labrador Retriever, Blaze? When he gets something right I give him a treat or throw his toy, but what do I do if he gets it wrong? If he breaks a wait, jumps off a contact or misses a weave entry, I don't want to yell at him or hit him.*

A I'm so glad to hear that! You should never use physical punishment. Mistakes are inevitable and an important part of the learning process. They'll happen even though you try to make it easy for Blaze to get things right. Mistakes also occur because our performance criteria change in different environments. A paw-perfect dog in training will break waits, miss weave entries and jump off contacts in competition.

Types of correction There are different types of correction. Not all mistakes are serious offences. Use what is appropriate. Fit it to fix the error. Here are various options:
* Ignore it. It might never happen again.
* Look the other way and shrug your shoulders. Withdrawing your attention cuts a dog right to the heart.
* Mark the mistake with a phrase like "Oh dear" or "Wrong" so that Blaze will learn where he went wrong.
* Withhold his praise and rewards. Don't give Blaze a treat or throw his toy if he gets it wrong. Try again and if Blaze gets it right, he gets his goodies.
* Halt the game. If agility is his thing, go to the end of the line in class. Or leave the building.

Above: *If your dog can't see your face, he won't be able to read your thoughts and feelings. Turn your back and you have hung up the phone. The line is dead.*

Right: *When you have a breakthrough, your dog needs a BIG reward. Tell him he's wonderful and get out the treats and toys. He will see how pleased you are by the BIG grin on your face.*

Get it right next time Mark the mistake and then show Blaze what you want. If he lies down when you left him in a sit-wait, put him back in the sit. If he pops off the contact, put him back on it. If he misses a weave pole, take him back to where he came out. You can do this at your local agility club or at simulated shows. But be aware that if you do this at a competition, the judge will eliminate you for training in the ring or touching your dog. He will ask you to leave his ring.

Balance If Blaze needs correction make sure that it is balanced with praise. Don't follow a strong "Wrong" with a weak, wishy washy "Good boy." And if Blaze is putting a lot of effort into trying to get something right, put a lot of effort into your praise. For example, if Blaze keeps missing his target at the bottom of the A-frame, he will need a big, big reward when he finally gives it a nose touch. You've had a breakthrough.

Drastic steps Don't let desperation lead you to desperate measures. Rattling a can filled with pebbles or squirting water will certainly get Blaze's attention. A puff of vapor from a remote citronella collar will stop him in his tracks. However, Blaze's misdeed must be pretty evil before you would want to take such drastic steps and resort to something so negative. You don't want him to be frightened of the agility equipment.

If Blaze makes a mistake, don't punish him. Correct him and show him how to win your love and approval next time.

Staying Put

Q *I am determined to teach my Boxer, Boris, a good start line stay. He always breaks the first time, but stays after I put him back. Sometimes he creeps forward but I'm so delighted that he is at least on the other side of the fence that I let him get away with it. Should I put superglue on his bottom?*

A Avoid the superglue. If Boris is really determined that won't hold him!
There are three components to a good start line stay. Don't compromise on any of them.

- The stay. This means do not move. Do not change position from a sit to a down or a down to a stand. Do not creep forward. Do not twitch a single muscle. Freeze!
- The release. If it is a word, like "OK," the dog is dying to hear it. It means he can move again. He can get to jump those fences.
- The acceleration. You want your dog to drive over the first fence when you release him, not yawn and trot his way round the course.

Away from agility Train your sit-stays in as many different situations as possible, away from agility. Agility will be the final test. Will Boris sit-stay while you put your coat on to go out for a walk? Will Boris sit-stay while your other dogs play fetch? When he is 100 per cent reliable in these situations, he is ready to try it in front of a fence.

Say it once Don't keep repeating your stay command. Boris heard it the first time and saying it over and over again will only make you sound distrustful and desperate. Have confidence in your training.

Keep an eye open Walk away from Boris, but look over your shoulder. How else will you know if he moves? If there is one paw out of place, go back and reposition it. One paw is only a few short steps away from getting up before you signal.

When he breaks If Boris breaks his stay at agility class, take him to the end of the line. Don't set him up again to start the exercise. He blew it. If Boris wants to get on the course, he has to do the sit-stay the first time.

And praise Boris has a stay problem, so he needs to know when he is getting it right. If he stays, tell him he is a good boy. Go back and give him a treat. He needs reassurance and rewards in order to continue doing what you want him to do.

It is worth mastering this exercise. If Boris can do a good sit-stay at the start, you will be able to leave him and position yourself on the course. You will be initiating your round in control and that will percolate through to the rest of the run. Remember that once your self-discipline slips for the start, it will probably start slipping for the contacts, the weaves and so on. Don't let your dog down. Have faith in your training.

Right: Such a tease! What dog wouldn't be tempted to break a sit-stay if his favorite toy was placed on the floor just inches from his paws? Not this Boxer!

But will he stay put when his toy is thrown up in the air?

Get Set, Go!

Q *I've watched handlers using different starting positions for their dogs. I can't decide whether to leave my dog in a stand, a down or a sit. Some handlers just break into a run and their dog follows. I have an eager Beardie cross called Purdy. Which one should I choose?*

A My position of choice is a sit-stay and that is what I would recommend. There are a number of reasons.

Ergonomic I think the sit is the best blast-off position. It's comfortable. The dog has his bottom on the ground, but is already halfway to stand. All he has to do is push and move his front paws so he doesn't fall on his nose.

Ambiguity The sit is a pretty unambiguous position. If your dog shuffles, creeps forward, or looks to the left or right, you'll be able to spot it. It is much harder to pinpoint changes or movement if the dog has been left in the down or the stand.

Wait and recall If your dog will wait, you have an advantage over the handler who drops and runs with his dog because you can pick the best place to position yourself on the course. And it's less likely that your dog will knock the first fence to beat you onto the course. With a wait you can take a few deep breaths to compose yourself before you signal "Go" to your dog.

Acceleration I like to motivate a dog to accelerate out of a sit-stay by making it an exciting game with the reward of a toy or a treat. The sit-stay shouldn't happen because the dog is bored and there is nothing else to do. The dog should be sitting

solidly but expecting good things to come. Handlers who run with their dog from the start can get into trouble if their dog loves to race. The dog runs so fast he overtakes, goes the wrong way and ends up with an elimination. In contrast, other dogs aren't so eager to get off their bottoms. They trot off and never catch up with their handlers. They get slower and slower and finally give up. Whether with a fast or slow dog, these handlers argue that their dog lacks enthusiasm and that a start line wait will shut them down. But not if they teach the dog to switch on with a sit and blast off with a release word!

The down Many of the dogs you see lying on the start line started their agility career in the sit. After the dog repeatedly broke the sit, their handlers downgraded in the belief that the down position would be easier to maintain. In reality, it takes a mere nanosecond for the dog to break and clear a fence from any position if he is eager. And many large dogs that are left in a down smash into or run under the pole of the first fence. They are so eager to get to the second obstacle, they don't see the first.

I nominate a sit-wait for Purdy. Practice till it's perfect!

Left: *A dog with a good sit-stay at the start line is both comfortable and alert. He is switched on and ready to blast off as soon as his handler gives the release command.*

Right On Target

Q *My first agility dog, a Schnauzer called Elvis, always missed his contacts. I have a new Schnauzer puppy, Poppy, and I don't want her to follow in Elvis's footsteps! I've been doing my homework – reading about different training methods and quizzing different agility handlers. She loves the clicker. What target behavior on the contacts do you recommend?*

A There are a number of target behaviors that you can teach Poppy while she is a puppy. All you need is the lid from a tube of chips or cookies, your clicker and lots of treats. When Poppy is older and starts learning the agility obstacles, she will be a step ahead. She'll see her lid at the bottom of the A-frame and know exactly what she is supposed to do when she reaches it. These are my favorite target behaviors.

Peck and go Hold the lid in your hand and teach Poppy to touch it with her nose on a command like "Touch" or "Target." Slowly lower the target to the ground and continue to click and treat when she gives a nose touch. Practice pecking in different places. The kitchen, the yard, the parking lot at agility training. Will Poppy run to the lid and peck it? Excellent. Try running on the left and right with Poppy to the target. She has to get accustomed to seeing you running by her side. What about if you run ahead of her? She still must peck and catch you up. No peck, no reward. Finally, if you command when the lid is in your pocket, will Poppy start pecking the ground like a chicken? Good! Quick click the pecking action and give her a treat.

Go to sleep You can also train Poppy to lie down and put her head on the lid. If she already has a nose touch, tell Poppy to lie down and place the target between her front legs. She will touch it with her chin as it is nearly impossible to touch it with her nose in that position, so click and treat. By withholding her click and reward, you can slowly

Above: *Teach your dog to "go to sleep" with a target. All he needs to do once his chin is on the ground is shut his eyes!*

extend the time she has her chin on her target. Teach Poppy a command like "Head" or "Chin" and get her to hold this position until she hears a release word. Dogs look so cute, as if they are about to say "night, night." Get her used to you running on either side and ahead. And fade her target. Will she put her chin to the ground when it's no longer there?

Teach Poppy both the "peck and go" and the "go to sleep." When you start agility training in earnest, you'll have a choice if you decide to ask for a target performance at the bottom of the contact. You'll never be able to take your lid into the competition ring, but if at any time you think Poppy is not performing well, you can reintroduce it to your training program.

Creeping Contact

Q *Scully, my Tibetan Terrier, wastes loads of time on the A-frame. He creeps down at a snail's pace while I twiddle my thumbs. And worse, sometimes as he is just about to put his paw on the contact, he jumps off! What am I doing wrong?*

A There are many reasons why a dog will descend the A-frame slowly. The dog knows that something is supposed to happen on the contact, but not what, so he takes great pains to approach it cautiously or avoid it altogether. Perhaps the chosen training method has been incorrectly applied or too many training methods thrown at the dog in quick succession. Let's try something completely different with Scully so you stop twiddling your thumbs and put them to good use – a hand touch.

Hand target Teach your dog a hand touch with a clicker. Most dogs will sniff the palm of your hand if it is held out to them. Click and reward Scully for each nose touch. Most dogs just can't believe that all they have to do is touch your hand in order to receive a treat. Keep repeating the exercise to convince him it's true.

Above: *A dog that drives confidently down the dog walk into the contact will reward his handler with a good time.*

Work harder Hold your hand out a bit further so that Scully has to stretch his neck out to touch it. Click, reward and repeat. He is having to work harder for his treat. Increase the distance a little at a time.

Movement Start moving your hand and have some fun. Will he zoom under a chair to touch your hand? Can he find your hand when it is held behind you? Will he jump over your cat to touch your hand? Look for drive.

Cue If you think Scully understands what he has to do to get a treat, add a cue like "touch" or "target." Your dog should be really eager to find and touch your hand with his nose.

Lure Now, you are ready to use your hand to lure your dog over a low A-frame. You will always have your hand in the ring – it's the sort of training aid that is impossible to leave in the car. No more creeping. Scully will be trying so hard to hit your hand that he will quickly descend the lowered A-frame to get to it.

Touch Gradually raise the A-frame, but don't lose your dog's momentum. Make sure you always use your hand to lure your dog right to the ground. If you take your hand away too soon, he will jump off the contact. Your hand must be moving all the time, but be just out of reach. When your dog gets to the bottom and has taken a few steps on the ground, stop moving your hand so your dog can catch it. He needs the opportunity to touch it and get his reward.

Stop twiddling your thumbs and try using your hand as a target instead. Good luck!

Making Contact

Q *My sheepdog, Clarrie, thinks contacts are a waste of time. I'm sure she thinks that they are put there to slow her down and she hates anything that slows her down! It's as if she thinks they are dangerous to touch.*

A Quite the opposite. They are perfectly safe to touch. It's jumping over them that is dangerous. If Clarrie flies off and lands badly, she risks hurting herself.

If you have a high-drive dog, I would suggest you train the two feet on, two feet off position at the bottom of the contacts. Start at home with a clicker and lots of treats.

1 Do you have stairs in your house? Place Clarrie with her bottom on last step and her front paws on the floor. Click and treat this position.
2 When she understands the position, use a command like "On it" or "Contact."
3 Don't forget to use a release command like "OK" or "Go." Clarrie must hold the position until you say it's all right to move. Get this part perfect before you move on to the next step.
4 When she is in the two feet on, two feet off position, put a treat about 24in (60cm) in front of her. If she is a good girl and holds her position, you can release her on to it. This will keep her looking forward. You don't want Clarrie looking up at you in expectation of her reward.
5 When you have become an expert on the stairs, place Clarrie on a lowered A-frame. Her back legs should rest on the bottom of the A-frame and her front two feet should rest on the ground. Click and treat. Clarrie is doing exactly what she was doing on the stairs so use the same command. Work through the progressions until she is being released on to a treat or toy on your command.
6 Back chain the A-frame. Make sure that each time you move Clarrie further up the A-frame that she drives into the two feet on, two feet off position.
7 Start the exercise from the other side of the lowered A-frame. And remember to run with

Clarrie on both the right and left. Sometimes run past the bottom of the A-frame. Look back to see if Clarrie is still staring at her toy and waiting to be released.
8 When you deem Clarrie's contact performance to be 100 per cent reliable, add other pieces of agility equipment like jumps and tunnels to make different sequences. You can dispense with your toy and use running on to an obstacle as a reward. She must still land at the bottom of the A-frame in a two feet on, two feet off position and wait for your release word before proceeding any further.
9 If Clarrie doesn't wait for her release word, place her back on the contact and praise her to reinforce the two feet on, two feet off position. Release her but do not allow her to continue over any other obstacles. Walk with her to a chair, sit down and count to ten. Now you are ready to start again.
10 You and Clarrie should be pretty good by now. Start to raise the A-frame until it is at full height and insist that Clarrie is paw perfect. You can always review your contact work or lower the A-frame if she looks confused or keeps jumping off.

If you make contact training rewarding and fun, Clarrie will learn that they are worth waiting on!

Last Link in the Chain

Q My dog walk contact is non-existent. Kaos, my bouncy Labrador, just bounces off the end every time. My instructor spent a whole lesson talking about back chaining. I didn't really understand what she was talking about, but was too embarrassed to interrupt her as the rest of the class nodded knowingly. What did she mean by back chaining?

A Back chaining is training the last behavior in a chain first, then training the next-to-last behavior, then the behavior before that, and so on. Working in reverse order may seem an upside-down way of doing things but it can be very effective.

If you are retraining your dog walk, start at the bottom of the plank. Place Kaos in his end position. This may be a two feet on, two feet off position, a sit or a down. All Kaos has to do is assume his end position. This is the place were he gets all his goodies and rewards when he is released from it. Back chaining will be successful as long as this end position is familiar and practiced. There should be no doubt

in Kaos' mind what happens at the bottom of the plank.

Next, start the exercise about 6in (15cm) up the plank and finish it in your end position. Slowly work your way up the plank a foot or two (30-60cm) at a time until Kaos can perform the whole dog walk from the start. It may take weeks rather than a few hours. Back chaining relies on the principle of the familiar behavior reinforcing a less familiar one. You will have done many thousand more repetitions of the end position than the start. Remember these key points if you back chain the dog walk.

Be thorough Do not move Kaos up the dog walk until he is delighted and overjoyed to be on the contact in his position. This is a key stage. Everything depends on it so it's worth spending lots of time here. Don't worry. Subsequent stages will not take so long to teach him.

Don't let your standards slip If you want a certain attitude or a certain position, don't accept less. Make sure you have the drive and enthusiasm you are searching for at each stage. You don't want Kaos to stroll to the bottom of the dog walk and have a snooze. You want him driving to get there and get into position for a treat and your praise. If you have trained a two feet on, two feet off position, don't accept a toenail less.

Don't rush Do not add to the chain until the stage on which you are working is exactly as you want it – perfect. If you have a defective link, your chain will fall apart. Take the time to get things right.

I hope that makes the concept of back chaining a little clearer. And perhaps it helps explains why many handlers walk the course in reverse.

Far left to right: *It is not enough to teach your dog to climb up and down the A-frame. He must also understand how to perform the contacts. Choose a training method that will persuade your dog to hit the contact confidently every time.*

In A Fix With Contacts

Q *When I started agility with Diesel, my Springer Spaniel, he was really fast; too fast on the contacts and he kept missing them. My trainer told me to slow him down or he would hurt himself. He made me make sure Diesel hit the contact by grabbing his collar and guiding him down. Needless to say, Diesel has never shown the turn of speed he did in the beginning and I'm sure I was given bad advice. I'm in control but there's no oomph! Please help.*

A Students expect trainers to know all the answers and that's a big responsibility. It's easy to see how a method has failed in retrospect. I would guess that your instructor was a hands-on type of guy. Many dogs can cope with having their collar grabbed. They don't take it personally. Other dogs, especially the sensitive types, hate it. They react by jumping off too early to avoid be snatched or they proceed very, very warily … just in case someone lunges at them.

Your dog's established contact behavior will be difficult to change and it may get worse before it gets better. Retraining is always an uphill struggle.

Above: *If your dog is sensitive, grabbing him by the collar to hurry him up may, in fact, slow him down. Consider a hands-off method of teaching the contacts.*

Ask anyone who has tried to give up smoking. But it's not impossible. Most retraining fails because the handler gives up too soon. So, don't be tempted to resurrect old handling habits if you do not see an immediate change in your dog.

Why? You seem sure that Diesel's lack of enthusiasm is due to your earlier instructor. It might be, but first rule out a physical problem that could be causing Diesel to slow down, before you start retraining.

Have a break The greater the distance between old patterns of behavior and teaching new ones, the better. If Diesel thinks he is learning a brand new game rather than playing the old game with a few changes of rules, he will be easier to retrain and eager to learn.

Lighten up Turn your attention to games that will inspire and motivate Diesel. What turns him on – a toy or a treat? Keep training sessions short and reward him frequently. And don't forget that your smile is just as important as a squeaky plastic mouse or slice of hot dog. Frown and training is hard work. Smile and it's fun.

Contact method Don't take a short cut. Although it may take longer, it is worth starting fresh rather than trying to doctor your existing contact performance. Pick a contact method that will allow you to continue to have fun together with your treats and toys. Diesel might find a two feet on, two feet off position depressing, but he might really like doing a hand touch and being lured down and through the contacts. Go back to the beginning and lower the contact equipment as far down as possible. You are not only rebuilding Diesel's confidence, but yours too.

Good luck with Diesel. I hope you succeed in energizing your contacts and putting the fun back into agility.

Running Contacts

Q *I have always taught my dogs a two feet on, two feet off position on the contacts and I have always been pleased by the results. However, I want to teach my new Staffy terrier, Pumpkin, running contacts as I think I'd be able to achieve better course times. How do I go about it?*

A A running contact is when the dog runs full force from the top of the contact equipment to the bottom and onto the ground. He doesn't jump off! There are a number of ways to train a running contact. Choose one that you can apply easily and it will give you the result you want.

Natural stride Some dogs have natural striding that turns into a running contact without any prompting from the handler. If this is what Pumpkin does, accept it as a gift and give thanks. Don't mess with it.

On the lead Put Pumpkin on the lead and run him over the contact equipment. The lead gives you the

Below: *Some dogs have a natural running contact. Their stride lands them in the yellow before they exit the obstacle.*

control to ensure that the dog maintains forward momentum but can't leap off into thin air. Repetition is the key. Pumpkin must achieve and maintain a good running contact performance without his lead.

Ball or toy Put a ball or toy at the bottom of the contact equipment to encourage Pumpkin to look earthwards and run to the bottom to collect it. You can allow him to carry his prize in his mouth over the course. This is a bonus for some dogs and ensures that drive is maintained. Fade out the toy slowly.

Physical barrier There are many strange contraptions fashioned by handlers – hoops, mesh tunnels and pipes – to shape their dog through the contact zone. Make one and practice running Pumpkin through it. When he is doing this happily, place it at the bottom of the contact equipment for him to race through. Don't let him jump over it. Eventually, Pumpkin will have to run to the bottom of the contact without the visible training aid that has been molding his performance.

Target Instead of teaching Pumpkin to stop on a target, teach him to run over one. Introduce him to a 2ft (60cm) square piece of carpet and teach him what you want him to do. Then, place it at the bottom of a contact. Insist he continues to step on it as he runs, not jump over it. He will adjust his stride accordingly. You can fade the target out by cutting it into smaller pieces until it is out of sight.

Quick release Teach Pumpkin a two feet on, two feet off position as you have taught your other dogs. Timing is of the essence. A good, quick release will make the halt at the bottom of the contact imperceptible – a running contact.

Contact performance needs to be deeply embedded in the dog's muscle memory and must be independent of physical training aids to be effective in competition. Whichever training technique you choose, don't let your standards slip.

Up Contacts

Q *I have received a lot of help at club training with the down contacts, but no one has helped me teach my Brittany Spaniel Bounty how to hit the up contact. And this is where he keeps getting marked at shows. Do I just do what I did for the down contact?*

A There are contact areas at both ends of the A-frame and dog walks so that these obstacles don't have to be lifted and turned around if the course is reversed. And having contacts at each end of the dog walk really makes the judge run!

Above: *Make sure that your dog does not leap onto the equipment and miss the up contact. Greyhound mixes and GSDs are the breeds most often faulted for this mistake.*

Shorten your dog's stride There are a number of ways you can do this, so experiment.
- You can place a pole on the ground in front of the obstacle so that Bounty has to step over it and adjust his pacing before he can mount it.
- Or you could teach Bounty a command like "Steady" which will cue him to decelerate. As he slows from a gallop to a trot, he will be less likely to leap the contact.
- Or you could say your dog's name as he is approaching the obstacle. He will momentarily take his eye off it and look at you. This is often enough to break his stride, but you must get the timing right – too early and it won't make any difference and too late and Bounty will have already leapt over the contact.

Teach your dog to step on a target with his paw. Place it just before or on the up contact so that Bounty will have to step on it before he mounts the obstacle. You will be able to find the best place for the target through trial and error. Some dogs are so intent on finding the target that they halt on it and then gather themselves up for a huge leap that takes them over the contact. Remember you do not want Bounty to stop, but to maintain forward momentum.

Shaping Teach Bounty to duck under a small arch or hoop. Place it in front of the obstacle so that he will have to hit the contact on his way up. This method can be very successful in training, but unless the behavior is well established in the dog's muscle memory, it will disappear when the visible training aid is removed. Alternatively, you can teach Bounty to duck under your arm. Obviously for this to succeed you have to arrive at the contact at the same time as your dog. Not always possible. And some dogs see an arm stretched out across their path as an invitation to jump rather than duck.

Whatever method you choose, make sure Bounty still has the power to get onto the equipment. Otherwise you will get five faults not for missing the up contact, but for a refusal.

Flying Off The Seesaw

Q *Have you ever seen a dog fly? Then you should see Petra, my Irish Setter, launching herself into space from the seesaw. How can I stop her? I'm sure she will soon leave Earth entirely and find herself in orbit!*

A Seesaws are not launch pads! Dogs become airborne because they have not been taught how to do the obstacle properly. They fail to find the point of balance and tip the plank. Or, they are afraid of the seesaw. They try to get the obstacle over and done with as quickly as possible and end up

scrabbling, airborne and scared silly. And some other dogs are so eager to complete the course, they dismount sooner rather than later.

Think of your ideal seesaw performance. It must touch the ground before Petra alights. She is a big dog so the seesaw will start tipping midway, near the fulcrum. You don't want her to creep up it, but to run, and work the tip. Then, run to the bottom of the contact and exit as soon as it hits the ground.

Above: *For a safe landing from the seesaw, this dog needs a parachute! His handler is too far behind to catch him in mid-air.*

The tip I like to see dogs finding the point of balance or the "tip" on the seesaw. The lighter the dogs, the higher up the seesaw they can go before it starts to move. Also, the tip will vary from one seesaw to the next, depending on the materials and manufacturer. Petra will notice a difference between the seesaw that she trains on at home and the ones she meets at shows. If you have played with Petra

on a wobble board when she was a puppy, she shouldn't have too much trouble finding a seesaw's tip. She needs to locate it and shift her weight back for a split second so that gravity can take over. Start her on the lead. With a big and heavy dog like Petra, stop her in the middle of the seesaw. When it starts to move, use your treat to lure her into a play bow so she rides it while the seesaw finishes its journey to the ground. She gets a treat. Then she can follow another treat along the plank to the bottom. I have seen some dogs so eager to stop in the middle that they slide the rest of the way onto the contact. And, tempting though it is, don't teach Petra to balance both ends in the air!

The contact Teach the seesaw contact the same way as you would your other contacts. It is painted there for the same reason. Have you taught Petra nose-touch on a target? Look where the end of the seesaw is going to hit the ground. This is where you should place your target. Work through the same progression as you would do for the dog walk or the A-frame. If you use your hand to lure Petra to the bottom, make sure you move your hand downwards as the seesaw falls so she follows it right to the ground. If you make Petra wait for a release on the other contact obstacles, continue to use it on the seesaw.

When Petra shows proficiency on the seesaw, start adding a few other obstacles. She needs to practice entries and exits onto it at speed. If she starts leaping off again, review her basics.

Light As A Feather

Q *My Papillon, Tinkerbelle, is too light to tip the seesaw. She is a bold, speedy dog and runs up no problem. Besides putting her on a diet of fattening food or sewing lead weights in her collar, what can I do?*

A Little dogs often have a problem tipping the seesaw. They fail to make it to fall because they don't run right to the end of the plank. And when they have gone past the point of balance, it seems to take ages for the plank to hit the ground. Tinkerbelle doesn't need fattening but incentives to run to the very end.

Fear Did Tinkerbelle give herself a fright? Did the plank hit the ground with a bump and bounce her into the air? Or did a gust of wind make it wobble? It's no surprise that she avoids going right to the end of the seesaw.

Climb It's a steep climb up the seesaw from the perspective of a little dog. Did Tinkerbelle get three-quarters of the way to the end of the plank and then worry about being able to make it tip? No wonder she turned around and started back down. At least that end was still on the ground.

Squished treats Teach Tinkerbelle to run right to the end of the seesaw, not just the contact area. You want her front feet an inch or two from the edge so her weight is as far forward as possible. Give her an incentive to get there. Leave Tinkerbelle in a sit on the ground at the bottom of the seesaw and go to the other side. Squish a piece of cheese or sausage meat an inch or two from the end. Hold the end of the seesaw up in the air with your hand underneath so that it doesn't fall and recall Tinkerbelle to you. She will be eager to reach the top for her squished treat. As she bends down to eat, let the seesaw tip and gently guide it to the ground. Tinkerbelle will be too busy licking up squished cheese to notice she is traveling downwards.

More squished treats As Tinkerbelle grows confident on the seesaw, you can start to let it fall a little faster each time. Soon you will no longer need to control the fall with your hand – Tinkerbelle will do all the work without your aid. Keep squishing a treat so she still has a reason to climb the plank right to the end. And instead of recalling Tinkerbelle, try sending her on to the seesaw while you run along it on the right and left side.

Less squished treats Start to vary the size of the squished treats and sometimes don't use one at all. Tinkerbelle will still check out the end of the seesaw, just in case there is one there!

Tinkerbelle sounds a feisty girl. She won't get too fat from all the treats and she will soon be tipping the seesaw like an agility pro!

Above: *Cheese is a great treat to squish onto the seesaw. It stays put until your dogs licks it off!*

Wiggly Poles

Q *I'm 12 years old and have a Cavalier King Charles Spaniel called Morgan. He's a year old and very smart. He can do lots of tricks like sit up and beg, roll over, and speak, but he will not weave. What should I do to make him weave?*

A I'm so glad to hear that Morgan is your best friend. He must be very clever to learn so many tricks and agility is another thing you can have fun doing together. The weaves are one of the most difficult obstacles to teach. Wiggling in and out of poles can be really boring so you have to make it an enjoyable and rewarding experience for Morgan. Try luring Morgan through the poles. Most Cavies like their food and will follow a titbit anywhere.

1 Put two poles in the ground about 2ft (60cm) apart. The poles should be about 12in (30cm) taller than Morgan at his withers.

2 Face the poles and start with Morgan on your left. Have a treat in your left hand ready to attach to his nose. Step with your left foot across to the second pole and lure Morgan through the gap. Agility dogs must always enter the weaves with the first pole on their left.

3 Step forward with your right foot, throw the treat ahead of Morgan as he passes the second pole with his right shoulder.

4 When, after a few practice goes, Morgan has a wiggle, give the action a command like "weave" or "poles."

5 If Morgan thinks two poles are easy, try a row of four. Keep luring him in and out and throw his treat as he exits the fourth pole. He'll have to keep running ahead to find and eat it.

6 Add two more poles until you have a full set of 12. But if at any stage Morgan looks confused, make it easy for him to get it right by reducing the number of poles.

7 When Morgan is happily weaving, try keeping his treat in your right hand. Go through the motions with your left and at the end of the row throw his treat from your right hand. Did you fool him? Slowly wean him off your left hand. Move it a little less each time, but keep rewarding him at the end of the poles so that he runs forward to get his treat. He will begin to look forward to the end of the poles and not up at your hand.

It is important to keep it light and fun. Don't do too many repetitions. Even though Morgan is very smart, weaving may take months to learn.

Have you thought of teaching Morgan to weave between traffic cones or plant posts? There are many things you can set up in the yard and weave around. And don't forget to teach him to weave between your legs – you'll always have those handy!

Left: *A dog that is play-orientated is easy to lure with a toy between two poles. But don't hold the toy too high or your dog will look up rather than straight ahead.*
And don't bend down too much or you may poke your eye out on a pole!

Weave Machine

Q *Where to start? I'm really having a problem with the weave poles with my Poodle Sonic. I started training two poles at a time and eventually gave up and moved onto channel weaves. Sometimes I clicker-train. Sonic is so variable it's difficult to discover what's gone wrong. Sometimes she's fast and accurate. Sometimes she's too fast and does two at a time. Other times she's slow and unmotivated. And she's started entering at the fourth pole and jumping out at the sixth!*

A It sounds as if Sonic is eager to learn but doesn't understand what you are trying to teach her. That's why her performance is so variable and why she is losing confidence and motivation. Sonic has put all the things you have taught her in a mixing bowl, stirred well and shoved it in the oven. Sadly, what she has baked is not delicious weave.

There are so many different ways that the weaves can be taught successfully. If you choose just one method, you must follow through even when the going gets tough. If you choose to combine different methods for teaching different aspects of weave behavior, you must be thorough with each and teach your dog how to combine them. Here are some little pieces to consider:

Entry Using only two poles, click and reward the entry. Make sure Sonic is attacking them with gusto and from any angle before adding another two poles. Continue to click the entry but reward at the exit.

Speed Use channel weaves to build speed through the poles. It should be fast and furious with a favorite toy or treat at the end. And yes, channel weaves can teach accurate entries and exits, but if you are breaking things down, you will have selected this tool to teach one specific thing (speed) – anything else will be learned incidentally.

Accuracy Attach the lead or hold onto Sonic's collar. Thread her through the poles. Not my favorite method of training, but it's how they used to do it in the good old days. And you will be ensuring every pole is performed perfectly from beginning to end.

Below: *Poodle perfect weaving. This poodle has got a check in all the boxes – entry, speed, accuracy and exit.*

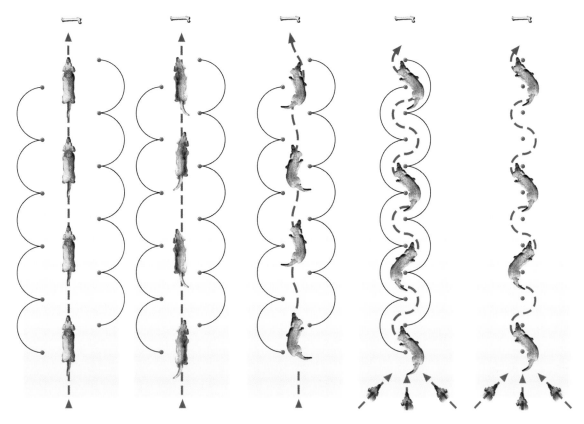

1 *A wide channel flanked by poles.*

2 *The two rows of poles move closer.*

3 *And then even closer together.*

4 *The poles are now in a straight line.*

5 *And finally the guide wires are removed.*

The weaves 1, 2 and 3 *When you introduce your dog to channel weaves, set them so that the channel is wider than his shoulders. At the start, he should be able to run straight to the end without touching the poles with his body. As the channel narrows, he will have to squeeze and bend.*

Exit Click and reward the last two poles. Start with four poles and gradually add two more until you have reached the maximum number of twelve. Continue to click and reward on your dog's exit, sometimes with a treat, toy or another obstacle.

Combining When you have broken the weaves down into little pieces, you have to think about what

The weaves 4 and 5: *When your dog masters the straight approach to channel weaves, try angled entries.*

order they will be taught and combined. For example, are you going to teach speed before entry? Entry before accuracy? Will you click both the entry to mark the beginning of weaving behavior as well as clicking the exit to mark the end? Plan it. And don't be surprised if, when you add a new exercise to an old one, Sonic forgets what she learned before. As Sonic becomes more confident in the new exercise, her skill in the older one will re-surface. Have faith. It will all come together.

Perfect Entries

Q *Zero, my big Dalmatian, always misses his entry to the weaves. As soon as he misses it, I call him back and we start again. Second time around he gets his entry no problem and does the rest of the poles beautifully. How can I make sure he gets his entry on his first attempt?*

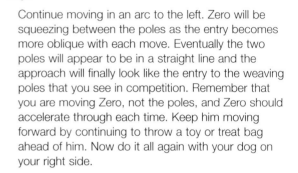

A By teaching him to get it at the first attempt! You are starting from a halt when you go for the second time and there is a big difference. Zero has not yet learned to nail his weave entry when he approaches the poles at speed. When he is running a course, Zero is accelerating from one obstacle to the next. He's a big dog and it isn't easy to squeeze himself between two poles when he is in top gear.

The first two poles Your first step should be to make sure that Zero understands weave entries. Set up two poles in your garden about 24in (60cm) apart. Position Zero so that the poles are in front of him – a big welcoming doorway. You can click as he goes through the gap but make sure he runs on to his toy or his treat bag to ensure that he continues moving forward. You don't want him looking back at you for his reward. Repeat until Zero is driving through confidently. Don't stand still. Accustom him to your movement. Run on his left and run on his right.

The squeeze Instead of starting the exercise with the two poles directly in front of Zero, begin by placing him a little to their left. The size of the gap between the poles remains the same, but it will look a little smaller from this angle.

Above: *The angle of approach determines the amount of squeeze needed to get a toy.*

Continue moving in an arc to the left. Zero will be squeezing between the poles as the entry becomes more oblique with each move. Eventually the two poles will appear to be in a straight line and the approach will finally look like the entry to the weaving poles that you see in competition. Remember that you are moving Zero, not the poles, and Zero should accelerate through each time. Keep him moving forward by continuing to throw a toy or treat bag ahead of him. Now do it all again with your dog on your right side.

More poles You should now have good entry to the weaves. Zero has learned to aim for the gap in the first two poles and to squeeze himself through. Add more poles a few at a time. Keep his rhythm going. Once he is in, there should be no problem. It's just one squeeze after another. Continue to run with Zero on the left and right.

More agility The weaves never stand alone in the middle of a course. It's time to practice them in combination with other pieces of agility equipment. Add a jump before the weaves. Does Zero still get his entry? Reward him with a jump after the weaves if he wiggles through each and every pole.

Above: *Put an obstacle like the tire in front of the weaves to test the dog's entry.*

Once you have re-taught and proofed your weave entries, Zero will be perfect on his first attempt.

Maverick Weaving

I am training my rescue German Shepherd, Maverick, on V-weaves. I'm so pleased with the result. He picks up the entry really easily and has a good paddle action. The poles are almost at an upright, but not quite. Problem is, Mav loses it completely when he sees the poles are vertical!

There is nothing more spectacular than a big, muscular GSD paddling through the weaves! V-weaves are an adjustable channel of poles. The poles are fixed onto a base that allows the angle of the poles to be moved from nearly horizontal to the ground to completely vertical. You've come so far, but Maverick is losing it at the very last hurdle. Let's review.

1 Start with six poles and bend them alternately outward until they almost touch the ground on each side. The first pole is bent to the left so that Maverick will learn the correct entry. As a gentle introduction, walk Maverick on the lead down the middle of the poles. Now get someone to hold Maverick while you walk down the poles and call him through to you. Give him a treat or a game when he makes it through. When he is happily doing a recall, let him watch you place a toy or titbit about 3ft (1 meter) from the end of the channel. Send him away over the poles to collect his toy.

2 Raise the poles until they are about 10-12in (25-30cm) off the ground. Repeat the recall. And this time when you send Mav away to his toy or treat, run alongside on the right or the left. Continue to raise the poles in increments of about 2in (5cm).

3 When the poles are about 18in (46cm) off the ground, start Maverick off a little to one side of the entry to the poles instead of straight ahead. Practice angled entries from the left and right.

Instead of placing a toy, try throwing it ahead of Mav as he exits the poles.

4 When the poles are about 24in (60cm) off the ground, begin to combine the weaves with Maverick's favorite piece of agility equipment. Add a tunnel or a jump to the end of the weaves.

5 Continue raising the poles until they are vertical. Make sure that Maverick maintains speed and enthusiasm. Don't be afraid to lower the poles if you hit a problem. If Maverick slows down or ducks out of the poles, you have raised them too quickly. The last 6in (15cm) up to the true vertical will probably be the most difficult and this is where you are struggling. Don't rush. You may only be able to raise the poles in 0.4in (1cm) increments.

Remember that you can lower all or some of the poles if Mav looks confused. If he is having difficulty with the entry, raise the other poles but not the first two. All the poles will be vertical in the end, but it will take a little longer to get there with these poles.

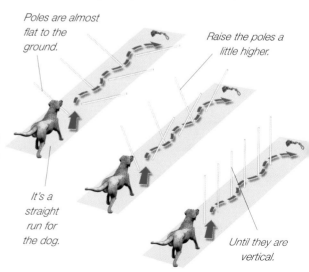

Poles are almost flat to the ground.

Raise the poles a little higher.

It's a straight run for the dog.

Until they are vertical.

The Last Pole

Q Please can you tell me why my collie Kite always misses the last two poles? She usually shoots out and does the next obstacle before I can call her back. It never happens in training, but always at competitions which is really upsetting when the round has been faultless till then.

A Take heart! Kite is making only one mistake instead of many for the judge to fault.

A question of time In class, you have all the time in the world but at a show you are trying to beat the clock. You push harder with your voice and your body. And out pops Kite. She is eager to get on and only too willing to miss the last two poles if it will help shave a few seconds off her time.

Voice If you are verbally encouraging Kite through the poles, listen to yourself. Are you repeating or holding onto one note that gets higher and more breathless as you approach the end of a line of weaves? Kite exits when you run out of air. In training, practice commanding Kite to "Weave" once and then say nothing.

Body language Make sure Kite has completed all the poles before you run on to the next obstacle. Stand still and upright. If you leave the weaves too quickly, so will Kite. And start training for independent weaves – recall, send away, left and right hand entries. When these exercises are solid, I would practice overrunning the weaves so that Kite will learn that even when her handler overtakes her, she must complete each and every pole.

Imaginary poles In order to help keep their voice normal and their body upright, some handlers visualize an extra pair of poles at the end of the weaves. Try this when you work Kite. It will stop you congratulating yourself for completing the poles too early.

Dogs can count If you only practice on six weave poles in training, Kite will be stupefied when she finds a set of 12 on the course. Teach your dog to weave right to the end no matter how many poles are in a line. Sometime six, sometimes ten and sometimes 12. If you want to be a contender for the Guinness Book of Records, you'll have to work your way up to 60!

Correction What do you do if Kite pops out of the weaves? If she is missing the last two poles because she is so driven to perform the next obstacle, you must stop her before she gets there. Not easy with a fast dog, I know. But if you mark the error with an "Oops" or "Wrong" the second she pops out, she will know where the mistake occurred. Call her back and guide her through the last two poles. Now she can reward herself with the next obstacle on the course. Soon that longed-for clear round won't be far away.

Where Mistakes Happen

Q *I'm fairly new to agility and will soon be entering my first show. Spud, my Collie/-Sheltie cross, is really good but sometimes makes a mistake in the weaves. I don't know how to correct him when this happens. Should I take him back and start all over again from the beginning or should I take him back to where he made the mistake?*

A Handler and dog can learn from mistakes provided they know where they made them. Think about the different kinds of mistakes that Spud makes in the weaves to determine a plan of action.

Random mistakes Is it impossible to predict where Spud will make a mistake? Sometimes he pops out in the middle, sometimes at the end, and sometimes he misses the entry? Spud's mistakes are random and it's not a case of correcting errors, but retraining the weaves. He doesn't understand what he is supposed to do when confronted by poles.

Last two poles Many dogs miss the last two poles because they are so eager to get on and complete the course. If this is where Spud is making mistakes, I would mark the error with an "Oops," call him back before he did any more obstacles and guide him through the last two poles. I would also do some remedial training to correct the problem. If you have clicker-trained Spud, click as he goes through the gap between the final poles to get a treat. And think about your body position. Don't be in such a hurry to move on to the next fence that you pull Spud out of the weaves.

In the middle If Spud is fast and excitable, he might be getting a hiccup in his weaving rhythm. Putting Spud back is problematic because it's difficult to tell exactly where he popped out. Moreover, it is unlikely that you would have been able to stop him carrying on after his error. When you can't mark exactly where the error occurred, go back to the beginning to start again and make sure that your dog does each and every pole.

Above: *A mistake in the poles can be difficult to spot, especially if your dog is a fast weaver.*

Metal feet Does Spud have twitchy toes? A dog with sensitive feet may be reluctant to step on the metal feet on the base and so may pop out of the weaves. An extra command at these points will encourage Spud to weave. Take out the poles and, as a separate exercise, work to accustom Spud to walking over and stepping on the metal base.

Motivation If Spud is a careful worker and only makes an occasional mistake, taking him back to redo a section of the weaves will demotivate him and erode his confidence. If the mistakes are one-offs, it will pay you to overlook them and do nothing.

But you must decide if it is a case of learning from a mistake or a case of needing to retrain the entire apparatus, or just a matter of going back a step.

Bending In The Poles

Q My Whippet Parsley is really fast over the course until he hits the weaves. We have had some good places at shows, but they could have been higher if Parsley could speed up in the weave poles. We lose so much time when we hit this obstacle. How can I get him to wiggle faster?

A Whippets, Greyhounds and their crosses all seem to have trouble bending in the middle! Parsley already knows how to weave, so try this game.

Below: *Whippets are born to run, not bend in the middle.*

1 Set up four weaves in the yard.
2 Leave Parsley in a "Sit" at the start and walk to the end.
3 Recall him through the weave poles and give him a treat when he reaches you. Most dogs move faster towards their handler. Especially if their handler is smiling. But remember, Parsley must do all four weaves to get his reward.
4 Do this enough times so that Parsley is keen to break out of his sit and wiggle his way down the weave poles to you and his reward.
5 Sit Parsley in front of the weaves and move to the next stage. Recall him as before, but just as he reaches you, turn away from the poles and throw his treat so that he has to continue running past you to catch up with it. The game now has a chase dimension that many dogs find irresistible. Make sure your treat will be easy to find in the grass and is something that Parsley can eat quickly.

6 Continue at this stage until Parsley is exploding out of the last two poles.
7 Is Parsley ready for a new twist to the game? While he is running after his treat, you run to the opposite end of the poles. As soon as Parsley finishes eating his treat and looks up at you, recall him through the weaves again for another titbit.
8 You can do this back and forth as many times as you like as long as your dog remains enthusiastic. You will both end up tired, but fit.

The difficulty can be increased in three ways:

Distance The further you throw the treat, the more ground your dog will have to cover to get back to the poles and the greater his speed of approach will be. Parsley will be more likely to miss the entry.

Number of poles The more poles, the more likely your dog is to slow down. Make sure he is traveling through four with energy before adding any more.

Angled entries If you throw the treat off to the right or the left of the weaves, your dog will have to perform an angled entry to return to you through the poles for his treat. Only try this if your dog has a good weave entry straight on.

This game has not only turned my dogs into fast wigglers, but it's made the weave poles their favorite agility obstacle.

Speeding Up

Q *My young German Shepherd Flash is steady but slow. We have been competing in agility for a few months now and always get a clear round or lower placing. I've taught him to go on. I can send him into a tunnel or direct him over a fan of fences from five yards. But he is reluctant to move too far away from me at shows. How can I help him live up to his name and speed him up?*

A German Shepherds are versatile and enthusiastic workers and much valued as guard dogs. They are on the look out for danger, intruders and titbits forgotten in your pocket. It's important for a German Shepherd to know what is

Above: *German Shepherds love to work. Their boldness allows them to attack agility obstacles with confidence.*

going on around them in order to protect their mistress or master. The farther you are away from them, the harder you are to guard. This can make German Shepherds less willing than other breeds to work at a distance from their handlers in agility. There are a number of things you can try.

Confidence breeds speed   You have a young dog with potential. As Flash grows more confident running agility courses, he will speed up. Give him time.

Independent worker   Flash is able to perform distance work in training. Build on this and teach him to negotiate the contacts and weaves regardless of where you are on the course.

Run faster   The tendency for many handlers is to hang back when they want a dog to work ahead. Yes, Flash will do it without you, but he would do it ten times faster with you by his side. Turn it into a race. That's much more exciting.

Experiment   Does Flash speed up if you cheer or clap? Does he get excited if you run with little busy steps or long strides? Does he like you to be in his face all the time (front cross) or does he prefer you in the background (rear crosses)?

Don't whine   Don't nag Flash to go faster. He'll know you are annoyed with him and slow down.

Encouragement   Don't put Flash in the position where he could mistake encouragement to go faster as praise for going slowly. Be discerning.

Praise speed   Make sure you are praising Flash for accelerating up a gear. Praise speed wherever you find it – when Flash is chasing a toy, running to you for a biscuit or simply having a case of the zoomies. Don't miss opportunities to let him know that it's not just a question of getting the job done, but getting it done fast.

Strengths   If Flash likes working close to you, I suspect your turns are nice and tight. He will be less likely to miss body signals or commands. Off courses and eliminations will be fewer. Speed will come.

   Speed is not everything, but attitude is. If Flash is enthusiastic and motivated, he will give you 100 per cent in training and at shows. Who can ask for more?

Tunnel Trouble

Q *My Brittany spaniel cross hates the collapsible tunnel. Beanie always pops out. I get all excited because he goes in and I rush to the other end to greet him only to find he's come out and is running up the side. Most dogs love the tunnel. Why doesn't Beanie?*

A Beanie loves you more than he loves the tunnel! When a dog goes into any kind of tunnel, he loses sight of his beloved handler. He figures that the quickest way out is to exit the way he went in. There are a number of things you can do to make sure you meet Beanie at the right exit.

Go back to basics Ask your instructor to hold Beanie at one end of the tunnel entrance while you go to the other end and hold up the chute. Bend down and when you have eye contact with Beanie, recall him through the tunnel. He needs to see your face at the other end, not your ankles. Praise and reward his efforts. Beanie gets treats and your reassurance at the tunnel exit – he'll want more of the same, so do it a few more times. Gradually allow the chute to lie flat. Beanie will no longer be able to see you and he will have to push through to get to you. It is worse for small dogs as it's such a long,

dark way to go, but if you progress slowly, Beanie will surprise you with his bravery.

Quick exit As above, but if Beanie likes to chase a ball, throw one as he comes out of the end of the chute. This will increase his speed and acceleration out of the tunnel. You don't want him to sit at the end of the tunnel anticipating a treat, but to drive on to the next obstacle.

Go it alone You won't always have your instructor handy to hold Beanie at the tunnel entrance. It's time to try running alongside the tunnel. Beanie will be eager to go through. Continue to throw a toy or treat at the end or send him over a fence. Practice running on the left and the right. If you make a bit of noise – clapping or cheering – Beanie will know that you are right outside, traveling the length of the tunnel with him.

Body language Make sure that when you send Beanie into the tunnel that you are pointing into it, not above it. You don't want him to jump it! But don't point with a treat in your hand or Beanie will stick with you rather than abandon his titbit. Your arm is not long enough to stretch from one end of the tunnel to the other.

Don't rush If Beanie thinks he can't catch you up, he will take a short cut around the tunnel rather than going through it. Make sure he is committed before you run by.

Tunnel entries When Beanie is happy going straight in and through the tunnel, practice some angled entries. When you approach the tunnel from the side, it will look different to Beanie. He won't be able to see the entrance and balk. Give him the opportunity to discover that the large dark entry hole is round the corner.

Tunnels are fun! Enjoy them and you'll have trouble keeping Beanie out of them, especially if it's dry inside and raining outside!

Left: *It's no good running around the course hoping your dog will take whatever obstacle is in front of him. He won't target the tunnel until he has learned to perform it confidently.*

Body Language

Q *My instructor keeps telling me that my body language is ambiguous. Shouldn't my collie, Billy, just do what I tell him? He's very fast and I'm sure he doesn't have time to see what I'm doing with my arms.*

A You'd be surprised how well Billy can read your body language. When you get up off the couch, Billy knows if you are going to make a cup of tea, if you are going to fetch your coat for a walk or if you are going to switch off the television. Dogs are very good observers and they practice reading their owner's every move. It's their preferred channel of communication most of the time. Think of all the occasions that you may have shouted tire and pointed at the tunnel (your dog did the tunnel) or yelled right and turned left (your dog turned left with you).

Expedient Many handlers with fast dogs just don't have time to spit out a long list of commands when they are running a course. Can you say "Billy left jump" before he has turned right and climbed the A-frame? These handlers act rather than speak. Especially those that don't know their left from their right. It's much simpler to use their dog's name combined with a body signal.

Body language You can cue Billy in a number of ways. You can make physical signs very obvious or very subtle to suit your dog and the course.

- Arms – an outstretched hand directs the dog to an obstacle.
- Face – your dog will look at whatever obstacle you are looking at.
- Shoulder roll – bring your arm across your body and roll your shoulder in and your dog will be pulled towards you.

- Feet – your dog runs in the same direction that your feet are moving.
- Movement – slow down or halt and your dog will slow down and stop. Change sides before your dog takes a fence and your dog will turn that way when he lands.
- Position – where you place yourself on the course will affect your dog's performance. Stand too close to the contacts and you might push your dog off them.

Above: *Can there be any doubt? The handler raises her arms in the air to call the dog up over, not down under, the jumps and straight to her.*

These are just a few examples, but they are enough to get you round a course. Body signals will help you traverse a box or snake down a line of fences. Don't think that because you are working Billy from behind that he will miss them. Dogs have great peripheral vision and he will pick them up and respond.

Experiment Try running a course without saying a word to Billy. Pretend you have laryngitis. It will make you work hard to sharpen your body language and make it meaningful. And, if Billy is the type of dog that barks his way round the course or gets very excited, keeping quiet will encourage him to focus on you and concentrate on your signals. Make sure those signals are clear and readable.

Some things like contact performance should be independent of body language, but as a means of directing your dog over the course, it's hard to beat the natural movement of your arms and legs.

Sending Ahead

Q *Silva sticks to me like glue. She is a Staffordshire Terrier and I always know where she is. The faster I run, the faster she runs. But I know she can run even faster. I would like her to work more independently and further away from me. How do I go about it?*

A Silva is a joy, but every now and again you wish she wasn't right at your feet? If you can't run any faster, you will have to teach Silva to work ahead of you.

Send aways Send aways are the foundations of distance work and are often overlooked. Handlers

Below: *Disappearing into a tunnel won't shake off this handler! She's doing all the chasing to try and catch up!*

practice recalls and working their dogs on the right and left. But send aways get left at the bottom of the barrel.

- Start at home. Sit Silva about 2ft (60cm) in front of her dinner bowl. Is she looking hungry? She'll be eager to get there so send her to it. After a couple of meal times, you can start commanding her with a "Go on" or "Away." Gradually increase the distance. Can she run from the living room into the kitchen to her bowl?

- Food bowls aren't just for meal times. You can use her food bowl as a target for send aways anywhere, anytime. Instead of putting her breakfast in it, use a single favorite treat. Send her to it from the top to the bottom of the yard or from one end of the drive to the other.

- Set up a line of three low jumps. Stand behind the last jump and send Silva over it to her bowl. Now stand behind the second jump and send her over two jumps to her bowl. If she goes on without any hesitation, try standing behind the first jump and sending her over all three. You can also throw a toy after the last jump but make sure she is committed to taking it before you chuck it. Be creative. You don't always have to use three jumps. What about trying jump, tunnel, jump? Your aim should be to get Silva to work the line of obstacles independently. It's you that varies your position.

Circles Stand in the middle of a circle of fences. Send Silva around to the left. You can make the circle bigger as she starts to flow and learns to work around you. Again, you can use different obstacles in your circle, but make sure they are things that Silva can execute competently. There is no point in putting weaves in the loop if she has a problem with her entry. Send her around from the right, too.

Lines and circles of obstacles will help Silva to work ahead with confidence. Initially, these exercises demand minimum movement from you. When you are competing, you will be running. So I would gradually introduce more movement when you have established some distance and Silva is driving away from you. She has to get used to you sending her ahead while you chase her from behind.

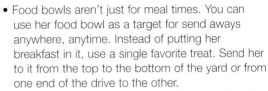

Changing Sides

Q *I have tried to tighten my Springer Spaniel's turns by doing front crosses. Yes, the turns are tighter, but Sassy ends up knocking the pole. Where am I going wrong?*

A Knocked poles are a sign of a badly timed maneuver or incorrectly positioned handler. Moreover, it indicates that the maneuver chosen was not necessarily the best one for the job. There are three types of crosses that enable a handler to change sides and turn his dog. Practice them so that you can execute all with equal comfort but, more importantly, learn to recognize which cross will be most effective in specific handling situations.

Front cross A front cross is just what it says. The handler changes sides by crossing in front of his dog – dancing face to face. A front cross will focus a dog on the handler and cause it to decelerate in order to make a tighter turn. But you must ask yourself if the loss of speed will be worth any seconds gained. And you must make sure that you give your dog enough space to land and take off. Stand too close to the fence and you will be too much of a physical barrier – your dog will knock the pole.

Rear cross The handler crosses behind the dog and the dog's bottom is always in view. To be effective the dog must work in front confidently. The dog is focused on the equipment and speed will not be compromised. However, turns may be wide and control can be a problem if the dog is too far ahead, misses the cross and then picks his own route. And position and timing is everything. You need to cross on the dog's take-off side of the fence, not his landing side. And, if you cross before the dog commits to the fence, you risk pulling him off it.

Above: *Agility is not all straight lines. The handler who can turn his dog tightly and keep the poles up will have a faster course time.*

Blind cross The handler crosses in front of his dog but instead of turning to face the dog, the handler changes sides with his back to the dog. As the dog finishes the turn, he is chasing his handler's bottom. Forward momentum is maintained. The dog must be comfortable with the handler ahead of him. If the handler is unable to get far enough ahead of his dog for the cross, he risks colliding with him when he tries to switch sides. Instead of allowing the dog to keep driving forward to the obstacles, everything comes to a halt while the First Aiders are called to the scene. Don't assume that a blind cross means that you don't have to turn your head to look where your dog is. The result can be an elimination or worse if you don't.

Decision time When you are deciding which cross to use, consider where you dog is coming from and where he is going to next on the course. Your handling of the first obstacle will have implications for the one that follows it. Also, think about the distance between the obstacles and the shortest path between them. Work not just the obstacles, but the spaces between them.

Select the right tool for the job. Practice all the crosses and use them where you think they will benefit you most on the course.

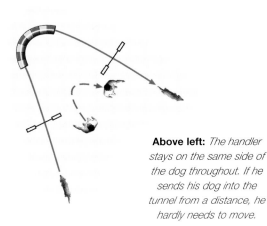

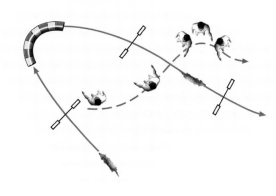

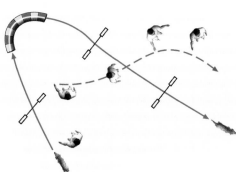

Above left: *The handler stays on the same side of the dog throughout. If he sends his dog into the tunnel from a distance, he hardly needs to move.*

Above: *This is a front cross. The handler sends the dog into the tunnel from his left side. He moves across the gap and faces the dog as he exits from the tunnel and collects him on his right side. Cut it too fine and he risks interfering with his dog's landing after the fence.*

Above: *A blind cross. Sending the dog into the tunnel from his left, the handler turns his back on him during the cross and needs to look over his right shoulder to see the dog.*

Right: *A rear cross. Sending his dog into the tunnel, the handler waits for him to exit and jump the fence before crossing behind and collecting him on his right to send him on.*

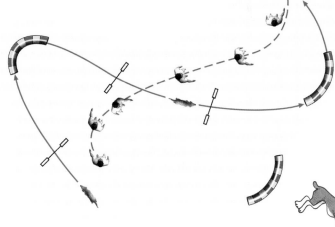

Dreaded Pull-Throughs

Whenever I walk a course and see three fences in a line, my heart sinks – pull-throughs. When it comes to my turn, sure enough, instead of running through the gap, my sheepdog cross Winnie back-jumps the second fence. I'm eliminated. Do you have any tips?

Handlers usually miss pull-throughs on a course because they start with a negative attitude. Inwardly, they sigh "I can't do this" and it turns out that they're right! Don't avoid pull-throughs. Practice them in training. Make them fast and fun and you will find that your heart will be soaring when you next see them on a course. You'll want to shout. "I can do this!" And you will!

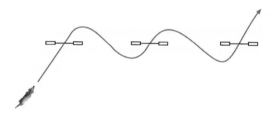

Above: *Pull-throughs are tricky if you don't practice them. Pretend your dog is a threaded needle and you are pulling him in and out of the material to make a hem.*

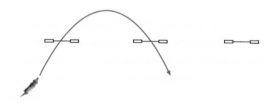

Above: *Ooops! It's all unraveling. If you don't give your dog a signal to run through the gap between the hurdle wings, he'll back jump the second fence and you will be eliminated.*

Pull-throughs A judge can set a pull-through between two fences in a line or through the corner of a box. There are three parts to the maneuver. You begin by sending your dog away from you over the first fence. Next, you turn your dog back towards you so that he comes toward you between the wings of the first and second fence. Lastly, you turn your dog away from you to send him over the second fence. Done well, a pull-through looks effortless. Done badly and it looks like you are trying to turn your dog into a pretzel.

Threadle A threadle is a series of pull-throughs on a straight line of jumps. It's a bit like sewing. You thread your dog in and out and hope your cotton doesn't break!

Through the gap Your dog needs to decelerate and change direction quickly in order to pull off a pull-through. And you need to learn to give Winnie the commands she needs to target the gap as well as the space to run through it. Reasons for failure are many.

Commit to the gap Treat the gap between the wings just like you would a fence. Make sure that Winnie has committed to it before you move across to turn her back into the second fence. Hold your position. If you move too soon she will back-jump the second fence rather than running between the wings towards you. In competition, you will be tempted to move too soon and hurry her, but resist it! There are three ways to commit and bring Winnie through the gap.

Directional commands The earlier Winnie is warned that a pull-through is coming the better. She needs a clear signal that she needs to come through the gap. You can use your directional

Above: *If your body starts to turn, so will your dog. Twist from the waist, use your shoulders and keep moving. Try putting your hands together in the shape of an arrowhead!*

commands to turn Winnie towards you between the wings and then to turn her away from you over the second fence.

Body signals Send Winnie over the first fence with your nearest arm. Then pull your outside arm into your chest which will turn your leading shoulder away from the second fence – a dummy turn.

As Winnie comes through the gap, turn, face the second fence and point to it with your opposite arm.

Hand touch If Winnie knows a hand touch, reach through the gap with your hand. She should come between the wings to try and touch it.

You can work commands and signals in combination to reinforce each other. But even if you use magic spells and potions, Winnie will back-jump fence number two if you fail to hold your position and allow her to commit to the gap.

Tunnel Traps

Q *If there is a tunnel trap on the course you can bet money that Vadar my Petit Basset will succumb. I can shout and threaten, but in he goes into the wrong end regardless. My trainer says to use my body and keeps telling me to do a "dummy" turn. Is he calling me dumb?*

A In agility, a "dummy turn" is also known as a "false turn" or "reverse flow pivot." The handler pulls his dog in towards him with his outside arm. But the poor dog is fooled; he's not going that way. The handler completes the maneuver by turning away from his dog and pushing him out towards an obstacle with his opposite arm. To be successful, the dog must be good at reading his handler's body language.

Turn tighteners Dummy turns will tighten turns. They are well suited to threadles when the handler wants his dog to be both tight and fast. The dog is sent over the first jump with the nearest arm, then called between the wings of the first and second fence as the handler pulls his outside arm into his chest, turning his shoulder inward. The dog is then sent back over the second fence as the handler straightens up, turns, and points with his nearest arm.

Discrimination aids Dummy turns can also be used as discrimination aids when there are obstacle choices on the course. If you use a dummy turn, it will be easier for Vadar to pick the right tunnel entrance rather than the wrong one. Shouting will not be enough! A dummy turn will direct Vadar to the entrance closest to you. Without the dummy turn, Vadar will run into the entrance closest to him.

Timing As in all agility handling, timing is important. If Vadar sees the dummy turn too soon, he is in danger of being pulled off the obstacle and missing it altogether. If he sees it too late, he will already be committed to whatever lies in front of him. Rather than being pulled in, Vadar will just keep going and be eliminated.

Above: *Nasty judges count on tunnel-happy dogs being sucked into the wrong end of the obstacle on their courses.*

Position Dummy turns can be very bold or very subtle. The longer you hold still as you pull your dog into you, the more you will get out of your dummy turn. The louder it will scream to Vadar to turn towards you and away from other tempting obstacles. Hold your position for a mere split second and Vadar will be better able to maintain speed and forward momentum. It's up to you to decide what is needed in any given situation on the course.

Dummy turns are a valuable handling tool. Practice them so that you can do them in your sleep. Vadar will be on the look out for your signals. But don't be a dummy! Learn to recognize when dummy turns are the most appropriate handling maneuver to apply on the course, and when to give them a miss. And you won't be the class dummy!

Turning A Corner

Q *My boy Ockley is a large Greyhound cross and I wonder if it's his size that makes it hard for him to tighten up his turns. He really drives down the straights but on the turns sweeps round in a wide arc. He looks as if he is about to come to a standstill. How can I help him?*

A It is always easier to run in a straight line than to turn the corner. Many agility handlers complain that their dogs slow down on the turns. And they are right.

- Dogs have to shift down a gear to negotiate a corner safely just like you do when you are driving a car. The trick is not to exchange safety for speed.
- Handlers have to wait for their dogs to turn corners. They perceive their dog as losing speed because they themselves are standing still.
- Dogs that dawdle on the turns fall prey to ringside distractions and actually slow down and widen their turns to get a better view of whatever has caught their eye.

Clear and consistent commands Does Ockley understand what you want him to do? If you variously shout, "Left!", "Back!" and "To me!", instead choose just one and he will respond more quickly.

Ever decreasing circles Set up a big circle of about six to eight fences. Run Ockley over these. Gradually remove fences and make your circle smaller and smaller until you have a tiny pinwheel of four fences with enough room for you to pivot in the middle. You must maintain your dog's enthusiasm throughout each decreasing circle while the turns get tighter and tighter. Repeat in the opposite direction.

Dummy turns The convention is to turn in the same direction as you want to turn your dog. By feinting a turn in the opposite direction, the turn sharpens. The dog is momentarily pulled towards you and then straightened up to continue on his way. This is called a dummy or false turn. Set up

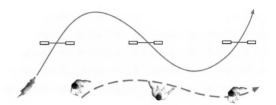

Above: *The handler performs a subtle dummy turn to call his dog over the middle fence in the snake. If he made the turn more pronounced, the dog would come through the gap as in a threadle.*

three jumps side by side and snake or threadle Ockley through them.

Front crosses If used correctly and at the right place on the course, a front cross will tighten Ockley's turns. Set up two jumps side by side. Send Ockley over fence one and recall him over fence two and redirect him back over fence one – a 360 degree circle. Don't get in his way or Ockley could refuse the jump or drop a pole. Make each front cross a little closer to the fences. How close can you get? Repeat in the opposite direction.

These exercises will help you. Use the appropriate tool to turn Ockley and he will tighten up. But remember that shortening the

Above: *Long-striding dogs can find it difficult to turn tight to the fences.*

distance that your dog will have to travel to turn will not necessarily result in a faster time. Don't sacrifice speed for tightness. You may find your time is better when you allow your dog to flow between fences.

Chapter Five

COMPETITION CRAFT

Don't let the fear of elimination put you off strutting your stuff in front of the judge. Fill out an entry form. Make some sandwiches and pack the car for the journey. Did you remember to stow a folding chair? Step up to the start line knowing that you have done your best to train your dog for this moment but don't be surprised if it all goes wrong. Your own nerves may turn your dog into a canine delinquent and there's a lot to think about. What if a loose dog runs into the ring? Who spilled all those treats by the dog walk? Not you! And why are you the only person with a Wolfhound in a line of Poodles and Papillons? Instead of your friendly instructor, a judge is standing in the middle of the obstacles waving his arms at the competitors. What does it all mean? The best way to find out is by volunteering your help at the ring. It's a good way to make friends, and you'll get a T-shirt too.

Turning Into A Canine Delinquent

Q *I have a problem with Hudson, my Springer Spaniel. He's great in training but at shows he runs by jumps, loops past tunnels and, if we are competing outdoors, he takes off over the fields. It's no surprise when we are eliminated. My well-behaved Springer turns into a delinquent. It's like he's a different dog.*

A It's not Hudson that's changed but his surroundings. And Hudson is indeed a different dog when he lacks confidence or is confused. His training venue is familiar and welcoming. There is his smiling instructor and fellow students. There are lots of treats and toys in the ring and you are relaxed. In contrast, an agility show has many new smells and sights. There are lines of nervous and noisy competitors. There are no treats or toys in the ring. And you are stressed and anxious! No wonder Hudson acts like a different dog.

You are not alone Sit by the side of the ring at a show and watch. Yes, some dogs are born agility stars, but others looked completely untrained. They run up to the judge or do a lap of honor before heading for the hills. Just like Hudson.

Relax Competition is stressful. The more you dread going into the ring, the more likely your Spaniel is going to find an excuse to leave.

Right: *De-stress yourself and your dog with a tug game. It may help you to forget your nerves.*

Have fun Don't aim for perfection. Ignore mistakes. Teach Hudson that the agility ring is not where he gets into trouble, but the best place in the world to have fun.

Togetherness Try to leave the ring together. If Hudson leaves the ring and you chase after him, he will think that you, too, have found a good reason to say good-bye to the judge.

Check-in Teach Hudson to check in with you at training. Stuff your pockets with treats or a portion of his dinner. Call him to you after the first obstacle, third obstacle, maybe the fourth and so on and give him a treat for giving you attention. He will acquire the habit of looking back to you – just in case you are going to ask him to check-in.

Different places, changing faces Give Hudson a chance to get used to different distractions. Train him in new locations and introduce him to new people. You should be the constant he can count on.

Thoroughness Make sure you have thoroughly taught the agility obstacles. If Hudson is a teeny bit unsure of how to make a seesaw tip in training, that flaw in his training may overwhelm him at a show. He would rather run by it than try and attempt to mount it. And your disappointment will just make it worse next time.

I believe that once the competition environment becomes familiar to him, Hudson will gain confidence and start enjoying himself (provided you, too, relax and have some fun). You don't want running out of the ring to become Hudson's way of coping with the unfamiliar or something stressful. Work now to show him what he'll be missing if he leaves the agility party early.

Are You Ready?

Q *I have been training Buddy in agility for about a year and I think the time has come to take the plunge and enter a show. My trainer says to wait a bit. How do you know when your dog is ready to compete?*

A I will never forget my first agility show! I didn't win anything, but I was so proud of how I handled myself and my dog on the courses. Your first time in the ring with Buddy will be a lasting memory. Make sure it is a good one.

Is your dog prepared?

Assess your dog's performance in class honestly. Buddy must be able to tackle all the agility obstacles and string them together on a course. Competition introduces new variables into the agility equation – different equipment, a strange venue, and a nervous handler. Don't be hasty to fill in your entry form.

- Proof your performance. Try running a course at a higher level than you will enter at a show. Can Buddy cope with increased difficulty? If he sails over the finish line with no faults and a fast time, you have nothing to worry about. If he struggles, it's back to the drawing board.
- Introduce Buddy to some of the things he will meet at his first show. Get a friend to stand in the middle of the ring as a judge and find someone else to stand at the side eating ice cream. Is Buddy still focused on his agility?
- Take advantage of practice rings and progress tests. Put your name down for interclub matches. Look out for simulated shows. These are the

Left: *Before you enter your dog for competition, prepare yourself by visiting an agility show as a spectator.*

closest you can get to the real thing and you can still correct Buddy if he goes wrong.

Are you prepared? Even the most seasoned agility handler will get nervous at a show. You and Buddy are a team and your dog will pick up on any negative thoughts racing through your mind as you stand on the start line. Can you cope with the extra pressure of competition?

- Offer to help at a show. It's a good way to learn the ropes and meet fellow competitors. You'll get an idea of what to expect when it's your turn to strut your stuff in the ring.
- Practice running different courses. There are an infinite number of equipment combinations and you should know where to go without reading the numbers on the jumps. Work the spaces between the obstacles.
- Learn to think positively. If you stand in the line wishing you had done more contact training, your dog will sense your doubts.

You can do Buddy more harm than good if you put him in the ring too early. If you have not adequately prepared yourself and your dog to meet the challenges set by the judge, you will leave your first show disappointed and frustrated. Buddy will wonder how he has let you down and the agility game won't be much fun anymore.

What To Take?

Q *I have entered my Kelpie, Kez, in his first agility show next month. I'm not expecting too much from Kez as we haven't been training for very long. But I want to have a good day out even if we don't take home a ribbon. What should I take with me besides Kez.*

A The more self-sufficient you are the better! Agility shows are held anywhere there is enough space for rings – playing fields, parks, equestrian centers or country houses. The amenities will vary so be prepared.

The dog Take everything with you that you would take to class – lead, treats, toys, water and a bowl. Check that everything is in your training bag – clicker and targets and diary. You'll need a stash of poop bags. And, if you don't know what time you will be getting home, pack a meal for him too.

Important documents These include the show schedule, running orders, directions to the venue and any club records.

Catering There may be a pricey restaurant, a deli or only an ice cream truck. So, rather than finding yourself with no lunch, pack a few sandwiches and fill a thermos. Don't be stingy. Shove in some cakes and cookies to eat on the way home. You might be stuck in traffic and need something on which to snack.

Toilets There are never enough of them and they always run out of soap and toilet paper. Pack tissues and stock up on hand-wipes to clean your fingers.

Weather The weather may well be unpredictable. You can get goose bumps, sunburned and soaked all on the same day. Pack an umbrella, hat and gloves. Add waterproof shoes and sun screen. Along with a spare set of clothes for you, don't forget Kez. Have you dog towels, his reflective coat and a crate fan with spare batteries?

Shoes Don't leave your running shoes at home. And if you have a favorite pair of socks to wear with them, they'll not do you any good at home in your bedroom drawer.

Time Most of us kill time between runs chatting with friends. Some knit. Why don't you take the opportunity to fill in your training diary – don't forget to bring it!

Money Don't leave your purse at home or you won't be able to buy anything at the stalls. How can you resist the giant tennis balls? But will you have room for them in your car to take them home?

Chair No one likes to be on their feet all day. Pack a folding chair and crate so you and Kez can sit by the ring in comfort and cheer your friends when they run.

Agility equipment Can you fit a few practice jumps in your car? You'd be surprised what you can squeeze in with a little determination.

Start with the bare necessities for your first agility show. You'll find the list of essentials will grow the more shows you enter!

Stand To Be Measured

Q *I have been told that my dog has to be measured before he competes. Is this true? Gnat is a little Chihuahua mix and I think he will freak out if someone tries to measure him. It's so obvious that he is small!*

A All dogs must be measured before the show. Even if Gnat was the size of an elephant, he needs to have an official measurement noted by the judge. It is the same for all dogs whatever their size.

Height is not always clear cut, especially if a dog is borderline. How would you feel if Gnat was fluffy and looked larger than he really is?

Measuring also ensures that dogs always jump in the same height category over the same height fences. Once upon a time, a medium dog could compete as "mini" one day and as a "standard" the next. And, there was nothing stopping a "mini" dog competing as a "standard." Size categories can vary depending on organization.

Sizes Gnat will not be measured for a specific height but for inclusion in a specific height category. Generally, here is how height categories are arranged:
• Large Dogs – over 17in (430mm) at the withers.
• Medium Dogs – over 12in (350 mm) and measuring 17in (630mm) or under at the withers.
• Small Dogs – 12in (350mm) or under at the withers.

Measuring There are two measures shaped like croquet hoops with feet at the bottom – a small and a medium size. The hoop is positioned above the highest point of the dog's withers. If the feet of the hoop do not touch the floor, the dog is too big for that height category. There are a number of things that you can do to prepare Gnat for his first measuring session.

Table Gnat can have his first measurement at 15 months but you can start getting him ready when he is a puppy. Teach Gnat to stand squarely and quietly on the table. It is much easier to measure a dog that is still than one that is a wiggly worm. You can click and treat him for a good stand. He should have all four paws on the ground and be neither stretched out or scrunched up. Gnat's head should be in a natural position, not tucked between his legs.

Gentle introduction If Gnat has never been measured before, he might think the person passing the hoop over his back is trying to staple him to the floor. However, if you have practiced with your own hoop at home and have asked your friends and family to do it too, Gnat will recognize a familiar procedure. He won't be frightened.

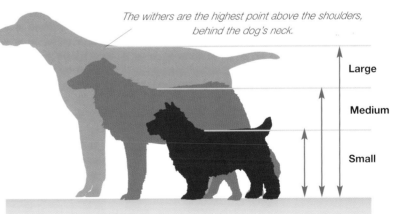

The withers are the highest point above the shoulders, behind the dog's neck.

Large

Medium

Small

A dog must be standing upright with the head held naturally when measured.

Volunteering To Help

Q *I want to put something back into agility and have put my name down to help at my next show. What sort of things will they ask me to do? They won't ask me to judge, will they? I've only ever been to two shows before!*

A They won't ask you to judge, but they might give you a packed lunch or a T-shirt as thanks for helping! Without volunteers like yourself, many shows would come to a standstill. There are a number of jobs that need to be done around a ring and many hands make light work. Here are some examples:

Pole setters/Tunnel straighteners
This is a great job because you can watch each dog run. Volunteers are placed around the edge of a ring. If a pole falls, you pick it up. If the collapsible tunnel twists, you straighten it up. Moreover, you need to keep an eye on any equipment that is pegged down. It might become loose and need to be hammered back into place.

Callers (gate steward)
My favorite. The caller controls the length of the line into the ring. Calling up to one hundred and ten! As the handlers book in to run, you can wish them luck and put faces to the names on your list.

Scrimers The scrimer keeps one eye on the judge who signal faults. It is quite a responsible job and many judges like to nominate their own scrimer who is accustomed to working with them and familiar with their signaling system. The scrimer keeps the other eye on the timing equipment and notes this with the score. And, in case you are wondering, "scrimer" is a new word that describes a person who is part scribe and part timer.

Leash runners Not a job for you if you have bad knees as there may be quite a lot of walking involved. You will be in charge of collecting the competitor's leash (lead) from the start and placing it at the finish.

Pad runners Pad runners check the information on the score sheet before the competitor goes into the ring. Is it the right handler's name, dog's name and so on? No one wants their score to be recorded on the wrong pad, especially if they go clear. The score pads are then given to the scrimer who will note the judge's marks. Then the runner will collect it and take it to the score tent. Often this job is done by two people.

Scorers Not for you if you have forgotten your glasses or hate math. You will be asked to record the results as they come in – time faults, eliminations, clears. You're guaranteed a chair and table and, best of all, shelter. Scorers usually have their own tent.

Ring managers The ring manager is usually appointed well in advance. He deploys the volunteers and makes sure all the jobs are done. If there aren't enough helpers, the ring manager does them himself!

Movers and shakers Everyone in the ring party will help to set up a new course or break up the equipment at the end of the day. Not for anyone who has recently had surgery for a hernia as it can be heavy work.

I hope you enjoy your day helping on a ring. I'm sure your ring manager will look after you. He'll probably want you to come back next year and help!

Judging Signals

Q *I took my daughter and her Cocker Spaniel, Tootsie, to their first show. I had a lovely time watching the dogs run and I was fascinated by the judge who appeared to be working very hard running around the ring and flapping his hands. What was he doing?*

A It's great that you were there to support your daughter and Tootsie at their first show. I'm sure they made you proud.

Keeping an eye on the dog An agility judge does have to work hard. He must not take his eyes off the dog that is competing in the ring. How active the judge is depends on the type of class, the design of his course and the judge. He needs to have a clear view of each piece of equipment and may have to move around a lot to see or he may be able to clock everything that happens from one spot. Also, he mustn't get in the competitor's way. Not always easy if the dog is very fast or the handler's maneuver is unexpected.

Signals If a dog is making a lot of mistakes, the judge's arms will spin like windmills as he raises one arm for a knocked fence and the other arm for a run-by. Yes, sometimes the judge looks as if he is bringing in a plane for landing rather than marking faults. Judging signals are pretty universal.

Left: *The judge is signaling faults for a knocked pole, not waving hello to the competitor.*

- Raised hand with open palm – one fault (for example, knocked fence, missed contact, popping out of the weaves).
- Raised hand with closed fist – refusal.
- Touching one hand on the other – handler touching the dog.
- Drawing a hand across the throat or crossing the arms over the chest – elimination
- Head nod – indicates to scribe that the judge is ready to start marking the next competitor.

The judge will brief his scrimer on his signals before the competition begins. Some judges have embellished existing signals or added their own creations. When I judge, I have a signal to indicate to my scrimer that I need a break and to ask the ring manager not to take any more dogs in the line. That way I get five minutes to visit the ladies room!

Scribe's signals You might see the scrimer signaling to the judge. If she raises her hand with three fingers up, the competitor has had three refusals and the judge needs to eliminate the dog. It's easy to forget how many times you have put your hand in the air if a dog and handler are struggling on your course.

It is always a good game if you are sitting outside the ring to try and mark each dog along with the judge. Would you have put your arm up for a refusal at that fence? Would you have marked the dog walk contact as missed? And what would you have done when the dog pirouetted on the seesaw before dismounting? It's a good way to learn how to judge and it can make you a better agility competitor.

Walking The Course

Q *I haven't entered a show yet, but I went to one with my friend and watched the handlers walking the course without their dogs. Some were gesturing and running around while others stood around talking. What were they all up to?*

A Time is set aside before each competition class starts to walk the course set by the judge. It can be anything from 15 minutes to the whole lunch hour. During that time, competitors must learn the route and plan their handling strategies. Once the class has started, they won't be allowed back into the ring unless it is their turn to run. And that might be some time. It is not unusual to walk a course at eight in the morning and run it at four in the afternoon.

Planning The people you saw on the course were not only learning the order of the obstacles but they were practicing their runs without their dogs. They

were trying out different body signals and positions and they may well have been muttering commands under their breath, too. It does look silly without a dog, but it is an effective way to remember where you are going and what you are supposed to do when you get there. And they will be walking it several times, not only to memorize it, but to come up with an emergency plan if things don't go as expected.

A social occasion The other people you saw on the course were just chatting. Agility people come from all corners of the country and it's great to meet up with old friends. It's inevitable that when you are walking the course you bump into old friends and stop to catch up on the latest news – who has a new puppy or who's had a baby. Traffic jams result and usually occur at the trickiest point of the course where another group of competitors have stopped to talk about handling strategies!

The crowd There can be hundreds of competitors walking a course all at once. Often you can't see the obstacles for the bodies. And it's made worse by competitors who push strollers around the course as they walk it. Cunning competitors wait until the crowds have died down a bit. There won't be as much time on the course before the class starts, but at least they'll avoid other people's elbows and be able to see where they're going. They will be lingering when the ring manager bellows "Clear the course please!" so that judging can begin.

No dogs or food Competitors must leave their dogs behind when they walk the course. It's crowded enough as it is. And I hope you didn't see anyone eating their breakfast as they walked the course. Think of all the crumbs they would leave behind.

I love watching competitors walk a course – swaying and swirling and peeling off into groups here and there. If I have time to watch the class later in the day, I like to see if these handlers run the course exactly as they have walked it!

Above: *When the course is being walked, it's best to catch up with your friends later outside the ring rather than in it.*

Disputing The Judge

Q *I came out the ring last week ecstatic. What a round! I came back to earth when I checked the score sheet and learned from my friends that I had been given five faults for missing the A-frame contact. My wife has the round on video and you can clearly see Timmy's paw on the contact. What should I do?*

Above: *Photographic evidence may clearly show that your dog hit the contact with a paw, but it's what the judge sees on the day that gets marked on your score sheet.*

A There is nothing you can do about this round. The judge can only mark what he sees at the time. On the day, a judge will have hundreds of dogs to work through and it's unlikely

he will remember you even an hour or so after your run. He certainly won't thank you if you try and stop his ring to talk to him. And, once he has hung up his judging hat, he'll want to concentrate on his own dogs. My advice would be to think of your next round. Teach Timmy the type of contact performance that will leave no room for doubt. Then, whether Timmy actually hit the bottom of the A-frame or not will not be up for discussion.

A match? What you see will not necessarily be the same as what the judge sees. Remember that you are working your dog against the clock, but the judge has all the time in the world to watch you perform. In addition, you may be right on top of your dog whereas the judge may be standing on the other side of the ring. Your perspectives are bound to be different and that can be reflected in the marks you receive.

Coming out ahead So this time you got five faults, but you may not next time. If you saw on your video that Timmy had missed the contact but had not been marked, would you have complained to the judge? It works both ways.

But, but, but ... Contact marking can be controversial but a pole is either up or knocked down. Nevertheless, if the judge didn't see it, he won't mark it. He is not going to change the score sheet on a spectator's say so. He won't be smiling if you march into the middle of his ring, halt the class and start arguing the call. And neither will the competitors waiting their turn in the line.

Decision The judge's decision is final. Your judge will do the best he can to mark accurately and fairly. If he is unsure, he will give you and your dog the benefit of the doubt and not mark you. But he is human.

I'm sure that Timmy's round was not a fluke. You did it once so you can do it again. Forget about what happened last week and concentrate on preparing for next time.

Running Surfaces

Q *I know that my Hungarian Vizsla Gladys is going to encounter all sorts of new sights and sounds at shows. It has just occurred to me that the flooring will be different too! What should I expect to find under foot?*

A A soft landing can make a big difference to the health and performance a dog. Ring surface is yet another variable that needs to be taken into account when walking the judge's course. The transition from one kind of flooring to another is not always easy as both dog and handler will have to make adjustments to work the surface. This is why handlers who are accustomed to working on grass include carpet work in their pre-event training program. Here are some of the surfaces that Gladys's feet will meet.

Above: *Long grass and flowers are perfect for studying the birds and bees but not so good for agility class.*

Grass field Nothing like it on a dry, sunny day. Unfortunately, the weather can be capricious and a nice patch of green can turn into a mud pool in a matter of seconds. Playing fields are carefully manicured and the ground is flat. But if the rings are located on Farmer Jones's farm, you'll find long grass and a few molehills. Pity the small dog handlers who lose sight of their mini dogs and make sure that you steer Gladys clear of the sheep droppings.

Mats, carpets and astro-turf These are usually laid over concrete or wooden floors. Thickness varies – sometimes the coverings are very cushioned and sometimes very thin. Be aware that carpet can be slippery and dogs might spend more time on their bottoms than on their feet. By contrast, astro-turf can provide a good grip, so much so that some handlers complain that it gives their dogs too much traction and takes the skin off their pads.

Dirt arena Horse arenas can be covered in anything from a clay and sand mixture to common garden soil. They may have a top dressing of shredded rubber or a filler of ground wood chips. Some dogs react to walking over a top dressing as if they are walking over broken glass. The bits get stuck between their toes and they hate it. A good surface should be moist enough so that it doesn't get dusty and it should be raked and turned so that it does not become packed. Arenas that are well maintained are a pleasure. But beware if you run behind Gladys. You could get a cloud of sand kicked in your eyes. Also, if Gladys is a particularly light-colored dog, she could finish an evening's training the same color as the floor.

Whatever surface you encounter, make sure that you choose the right shoes and handling strategy. For example, if Gladys is a big, fast dog that is likely to slide on carpet, don't rush her through her turns. Hold your position a little longer to make sure she has her balance and footing before moving onto the next obstacle. The more shows you attend, the more experience you and Gladys will gain of working different surfaces. It always pays to look beneath your feet.

A Pocketful Of Treats!

Q *My Cairn Terrier, Elsa, would never come back to me at the end of a round in class so I have started to carry a few treats in my pocket to give to her. She nibbles them while I attach her lead. This works, but will I be able to continue doing this at a show?*

A The rules for most organizations say that food should not be carried in the competitor's hand or be fed to their dog while it is in the ring. It says nothing about food being in pockets or being given to the dog when it is outside the ring.

Pockets Whenever I unload the washing machine and fold the laundry, I find cleansed and sanitized dog treats in the linings of my jackets and trouser pockets. It's a fact of life for dog owners. I bet many handlers unwittingly compete with bits of liver stuck in their seams. Or simply forget that they are there nestled amongst poop bags and tissues in pockets.

Body search Competing in agility is not like going through security at an airport. The caller is not going to give you a body search when you join the line. But he might query you if you reek of garlic sausage, you squeak with each step or your pockets bulge unnaturally.

Litter bug Think how embarrassing it would be to bend over Elsa at the bottom of the contact and see all of her treats tumble out of your breast pocket. The line would curse you. Their own food-orientated dogs would make a beeline to the contact instead of jumping the first fence. It's not a good idea to rely on zippers, snaps or buttons!

Alternative plan To avoid embarrassment and eliminations, leave your treats in a jar outside the ring with your fanny pack or jacket. Or ask a friend to hold it for you. As soon as you finish your round you can leave the ring and go to the treat jar. Elsa won't be far behind you. But be careful. If the treat jar is in plain sight, another dog in the line might get there first or Elsa might leave the course to find it before she has finished running it.

Keep rewarding Elsa with a titbit in training. You may find that by the time you enter your first show that Elsa returns to you each and every time you call her whether she gets a treat or not.

It is so obvious to the dog. I sit. You treat.

Left: *There is an unwritten contract between handler and dog that if the dog works hard, he gets a treat. Build anticipation and your dog will be able to wait for his pay off at the end of the round.*

Multi-Dog Handling

Q *I have two dogs. A small Jack Russell called George and large Labrador Retriever called Gwennie. They both compete in agility in different classes – one is a novice and the other is a senior. Sometimes I feel like a headless chicken running from one ring to another. Is there a trick or two that would help me manage the situation better?*

Above: *Even if your dogs are best friends, they will almost certainly need different handling strategies depending on their size and ring experience.*

A You have doubled your work load, not to mention the amount of dog hair on the sofa. You have two classes to walk, two courses to remember and two different handling strategies to apply. How to simplify?

Parking Park as near to the rings as you can. That reduces the amount of walking you'll have to do back and forth, fetching George from your vehicle, putting George back in your vehicle and then starting all over again with Gwennie.

Friends They can be roped into saving places in the line for you at one ring while you walk the course in another. But don't abuse them. They'll probably have their own dogs to run too!

Every dog has its day Look out for shows that cater only for small or novice dogs. Enter those and George will receive all your attention and treats that

Right: *Some shows restrict entry to a specific height category. If you enter your Jack Russell at a Small/Medium Show, your large retriever will have to have a day off.*

day. Look for shows that accept only large novice plus dogs on another day. Fill in your entry form and you can focus all your attention on Gwennie. If you do this, you will never warm up George and take him to the ring only to discover that you are trying to book into Gwennie's class. Didn't the size of the dogs in the line give it away?

Consistency Aim for consistency with both your Jack and your Lab. Don't use different commands for each dog. If you say "target" for George's contact, but "touch" for Gwennie's, you'll find yourself at the bottom of the A-frame tongue-tied and saying neither. If an independent weave performance is your aim with your Lab, it should be your aim with your terrier too. Make sure both dogs are familiar with all your available handling skills. If you go on autopilot and suddenly whip out a blind turn, Gwennie will oblige since you've been practicing with her. But George will put his paws in the air in horror – he's never seen you do that before.

Multi dogs Some handlers are really good at running lots of dogs. They switch effortlessly from one dog to another with relish. They never forget the course they walked five hours ago, even though they have already run three bafflingly similar ones earlier that day. You'll find out that the more you do, the easier it will become and the better you will be at it. It comes with practice. Really!

Are you considering getting a third dog – a medium-sized one? Then you'd be a real all-rounder!

A Friend In Need!

Q *Help! My best friend Cathy has broken her leg and has asked me to run her Cocker Spaniel, Murray, while her leg is in a cast. I already have a Cocker, Twister, that I compete with so I'm hoping running one more won't make too much difference. Any tips?*

A I'm sorry to hear that Cathy has hurt herself. She must have a great deal of faith in your handling abilities to entrust Murray to you and I know you'll do your best not to let her down.

Will he? Some dogs love agility so much that they will run for anyone. They really don't care who is shouting directions as long as they are allowed to have fun. They are happy to pass on the buzz they get from agility to any lucky handler holding their lead.

Won't he? Some dogs won't run for anyone else for love, money or hot dogs. They are real Momma's boys. For them, agility is something special and they only do it with the person they love and trust the most. If Murray doesn't want to run with you, don't take it personally. You don't live with him and it is Cathy, not you, who has fed, walked and cuddled

him since puppyhood.

Decide if it is worthwhile working through this or if it is better just to wait till Cathy's cast comes off.

Training I hope that you are not just going to run Murray at competitions. If you attend training classes together it will help you bond and give you better results at shows. You'll learn a lot about his personality and will be able to build a working relationship with him. Don't assume that just because he is the same breed as Twister that he has the same strengths and weaknesses. And he will learn a lot about you too. In addition, if he does run back to Cathy, it's better that you find out here and not at your first show.

Communicate Although Cathy is going to sit on the sidelines, she needs to be involved in Murray's training. Don't introduce new commands or attempt different contact strategies without consultation. When Cathy is back on her feet, she needs to be able to pick up where you left off so discuss with her how you are going to handle problems on the course. You could learn a lot from one another.

Stay friends Decide in advance who sends in show entries, who keeps the ribbons and who pays for training. Disagreements can escalate and you don't want your friendship to suffer on points of technicality. Don't blame any of Murray's errors on the course on Cathy's training and she won't blame your handling for Murray's eliminations.

Above: *How will your friend feel if your trainer says that her dog runs better for you than he does for her?*

Loose Dog In The Ring

Q *My cross breed, Yettie, is a real babe magnet. I don't know why other dogs find him so attractive but they flirt with him in the line and, once at training, a dog that really loves him ran into the ring while he was working. What should I do if this happens at a show?*

A Just keep working Yettie unless the judge asks you to stop.

Above: *I know I'm irresistible, but I should to be jumping fences not kissing you. Get to the back of the line!*

Distractions Yettie should be so focused on you and his agility that he doesn't notice any canine interlopers in the ring. Dogs visiting are viewed in the same way as cigarette packs that blow across the ground in front of jumps – just another distraction to be ignored. And I know that's unfair. But it is also unfair when half the competitors run their dogs in the sun in the morning and the other half have to run in the rain in the afternoon. As a rule of thumb, keep working your dog unless the judge tells you to stop because he'll keep marking you.

Calling a halt Yettie's visitor in the ring might follow Yettie as he makes his way round the course or she might settle down by the tunnel to adore her hero. Yettie might not even be aware that he has a visitor. However, the judge will call a halt if he thinks that the interloper is going to actively interfere, impede your dog or pose a potential danger. For example, if the other dog takes up residence in front of the weaves, you haven't a chance of making the entry. Or if the visiting dog is raising her lips and her fur is standing straight up on her back, it's not love but a fight in the offing. Someone will collect the loose dog and you will probably be awarded a re-run.

Your call You know your dog best. If Yettie is a shy dog, easily frightened and lacking in confidence, you might decide to quit the course before the judge calls a halt. You might decide that it's not worth risking Yettie colliding with the other dog or getting involved in a fight. It's your call, but you will be eliminated for leaving the ring and not finishing the course. No re-run will be offered but you know that there will always be another show tomorrow.

Loose dogs The only time a dog should be off-lead at an agility show is when he is in the exercise area or working in a ring. But accidents do happen. It is not uncommon for a handler's second dog to escape and join him with his first dog – at least he knows they will get along but it is so embarrassing! Yettie shouldn't be bothered by a loose dog, but if he is, the owner will be terribly apologetic and will take steps to make sure it doesn't happen again.

Staying On Your Feet

Q *I'm a bit of a clumsy type and always tripping over my big feet or running into pieces of agility obstacles. What happens if I fall over in the ring when I compete? Will I be marked if I knock the pole instead of my Jack Russell, Spud?*

A Oh dear! You need to watch where you are going. Keeping one eye on Spud, the other eye other on the course and standing up at the same time is not always easy.

Falling over You will not be marked for falling over, but it will cost you time on the course. Unless you have hurt yourself, get up as quickly as you can and keep going. Spud may come over to investigate your prostrate body out of curiosity or concern. On the other hand, Spud may take no notice of you writhing on the ground in agony and he'll keep driving forward over fences. If so, you'll have no trouble picking up where you left off. It depends on the type of dog.

Shoes Make sure that you are wearing the best running shoe for the ground and weather conditions. If you step into the ring in a pair of galoshes, I'm not surprised to hear that you sometimes end up on your bottom.

 Knocking over the equipment You will be penalized for caressing, hitting or beating the equipment. Don't touch it! It doesn't matter if it is an intentional or an accidental touch. If a pole hits the ground, it's still a fault regardless of whether you or Spud knocked it out of its cups.

Handling When you walk the course, look at the equipment and the surrounding space. Are you too big to fit through a narrow gap? Will you be dangerously close to fence ten if you do a reverse turn after fence nine? If you step back after fence eight, will your foot hit the tunnel behind you? If you do a pivot turn after the A-frame, will you become dizzy and collapse in a heap on the ground? These are valid handling considerations. Take them into account when you plan your route.

Everyone falls over at some time – some more gracefully than others. And everyone has been in the middle of at least one winning round until they knocked over the wing of the last fence. Happily, there is always the next time to get it right!

Left: *Avoid reaching across the agility equipment. If you lose your balance and accidentally touch it, the judge will mark you down!*

Contact Failure

Q *My Poodle Travis loves agility. At training, he is fantastic and never makes a mistake. But the minute he puts a foot into the ring he steps up a gear and forgets everything I've ever taught him, especially the contacts. I invested a lot of time teaching these and Trav is usually really reliable. Maybe he's a jumping-only dog? Why doesn't he do his contacts?*

A The ultimate test of any training is competition. You will never get the same rush of adrenalin at your local agility club as you will standing under starter's orders at a show. When you are running under the watchful eye of a judge, nerves usually combine with anxiety to produce a performance that isn't as good as it is when you are being assessed by your instructor. Contacts are a prime example of good training that flies out the

Above: *All four feet in the contact zone. Any handler would be pleased with this performance in training. The next challenge is to get the same result in the adrenalin-charged atmosphere of a show.*

window the minute there is a possibility of a ribbon. Consider the following points:

Was Trav's contact performance trained as static exercises? It's easy to hit the contact when nothing follows it, but there can be up to 20 obstacles on an agility course. Dogs pick up speed and excitement as they travel from start to finish. Their striding as well as their entries and exits on equipment is bound to be less exact, sometimes non-existent. Start practicing your contacts in sequences of equipment.

Perhaps Travis has not generalized his contact training? The dog doesn't understand that he is expected to tackle the A-frame at a show in exactly the same way as he tackles the A-frame at his local agility ground. The A-frame may be in a different part of the ring, painted a different color and embedded in a different sequence of obstacles, but it is still an A-frame. Help him to learn that an A-frame is still an A-frame by taking him to different venues and by always maintaining your performance criteria. Be confident in your chosen training method and remember to apply it. Don't rely on luck.

Do you get nervous and lose confidence in yourself? Nerves can make a handler forget his own protocols. Do you plan to pause at the foot of the contact, but keep running? Do you always say "On it" in training but shout "Stop" at the show? Does your voice sound pleading instead of commanding? No wonder Travis jumps off the contact.

You need to develop your training program to include competition work. Your dog is not the only one that forgets everything when stepping up a gear at a show. In addition to learning the judge's course, you need to master your own nerves. Give Travis 100 per cent wherever and whenever you work him. Be consistent and Trav will know what you expect and produce the goods. If you don't accept one toenail on the contact in training, don't be tempted to accept it in competition.

Catch A Falling Dog

Q My terrier cross Daisy fell off the seesaw sideways at a show the other day. She caught sight of a bird overhead and was looking at that instead of where she was putting her feet. It frightened her a bit when she fell off so I took her to the front of the seesaw and did it again with lots of praise and encouragement. I finished the course but was so surprised to learn that I had been eliminated. But she fell off! How can this be?

Left: *A confident seesaw performance is the result of careful training. If your dog has a fright on this obstacle, you will have to work hard to convince him that the seesaw is great fun and not an instrument of torture.*

A I think you were right to reassure Daisy and repeat the obstacle despite being eliminated for doing so. You have to learn to live with the judge's call.

Seesaw marking The seesaw is divided in two equal halves at its pivot point. If a dog jumps, falls or slides off the seesaw after passing the pivot point that dog will be faulted for missing the contact on the down side. If the seesaw is not touching the ground before the dog dismounts, that dog will be faulted for exiting too early. And further, if the dog jumps, falls or slides off the seesaw before reaching the pivot point that dog will be marked with a refusal. The dog will have to try the seesaw again and complete it correctly before moving on to the next obstacle. If he doesn't or refuses twice more, the dog will be eliminated.

Performance The judge is only interested in marking performance. He is not interested in the whys or wherefores of your dog's behavior. On the other hand, you are. It is your responsibility to make sure that Daisy executes each obstacle competently and happily. If she is worried or fearful, do something about it.

Elimination I didn't see your run but I think Daisy probably fell off the seesaw after she had gone past the pivot point but before the contact in which case you would have been faulted. Even if a flying saucer had flown by, the judge's mark would be the same. Having completed the seesaw, albeit badly, the expectation would be to proceed to the next obstacle. When you repeated the seesaw, you were eliminated for taking the wrong course (doing seesaw and then the seesaw again instead of seesaw and then jump).

Thinking forward So, you may have been eliminated on the course but you took steps to ensure that Daisy won't spook next time she gets on the seesaw. That's an investment for future agility. And, although they don't give out ribbons at shows for considerate handling, you would certainly get a pat on the back from me!

Jumping Out Of The Ring

Q *At a show today my dog Clover jumped out of the ring. She is a big, long-striding cross-breed. She cleared a hurdle, landed and found herself directly in front of the ring rope – so she jumped it! She immediately turned and we were back on track on the judge's course. How should I have been marked? Should I have lost points?*

A I wish I had seen Clover in action! I'm sure your judge was as surprised as you were and was scratching his head. The organization's rules and regulations are very clear in most instances; for example, if a dog pees in the ring, it's an elimination. But there is no specific ruling on jumping ring ropes. It doesn't happen as often as peeing in the ring!

Course design and safety A good course will be fun and testing for the competitors. It should also be safe for the dogs to run. Jumps positioned too close to the ropes are asking for trouble. What if Clover had caught her leg in the ring rope, fallen and hurt herself? Poor Clover had no alternative but to jump it. It was either that or garrotting herself. The ropes should not be another obstacle for the competitor to negotiate and a considerate course designer will steer clear of them. I suspect that when Clover did her leap, the judge kicked himself for putting equipment too near the edge of his ring and will give more thought to his course design next time.

Marking The price you paid for Clover's leap was time wasted and extra seconds on the clock. Depending on your dog's speed elsewhere on the course, you may have incurred time faults.

Elimination Clover would not have been eliminated. Despite the hiccup of jumping the ring rope, Clover picked up where she left off immediately. She worked the course and responded to your commands. On the other hand, dogs that jump barriers and leave the ring to heckle the line, chase rabbits in the adjoining field, or beg at the lunch truck **will** be eliminated. These dogs have something other than agility on their mind and their handlers have lost their grip on the situation. Unlike Clover, the dogs are out of control and they will be eliminated.

Walking the course Jumping the ring rope is probably a one time incident and Clover will never do it again. However, it's a good idea to check how near the ring ropes are to the jumps when you are walking your next course. If you think Clover is going to land on top of them, mention it to your judge before his briefing. He may not realize that there is a potentially dangerous trouble spot and will in all likelihood adjust his course or move the ropes before the class starts.

Below: *A jumping dog needs room on both sides of the hurdle.*

We have lift off!

And a safe landing!

Double Handling

Q My German Shepherd, Fudge, loves my boyfriend Steve. In class, I get Steve to stand at the finish line with Fudge's toy and Fudge beats it down the home stretch to see him. If Steve encourages him, Fudge really steps up a gear! I'm hoping Steve will be able to come to the shows with me when I start competing, but he likes to play golf at the weekends. What should I do?

A It's good to hear that Steve comes to training class with you and lends a hand, but he won't be able to do that at an agility show. When you are competing, it's up to you and Fudge to run clear and within the course time all on your own.

Double-handling Getting outside assistance when you are in the ring is known as double-handling. It can be hard to spot, but if the judge notices, he will reprimand or penalize you. Double-handling is frowned upon and some people would simply call it cheating. I'll give you two examples.

Start line You set your dog up on the start line and tell Fudge to stay. Steve is just outside the ring, but only a few feet behind Fudge. You move away from your dog to position yourself past the second fence for a recall. Fudge shuffles and your boyfriend tells him to sit and then commands him to stay. Who is working the dog? The person in the ring or the person outside the ring?

Finish line Steve stands at the finish line playing with Fudge's toy to encourage him over the last fence. He says, "Ready, steady, get it!". Fudge runs to him for a game of tug. Would Fudge have been so fast if he had not received this incentive from the wrong side of the ring ropes? Did he jump the last fence because you sent him over it or because your boyfriend called him?

Training Two people working together can accomplish a great deal, especially in the early stages of learning, for example, by practicing restrained recalls. Indeed, double-handling may be the safest way to proceed in some instances. A person either side of the dog walk when your dog trots along its length for the first time is a good safety measure. It means that if he falls off, there's someone to catch him. But if you enter a competition, your training should have advanced to the point where you alone are enough.

So, let Steve go to the golf course! But if he does come to watch you run Fudge, explain that you could be eliminated for double-handling. Do be careful and keep your fingers crossed that Fudge won't run out of the ring to your boyfriend in the middle of the course instead of finishing it!

Below: *A game of tug with your boyfriend after the last fence could get your dog eliminated.*

Grooming For Success

Q This may sound silly, but my husband is coming to an agility show with me this weekend. I worry that he will be bored unless I can think of a way to involve him. He doesn't want to run one of my two Collies and he doesn't want to help on a ring. Any suggestions?

A You certainly don't want your husband bored at an exciting event like an agility show. Employ your husband as your groomer – there'll be plenty for him to do.

Above: *Your husband can walk the dogs while you line up to collect your ring numbers and running orders.*

Above: *Watching two agility dogs at a show will never be boring! They will need exercising, toileting and brushing.*

Driving He can chauffeur you to and from the show. This allows you to catnap in the passenger seat and you will arrive fresh and ready to compete.

Exercising the dogs While you are walking the course, he can take the dogs for a walk and toilet them. He may not want to run a dog in competition, but if he loves the dogs as much as you do he'll be happy to warm them up by jogging up and down the field a few times or playing a game of ball with them.

Lining up This is such a help. If you have forgotten the course, your husband can hold the dog in the line while you walk around the ring and study the equipment from different angles to refresh your memory. How is it running? Are all the eliminations in the same place? Where is the judge standing? You can do all this and never lose your place in the line. And the reverse works. If your dog is easily excited, he can take the dog away from all the excitement of the ring while you stand in line. When he returns the dog to you near the start, the dog will be cool and calm.

Timing It is not always possible to be in two places at once. He can keep an eye on how classes are running and alert you if you should be at a ring rather than standing in a line for hamburgers.

Above: *Your dog is your best friend – so is your husband so share the highs and lows of the day with him!*

Coat stand He can hold your coat, your fanny pack, your dog's toy and so on when you go into the ring and give it all back to you when you come out. You'll never have to dig your jacket out of a pile of competitors' clothes thrown on the ground again.

Shopping If there are stalls at the show, take your husband shopping. You might find those matching T-shirts irresistible.

Being a groomer is an important but undervalued job. Your husband will be supporting you and your dogs and, if you work together, you can become an indomitable team. Talk to him about your successes, your difficulties and your failures. He can give you an objective view and offer valuable advice. Even if he only listens and nods his head in the right places, he will be helping to keep you sane.

Chapter Six

FIT FOR THE RING

Once hooked on agility, neither you nor your dog will want to miss a single training night or show. But when should you take a break and for how long? Can you run with your dog with the same style and panache when you are nine months pregnant? Can you handle your dog from a wheelchair? How long should you wait after your dog is neutered to return to class? Will your dog ever be able to jump again if he has been lame? Don't be impatient! There are some things you just need to learn to work around. Deafness and old age won't stop your dog from enjoying the obstacles. Keep yourself and your dog in tip-top condition and you will have a long-lasting working relationship. Remember, when it comes to your pet's health, it's more important to play safe than jump hurdles. Always ask your vet for his opinion.

Canine Callisthenics

Q *My friends at agility class keep calling my terrier "Toby the Tub." They love to tease me and Toby isn't tubby, he's just big boned! Nonetheless, I want Toby to be in top condition, a real canine athlete. What exercises and fitness routines do you recommend?*

A Many handlers think that their dog is fit because he does agility. Running over jumps is good exercise, right? But think how much faster and better the dog could jump if fitness was a prerequisite for his agility training. If Toby's exercise regime is varied and fun, he will relish working out with you and you will see an improvement in his performance over courses.

Above: *Time for a wet kiss? Turn your pet into an aqua-doggy. A session in the pool is a great way to maintain fitness or regain condition after injury.*

Is your dog out of shape? Have your vet check Toby's general health before embarking on a new fitness regime for agility. Is Toby a bit overweight? Does he suffer from any medical conditions. Does he have an old injury? Is he getting on in years? All these factors should be taken into account before you start exercising your dog.

Left: *A vet can help you determine your pet's health and fitness and suggest appropriate exercise levels.*

Strength and stamina When you take Toby to the park, alternate between walking, jogging and running. You'll lose weight too. Throw a ball low to the ground for him to chase. Check out your local hydro-therapy pool and arrange a swimming session for your dog. They might let you join him in the water!

Don't be too ambitious Do not attempt to jog ten miles with Toby on your first day. Build up gradually and remember that exercise is not just for Saturdays. Doing a little bit every day is what will get you results. Increase duration and intensity slowly.

Flexibility Toby needs to be agile to be an agility dog. Just watch him wiggle through the weaves. Find activities that will keep him supple. Put on the radio and teach him to do the twist!

Static exercises Static exercises don't take up much space. Teach Toby some tricks. Can he walk backwards? Do a bow? Sit up and beg? Tricks are valuable tools that teach your dog spatial awareness, strengthen muscles and enhance flexibility.

Warm up and cool down When Toby is in prime condition, make sure he can make the most of it. Always give him a warm-up before you step into the ring. A quick jog or game with a tug toy will kick-start his heart and get his blood pumping. He'll be

Above: *Jumping through your arms is a trick that will impress your friends and keep your dog strong and supple. Start with your arms low and gradually raise them higher.*

ready for action. A gentle massage after a run will help Toby to cool down and give you the opportunity to check areas for tenderness. Treat to compete.

Keeping Toby fit to meet the requirements of competition takes time and effort, but the results will be worth it. Be creative in designing an exercise plan so that Toby enjoys keeping in shape and make it relevant to the demands of agility. In addition there are a growing number of canine fitness specialists ranging from chiropractors to physiotherapists. Toby has no excuse for being tubby. He soon will become Toby the Tiger!

Performance Diet

Q *I don't know if you can help, but my Boxer Sidney has just started agility training. He had colititis as a youngster and has been on a special diet available only from the vet ever since. His stools are fine and he bounces around happily, but I'm wondering whether, now that he is an agility dog, he needs a diet for active dogs. Any advice?*

A The only way that you can tell if the food you are putting into your dog's mouth is the right stuff is by what comes out the other end. If Sid is bouncing with good health and producing stools of an acceptable smell, color and consistency, then the diet your vet has prescribed is doing what it is intended to do. It is a successful feeding regime. I would be loath to mess with what your vet has prescribed without discussing it with him. Changing

Above: *Good quality food will taste yummy and provide the nutrients and calories your dog needs to be fit and active.*

Above: *If your vet has prescribed your pet a special diet, please don't change it without consulting him first.*

a dog's diet suddenly or introducing a new food is not without consequences. Some dog's tummies are so sensitive that even a minuscule titbit of something different can spark a bout of diarrhea or sickness.

Agility is a high energy sport and there are a number of dog food manufacturers that cater especially for active or sporting dogs. The food is not only well-balanced but a calorie- and nutrient-dense product that the manufacturers claim can make your dog a champion. Price and availability varies. Some brands are found at the supermarket and others are available only through special outlets.

It is not only the choice of food that is important for the agility dog but when it is fed. To benefit fully from a calorie- and nutrient-dense food, a dog should find it in his food bowl for about two months before starting a busy, competition-filled season. A single meal of the stuff the night before the show won't make much difference. Moreover, off-peak energy demands will be lower. An agility dog that is rested over the winter does not need food that is packed with calories as he is likely to return to training in the Spring carrying some extra weight.

Your dog is just starting his agility career and is still a long way away from entering his first show or a hectic season on the circuit. Discuss your diet concerns with your vet. It is as important for you to enjoy peace of mind as it is for your pet to have good bowel movements.

Female In Season – Hey Boys!

Q My little female, Flash, has just started her first season. Does this mean I have to stop taking her to agility training? We are halfway through a course of eight classes and I paid in advance.

A Unless you want puppies, stop taking Flash to agility classes until her season is finished. Her presence will be disruptive and it will be unfair to the other dogs in the class who are there to work.

When Flash is in season (in heat), she is fertile and may become pregnant if mated. You can start looking out for a female's first season when she is six months to a year old; larger breeds of dogs tend to have their first season later than smaller breeds. During her season, Flash will have a bloody discharge and her vulva will swell. A season will last for approximately three weeks and occur every six months or so. You will need to give Flash extra care and be extra vigilant when other dogs are around.

A female in season will attract the attention of every male dog in your agility class Leave Flash at home, rather than risk an accidental mating that will result in unwanted puppies. There are a number of sprays on the market that claim to mask the scent of a female in season, but many dogs recognize the

Left: It's not fair to the other participants to take an in-season female to agility class. The male dogs will probably be distracted and chaos may ensue!

odor as a signal that love is in the air. They become even more determined to find a mount. And you may discover that Flash is only too willing to oblige.

The dogs in your agility class will turn into canine Romeos who only have one thing on their minds They will no longer think of the thrill of jumping hurdles but the excitement of fulfilling their sexual desires. And worse, they may start to behave aggressively in the hope of seeing off any rivals for Flash's affections. Macho males with one-track minds will be a real handful.

A female in season will leave a delicious olfactory trail for dogs to track Flash will leave her mark all over the agility ring. Even though she trained in the morning, the dogs in the afternoon classes will be looking for her. "Hurrah! a female in season has gone through the tunnel. Is she still in there!" It will be difficult for their handlers to convince them that they are in class for agility, not speed dating.

Three weeks is not too long a time to miss your agility classes and if you explain the situation to your instructor, he may reimburse you or put your fees towards the next course. There are plenty of agility exercises you can practice in the privacy of your own yard. And if you are thinking of entering shows, study the conditions outlined on your entry form. Females in seasons are not allowed to compete at most shows. Is it time to think about having Flash spayed?

To Spay Or Not To Spay

Q *I'm thinking about spaying Ellie, my three year old Golden Retriever. She loves agility and is getting a lot faster. However, unfortunately her seasons usually arrive in August/September and we have to miss the summer shows. Also, I'm worried that spaying may affect her confidence in the ring. If I decide to have her spayed, how long until we can do agility again?*

Left: If you have your dog spayed, give her time to recover from her surgery before you return to agility.

A Such a nuisance! You can't take a female in season to training or shows without risking a big male dog jumping on her. And worse, you have to stay at home to keep her company.

Talk to your vet Your vet will be happy to discuss the pros and cons of spaying with you. If you are certain that you will never want puppies from Ellie and she is fit and healthy, there is no reason not to have her neutered. Some vets will spay a female as young as six months before the animal's first season. Older animals are usually spayed when they are mid-cycle, halfway between seasons. The advantages of early spaying include a reduced risk of mammary cancer, uterine ovarian cancer, false pregnancies and pyometra (infection of the womb). On the down side, a few females develop urinary incontinence as a result of spaying but this is easily treated with daily medication. Also, the coats of some dogs get a little more fluffy after neutering.

Will my dog's personality change?
Personality is difficult to measure objectively, but you may find your dog becomes less moody. Females can be so hormonal – up one minute and down the next. They brood or they pout to get their own way. Sometimes spaying can help a dog settle down and stay on an even keel. If Ellie is getting more and more confident in the ring and producing faster and faster course times, there is no reason why this trend should not continue after she is spayed.

How long before returning to agility?
This will depend on the surgery and your dog. Most vets will recommend leash walks and no jumping up on the sofa or climbing the stairs for the first two weeks followed by a gradual reintroduction of normal exercise. Take your time. Just because your dog looks fit doesn't mean that she is 100 per cent. Start with mini-jumps and slowly work up to full height. Don't rush. Your dog may be sore. If she feels an odd pinch when she is jumping a hurdle during her recovery, she will approach the next one with some trepidation.

I am always surprised by how quickly many dogs return to competition. The fur has barely had time to re-grow. Get out your calendar and have a chat with your vet.

Motherhood And Puppies

Q *My female Teasel is a gorgeous Border Collie and a star agility dog. Whenever I come out of the ring, people ask me if I am going to let her have puppies. I don't think I would have trouble finding good homes for her offspring, but I am worried about my agility. Would I have to stop agility training and for how long?*

A Agility is like riding a bicycle. It will not be something that Teasel forgets because she has taken a break to have puppies. Give her time off during her pregnancy and while she is nursing her pups. Don't rush her recovery to return to agility training.

To be absolutely safe, halt agility training as soon as Teasel is mated. Some handlers carry on for a little while longer. Your dog's size, condition and changing shape will be deciding factors. Agility is a high energy, high impact exercise. The longer you continue training, the greater the risk of compromising the pregnancy or injuring your dog. Exercise is still important, but choose something less stressful and more gentle than jumping hurdles. Walking is ideal. Let Teasel pick the pace. As she becomes big and heavy with pups, she'll tire easily and will probably be happy with a saunter around the yard.

Although you have stopped agility training with Teasel, there is no reason why you can't do a few less demanding exercises. She will need to continue to feel special and have quality time with you. If she is up for less strenuous static training, go ahead. Review your target work and hand touches.

Don't hurry back to agility training. Let Teasel guide you. She may not want to leave her babies and they need lots and lots of nursing. When the pups have been weaned and gone to their new homes, you can start to build up Teasel's fitness. But do it gradually. Start by training over mini height jumps. Nothing too demanding to start with – keep

it short and simple. Every dog is different, so read your dog. You know her better than anyone else. Some females make a quick comeback and others take a little more time to regain condition. I know of some dogs that are back at agility competitions by the time the puppies are 12 weeks old.

If you are going to breed from Teasel you need to have a chat with your vet about her care during pregnancy as well as whelping and weaning the puppies. Motherhood can be an expensive and time-consuming business. There's more to it than a simple act of nature. Agility should take a back seat. After her time off, Teasel will return to the circuit the gorgeous agility star that she was before.

Above: *Make the transition from motherhood back to agility gradual. Build fitness and start small with mini jumps.*

Deafness and Agility?

Q *I already do agility with my Golden Retriever, Ace, and I have just rescued a three-year-old deaf Border Collie, Kermit. I would like to do agility with Kermit, too. He needs to let off steam. Will I be attempting the impossible?*

A Kermit's deafness will be a problem only if you let it be. There are a number of deaf dogs that do very well in agility. Watching them race around the ring, you would never suspect that they can't hear a thing their handlers are saying to them. This can be a good thing, especially if the handler gets the verbal commands for right and left mixed up or calls the tunnel the tire by mistake! A deaf dog relies on visual communication. Body, hand and facial signals are important in agility, but they are even more important for the deaf dog.

Make sure your signals are consistent Don't sign to your dog to stay still with an outstretched hand and open palm one day and then change it to an outstretched hand and pointed finger the next. He'll see the difference.

Make sure your signals are clear and visible Remember your dog will have to see you in order to react to your commands. Don't sign to him to come to you unless he is looking at you. Make your body signals as clear as possible. If your dog is behind you, he will not be able to see you point across your body to a jump.

Treat your signals as a language You will be able to amplify some signals to make then louder or urgent. If smiling at your dog means "good boy"

Above: *Stay – The handler holds the flat of his hand in front of his dog's nose. Don't move until you are released! It's an important exercise if a dog can't hear traffic.*

Above: *Sit – The handler stretches out his hand to his dog and then bends it with an upward motion to his shoulder. It means put your bottom on the ground!*

Above left: *Down – Start in the sit position and the dog is already half way into a down.*

Above center: *Now point to the ground and your dog's nose and body will follow your finger downward.*

Above right: *The dog is securely in the down position. Now it's time for thumbs up for "good boy!"*

then smiling at your dog till your cheeks hurt and the sun comes out of your eyes means "what a superstar!" If you want to turn your dog to the right, drop your right shoulder and twist your left one to the right. If you want to really tighten the turn, twist it even more bringing your arm across your body.

Try different training methods on for size It is your responsibility to tailor the training method to fit your dog's abilities – take in the cuffs or let out the hem. Kermit can't hear a clicker, but he will be able to sniff out a hot dog. Find a way of giving your dog the thumbs up and marking good behavior that isn't dependent on sound.

Don't stop talking People who stop talking to their dogs can look insincere or wooden. Your facial expressions and body movements will flow more freely if you continue to speak to Kermit, even though he can't hear you.

Don't use your dog's deafness as an excuse Your dog can do anything that you decide to teach him … except hear. Provided his training is fun, Kermit will want to learn.

Training a deaf dog in agility is not impossible, but it can be a challenge. One day Kermit will thank you for your efforts by going clear on the course.

Left: *Come – First make sure the dog is looking at you. Give your dog a big smile and open your arms. This is an irresistibly warm welcome!*

Getting The Snip

Q *I have a lively, two-year-old male Border Collie called Blue and have been having agility lessons for the past couple of months. He is getting really good and we are enjoying it. The problem is he loves the ladies! I am considering having him neutered as I will not be breeding from him. Would castration calm him down too much for agility?*

A You can't blame Blue for looking at the ladies, but you would be upset if, instead of going through the tunnel, he left the ring to introduce himself to a pretty poodle in the line. Your boy has just grown up.

As a dog matures, the male hormone testosterone starts to be released in his body. The testicles are the main source of this hormone and they are responsible for stimulating the development of macho male characteristics. A male dog may start roaming the countryside looking for females to have his puppies. He may start cocking his leg on the gate post thus marking his territory with a big sign that says "MINE." And he may begin to show aggression to other dogs and proclaim himself king of the castle. Woe to any dog that comes near his gate post.

Castration halts the production of testosterone and it may eliminate some of the more undesirable male behaviors in your dog. The hormone is only the trigger and if Blue now spends every night out chasing females, losing his testicles won't stop him trying to spread his favors. He is already in the habit of eyeing up the ladies and habits are hard to break. For the best chance of castration changing a dog's outlook on life, the earlier he is neutered the better. But there are no guarantees.

Although castration may not change Blue, it will probably affect how other dogs react to him. Your dog may strut around like he is the king of the castle, but no one is going to take his bluster seriously. The dogs on the exercise field will give him a sniff in greeting but no longer see him as a threat or rival.

Some people argue that castration makes dogs fat and lazy. They insist it takes the edge off an agility dog. Clowning rather than jumping become the business of the day. But perhaps the day would be like that anyway? It is impossible to tell as so many other factors play an important part influencing a dog's behavior. Next time you are at an agility show, check the dogs in the line at the ring. You will find that many of the dogs have lost their manhood but not their lust for agility. They will be fit and lively and because they have been castrated they will be less likely to develop prostatic disease or testicular cancer in the future.

Castration may make no difference to your dog at all, but it will certainly do him no harm and could do him a lot of good.

Above: *Male dogs cock their legs on just about anything – trees, posts or even you.*

Below: *The message is clear. You are nothing and I am king of the castle.*

Eye Care

Q *A few weeks ago I discovered that my poodle Yogi had an eye infection. He is receiving treatment from our vet but I'm so worried that Yogi will lose his sight in the infected eye. Yogi loves his agility. Would he be able to continue training if he is partially sighted?*

A There are many causes of eye infections ranging from the simple to the complex and you should discuss your worries with the vet who is treating Yogi. He will be able to give you the full picture and allay your fears.

Eye disorders will present in a number of ways. Signs of a problem include excessive tearing or discharge. A dog that squints in bright light or continually rubs his eye with his paw is trying to tell you it hurts. The sooner the dog is under the vet's care, the sooner he can be diagnosed and his symptoms treated.

If your vet gives you the OK to return to agility, remember that dogs do not see or understand the world in the same way that we do. Agility dogs will never be able to read the numbers on the course or tell the difference between a green hurdle and a red one. They aren't very good at judging distance but they have great peripheral vision and are very sensitive to movement. It is these visual characteristics that enable the dogs to read a handler's body signals and to work ahead. And they often override the verbal commands.

Medication If Yogi has drops or creams for his eye, his vision may be blurred for a while after you administer them so hold off training until they have been fully absorbed and he can see clearly again. Also, some topical ointments leave a sticky residue around the eye so avoid working Yogi in dusty environments or sandy riding schools.

Bumps Take extra care when you return to training as Yogi's eye may still be sensitive. Leave out any equipment that comes into close contact with Yogi's face like the weave poles and collapsible tunnel in case he accidentally knocks his eye.

Light and dark Yogi's eye may not be able to respond to changes of light as quickly. He might find the bright sunlight that hits him as he exits the dark rigid tunnel temporarily blinding. Give him help to get his bearings if he looks unsure.

I hope that Yogi's vision is not permanently affected by his eye infection. If it is, whether he continues in agility will depend on how significant the loss of sight proves to be for him and how well he adapts. I know of a one-eyed dog that runs for fun in Veteran classes over mini-jumps and there are many partially sighted dogs competing on the circuit. The dogs have adjusted and their owners have modified their handling techniques to take this into account. Remain confident in your vet and follow his advice. Worry about agility later.

Below: *Eyes are delicate windows on the world. An eye check by your vet will make sure they stay open.*

Three-Legged Agility

Q *My collie, Gem, was hit by a car and we are lucky still to have her. But Gem had to have her right foreleg amputated to save her life. She is managing amazingly well on three legs and I would like to continue training and competing in agility. I realize that some of the equipment may be out of the question, but what about working her over mini-jumps? Any reason why I should not take her to a class and see how she copes?*

A I am sorry to hear that Gem has had such a horrible accident but glad that she has made a good recovery. You have a responsibility to Gem to ensure that she continues to enjoy life on three legs. Much of what an amputee dog would like to do and should be allowed to do will clash. It's up to you to have the last word.

Above: *Some dogs are so active and boisterous that it is hard to believe that they are amputees. But agility?*

and motor skills to keep them on their feet. Gem's remaining legs are already compensating for the loss of her foreleg and I think agility would put added stress on her joints and accelerate deterioration in their condition.

Is agility necessary to Gem's happiness or yours? I suspect that you both miss the partnership you gained through agility training and the exhilaration of working as a team in competition. You both love agility and, even on three legs, Gem would give it her best shot. However, I think this is one of those occasions when your head should rule your heart (and hers) and you should say no to more agility training. Try other activities that you and Gem could do together that are less demanding and more achievable. And, if you want to continue in agility think about getting a puppy.

Future risks When considering a three-legged dog's future training, there are a number of things to take into account including the dog's build, weight, muscle tone and the amount of time passed since surgery. But the most important thing to consider is how would you feel if disaster struck again. Fit and healthy four-legged dogs have accidents in agility. They tumble off A-frames, trip in the weaves, or crash into jumps. What if one of her remaining good legs was injured? The consequences for a three-legged dog would be dire.

Confusing confidence with ability Gem may be very confident and self-assured on three legs. She can manage to climb stairs and to jump on and off the living room chairs, but this is not agility. Agility asks a dog to perform these actions repeatedly and at high speed. Agility dogs need good co-ordination

Old Age Pensioner

Q *I got the taste for agility with my first dog, a Belgian Shepherd named Taz. He got me hooked on the sport and I have added two more dogs to my agility pack. Taz will have his ninth birthday next September and still barks on the start line in anticipation of the jumps. When should I retire him?*

A It sounds as if Taz is still up for a round of agility. If he is fit and healthy, there is no reason why he should not continue to compete for a little longer. It's good exercise and although Taz may be a little grey around the muzzle, you don't want him to lose his waist line.

Dogs age at different rates. The older they become, the more likely they are to suffer age-related ailments like arthritis. They don't see or hear as well and they sleep more. It takes a little longer to walk to the park in the morning. Many of the signs of aging are symptomatic of other medical conditions so have Taz checked by a vet who will prescribe the appropriate treatment. Be vigilant and look out for:

Slower course times As Taz gets older, he will get slower. His turns will be looser and his course times won't be as fast. He might incur the odd time fault. You can help him by giving him a little longer to warm up before a round.

Did you say "go" or "no"? Many older dogs suffer a degree of hearing loss. Taz was not being naughty when he went into the tunnel instead of turning towards you when you called his name. Work on your body signals and make sure your verbal commands are well timed and clear.

Measuring the jumps Older dogs knock more poles. They measure their strides approaching a fence and often rock back forth when they get there. Taz may have trouble seeing the hurdle, finding his take off spot and gathering the strength to clear the pole. If Taz knocks a pole, don't rush him. Run with him. Don't get ahead of him.

What will you find acceptable on the course?
A few time faults and knocked poles is one thing. A dog that trots instead of runs, looks disorientated and trips over every hurdle is another. Extra help on the course and sensitive handling, won't make any difference to performance. The dog may love agility, but it's time to retire before he is injured.

There are Veteran classes that cater especially for the older competitor. The courses are simple and flowing – no tight turns – and course times are generous. Jumps are set at the minimum height and contact equipment and weaves are removed. The idea is to give older dogs a blast. Taz would love it!

Compete with your other two dogs, but run for fun with Taz while he is still enthusiastic and fit enough to enjoy agility with you.

Above: *Old dogs can continue a love affair with agility, if they are fit and their handlers don't expect miracles.*

Big Boys!

Q *Do Rottweilers and agility mix? My boy Ronnie weighs 100lb (45kg) and is quite lean but that's still a lot of Rottweiler to maneuver through the weaves. The earth shakes when he lands after a jump and he hits the A-frame like a sledge hammer. Are his joints going to hold out if I continue training?*

A The short answer is if your dog is sound and loves agility, there is no reason to stop doing a sport you both enjoy. But I would take sensible measures to ensure that Ronnie can continue training for as long as possible. Keep your eyes peeled for any signs that might indicate that agility isn't as much fun as it used to be.

Weight Everything works better when your dog is the correct weight – heart, lungs and muscles can operate at full capacity. Ronnie is nice and lean and that's good. He will be able to give you his optimum performance and he'll live longer.

Equipment Ensure that the agility equipment at your training venue and at competitions is strong enough to withstand the force of a turbocharged Rottie. Look out for poles that may splinter or planks that could give way under Ronnie's weight. Most equipment is reinforced, but it can lose flexibility and strength if not adequately maintained.

Noise factor The sound of a dog hitting a pole or the upside of the A-frame can be extraordinarily loud. Listen to the featherweights, like the terriers or shelties, when they are running. Is the noise just as thunderous?

Pain threshold Many dogs have high pain thresholds and will train through an injury without raising a single objection. The thrill and excitement of agility keeps them going. Would Ronnie keep jumping for the sake of it or would he be sensible and ask for his lead? Watch him carefully so you don't miss the signs of an injury.

Reduce the stresses and strains of agility, not the fun

- Lower the jumps and lower the A-frame. You don't need to train at competition height all the time. If you are going to retrain your A-frame so that Ronnie runs up it rather than jumping through it, you want to lower this obstacle anyway. You can bring everything back to full height before a show.
- Keep Ronnie fit by doing work on the flat – practice turns, send aways and recalls. Play games of fetch and work on your obedience basics.
- Train one night a week instead of two or three. This will cut down on the number of repetitions that you do with Ronnie over the equipment. Aim for quality of performance rather than quantity.

If you and Ronnie are sensible, there is no reason why you shouldn't jump around to your heart's content for a long time yet.

Vertical Take-Offs

Q *My dog Luka is a terrier mix and has an unusual jumping style. I have never seen another terrier jump like he does so I guess his method is not a breed specific. Luka takes off vertically with all four feet pointing straight downwards. Is there something wrong with him? Although he never knocks a pole, I'm sure that his jumping method costs me time on the course and I worry that if he persists, he could injure himself.*

A Luka must be something to see on the agility course. Have you explained to Luka that the judge does not award bonus points for innovative

Bounce jumps Set up a line of low fences quite close together. If Luka is unable to take a stride between fences, he will have to bounce between them. As soon as he lands, Luka will have to lift his front feet to jump the next hurdle in the line.

Arc of the jumper Luka needs to learn to arc over the hurdles. Going vertically up in the air means that he will come straight back down again. There's little margin for error. Set up some gentle spreads to jump over so that he has to lengthen and arc his body. The shape of his jump will improve.

You can't say to a dog, "You have to stop jumping off all four legs to clear a jump. You need to raise your front paws and push off your back legs and arc in the air." He won't understand. But he will learn through experience so give him the opportunity to improve his jumping style and he will reward you with improved times on the course.

technique? Unfortunately a dog's natural jumping action may not always be the most economical one. It is your responsibility as Luka's handler to take steps to change and improve it.

Peace of mind Before attempting to correct Luka's jumping style, visit your vet for a check-up. Rule out any physical reasons for his vertical take-offs.

Defensive jumping You often see young or inexperienced dogs jumping like this. They want to make sure that their take-offs and landings are perfect. They want to jump straight over the middle of the pole, not the sides. And they may have lost confidence because the jumps have been raised too quickly. They are afraid of knocking a pole. It sounds as if Luka is jumping defensively. He wants to do it right, but he doesn't want to hurt himself.

Lower jumps Set up lines or circles of low jumps – the lower the better, just a few inches off the ground. Race Luka over these and cheer him on. He will gain confidence with speed and it is really difficult to knock a jump that is almost on the ground already! The faster you go, the harder it will be for Luka to pause for a vertical take-off.

Above: *What goes up, must come down. Examine your dog's jumping style, especially take-offs and landings. Study his mid-air body shape. Could it be improved?*

Limping Occasionally

Q *Sheba woke up one morning after agility training and was lame. I took her to the vet who gave me some tablets and told me to rest her. He said it was a soft tissue injury and nothing to worry about. Ever since, Sheba has had brief spells of lameness. She will get off her bed, limp a few steps and then all is well. Months will pass before she has another episode. Is agility the cause of her problem? What can I do to help her?*

A I would make an appointment with your vet so that he can have another look at Sheba. Tell him about her occasional episodes of lameness. He is the best person to diagnose and treat your dog.

Put your vet in the picture As well as Sheba's symptoms, you must tell your vet that Sheba is a competing agility dog. He needs the full picture of your activities with your pet. You might not be representing your country at the World Agility Championships this year, but that doesn't mean your training is any less intensive or dedicated. Explain your expectations as an agility handler and be honest about how many hours a week you spend training contacts. Your vet probably thinks that after dinner Sheba curls up with you on the sofa to watch TV. Not likely! You're off to your agility club.

Return to training When Sheba's treatment is complete and your vet has given you permission to return to agility training, don't rush. Build up Sheba's general fitness before you start training more specific agility skills. Take it slow and steady. Put the jumps down. Lower the A-frame. Avoid twists and turns. Don't overdo it. Five minutes can be a long time for a dog that is returning from injury. You are back in the agility saddle so make sure you stay there by working one step at a time – otherwise you could find that Sheba's old injury flares up again or, worse, she incurs a new one.

Minimize the risk of injury Like any sport, agility is not without risk of injury. Minimize it by making sure that Sheba is always physically fit and healthy. Regular exercise, like walking or jogging combined with games of fetch or tug, will keep her in peak condition and she will be able to meet the rigors of challenging agility courses that demand speed and flexibility. And, always give Sheba a warm-up before you go into the ring. She needs to prime her muscles for a burst of activity. Walk her briskly or trot her around. Do some tricks that will stretch her back and legs. A dog that is in good physical condition and is adequately warmed-up before it goes into the ring is less likely to have an injury than the dog that is overweight, unfit and has just woken up from a nap.

Below: *A controlled game of tug will help a dog keep in shape, maintain fitness and minimize the risk of future injury.*

Poorly Pads

Q *My dog, Quiz, keeps getting contact burns on his pads. He is a very fast collie and when I get home after training, his pads are grazed from the surface material of the contacts. How can I stop him from getting sore feet?*

A Check Quiz's pads regularly. They should feel rough and look like fine sandpaper. Worn pads feel smooth and they may have little dots on them. Cracked, swollen or bleeding pads can lead to prolonged pain or lameness. Does Quiz lick or chew his feet? It's worthwhile having a vet check Quiz's feet to make sure there is no medical reason why they are suffering from wear and tear.

Above: *Cracked or grazed pads can make walking painful. Get a vet to give your pet's feet a full examination.*

Salves and lotions There are a number of commercial products available on the market claiming to help toughen and protect pads if applied routinely. Some agility handlers smear a thin coat of Vaseline before the pads are worn badly. However, care must be taken to remove this coating once training has finished. It does form a protective layer on the pads, but it will also inhibit a dog's ability to sweat through his feet.

Boots Boots can help stop trouble developing in the first place and will guard pads while they are healing. They are designed for sled dogs or hunting dogs that work over tough terrain, especially snow and ice. However, I think booties would impede an agility dog during training – a bit like asking a ballet dancer to pirouette in clogs.

Agility equipment Has your training club recently overhauled its agility equipment? Usually sand is mixed with paint to roughen the surface of the contact areas and give the dogs some traction. It could be that the grade of sand chosen is too abrasive for Quiz's feet. I know of one agility club that opted for a softer alternative and mixed bird seed in the paint for the contact areas. This worked fine and, despite expectations, the sparrows did not roost on the dog walk.

Training method If you are using a training method that results in Quiz screeching to a halt in a two feet on, two feet off position at the bottom of the contacts, perhaps it is time to consider something different? You could teach an alternative contact behavior that won't be so harsh on his paws. Many people are now advocating running contacts because they are faster and kinder to a dog's shoulder joints. And kinder to your dog's feet!

You can always take a break from agility to give Quiz's pads time to heal and when you return, limit your contact training.

Finding The Itch

Q *Last week, I stood in the line next to a handler with a little crossbreed hound that was bald in patches and kept scratching (until it got on the course and then the dog went on to win the class). Do you think it had fleas? My dog Clarrie is scratching now and I'm worried she might have caught something nasty. And what should I do to make sure it doesn't happen again?*

A Dogs will scratch because they itch and they could itch for any number of reasons. Itching may be because the dog has fleas or other parasites, or an allergy to something in his environment. It could be the result of a fungal or other infection. A dog may scratch his ear once, or his scratching my be chronic

Above: *The more a dog nibbles and scratches, the more he itches. Persistent scratchers can do a lot of damage. The skin breaks leaving the wound open to secondary infections.*

and persistent. He may itch in just one spot or he may itch all over. It can be simply irritating or extremely painful. Scratching can be the sign of a problem that your vet should know about or it may be something completely innocent. For example, if your dog is not groomed regularly, he could have a knot of hair behind his ear and he is trying to dig it out.

You could have asked the handler what was wrong with his dog instead of speculating. If his dog had something contagious and he is a responsible owner, he would not have attended the show. Most people love to talk about their pet's health and medical histories. It is this exchange of information that makes all dog owners amateur vets. You may discover that his dog does indeed have problems, but that they are nothing for you worry about.

It is your responsibility to make sure that Clarrie doesn't itch and is parasite-free. She should regularly receive worm and flea treatment. Choose a product that suits your pocket and is easy for you to apply.

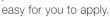
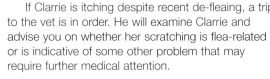

Read the label. You will find that most products will not only get rid of parasites but will give your pet protection against future infestation for some weeks. So, if Clarrie has been treated she won't catch fleas from mixing with other dogs that are carrying a few "friends."

If Clarrie is itching despite recent de-fleaing, a trip to the vet is in order. He will examine Clarrie and advise you on whether her scratching is flea-related or is indicative of some other problem that may require further medical attention.

Poop Picking

Q *I have a ten-month-old crossbreed called Ted. His only interest in life is eating poop. When I let him out in the yard he poop-picks after my five other dogs. I have just started agility training and he is more interested in poop than in me! I never had this trouble training my other dogs. Help!*

A The scientific word for your dog's behavior is "coprophagia," the consumption of feces by animals. "Autocoprophagia" is when an animal eats his own poop. Puppies often do this, but usually grow out of it. "Intraspecific coprophagia" is when an animal eats the feces of animals of the same species. This is what Ted is doing when he cleans up after your other dogs in the garden. "Interspecific coprophagia" is when an animal eats poop indiscriminately – sheep droppings, horse manure, bunny balls. It's all good stuff.

Why do dogs eat feces?

- Coprophagia may be a result of a medical problem. Discuss Ted's eating habits with your vet to rule out any conditions that may make your pet unusually ravenous.
- Dogs are scavengers and eat the most disgusting things, including poop, to survive in the wild. If they had insisted on a sanitized diet the canine race would have died out years ago.
- Many of the things we feed our dogs still smell appetizing after being digested and excreted. Feeding your dog a bland diet that won't smell at all attractive the second time around can help.
- Poop-eating gets your attention. Your dog lowers his head to sniff some droppings and you race to stop him. Good game!
- Your dog likes the taste and can't help himself. When was the last time you left the last chocolate in the box for someone else?

What you can do

- Pick up after your other dogs have toileted. Ted will stop looking for the stuff if he never finds any.
- Teach your dog a "Leave" command. Ted's reward for withdrawing from the feces should be of greater value than the poop itself. Would you leave a five dollar bill note on the pavement if someone offered you a quarter? No.
- Remote punishment can be effective. Rattling a tin or squirting water can interrupt poop snacking. Time it so that Ted thinks the interruption comes from heaven above or the surrounding environment, not from you.
- Ted won't be able to eat feces if he is wearing a muzzle *(below)*, but he will try. Beware. When his muzzle is coated with the stuff, he'll try to rub his nose on your pants.

- Forget agility training in a field where horses, cows or sheep have been grazing. Build a relationship with your dog in a poop-free environment.
- Switch your dog onto a toy. If Ted becomes obsessed with a tennis ball, he will lose his interest in feces.

You must accept that eating poop is something that dogs do. If your dog gets excited by a pile of horse manure, my final advice is to quickly look the other way!

Bringing It Up Again

Q *My two-year-old Sheltie, Vanya, gets so excited about going to agility class that she throws up. It's either a bit of bile or a treat that I've just fed her. I don't know if it's because of standing with the other dogs waiting for her turn. She doesn't do it any other place and it hasn't put her off, but it's not nice for the other people in our class. It's unpleasant to clean it up and I'm worried about her health. What should I do?*

A The excitement of agility affects dogs in different ways. Vomiting is a rather anti-social habit, especially when you are standing with a group of friends waiting for your turn in the ring. Here are some things to think about.

Have Vanya checked by a vet Rule out any medical reasons for her behavior before you try other remedies.

Vanya may be vomiting because she is excited
The prospect of a few agility jumps and her stomach

Above: *Your dog may vomit because he has an intestinal blockage, has been poisoned or has worms. Perhaps he is suffering from a metabolic disease? Consult your vet.*

starts doing back flips – which means she empties it at your feet. Try to be cool as a cucumber at agility class. If you remain calm, your dog might too.

Many dogs like to make sure that their stomachs are emptied before taking part in any activity that requires total concentration
Nerves affect us all in different ways. Vanya may feel she performs better when her digestive system is on standby – not finishing off the remnants of a treat or sloshing with water. And there are a few agility competitors who have lost their breakfast before an important run.

Keep Vanya on empty I would reward Vanya with play, toys, and her favorite agility obstacle instead of treats. She is probably too excited or stressed to eat and digest titbits and they won't stay down her very long. If she is training in the evening, feed her in the morning so that there is nothing left in her stomach when she goes to class.

Stop worrying If there is no medical reason for Vanya vomiting, learn to ignore it and start concentrating on your agility. Stop giving her attention for bringing her treats back up. It may be that your concern has reinforced the behavior rather than helped eliminate it. The words "Oh no! Vanya has been sick AGAIN" may well be music to her ears.

Vanya may grow out of it Puppies are prone to travel sickness, but it becomes a thing of the past as they become big enough to keep their balance and dinner. They become accustomed to car journeys. Vanya will probably always be excited by agility, but her initial enthusiasm will lose its edge the more she does and she could stop being sick.

Consider a few private lessons Vanya would be more comfortable and so would you. No other dogs and not too long to wait between turns, so less reason to throw up.

Too Hot For Agility

Q *If I go to a show and the sun is shining, my heart sinks. My dog Silva hates the heat. She slows right down to a walk and putters around the course. She's black and her coat absorbs the sun. What can I do to keep her cool? Should I give up competing in the summer?*

A There's no way around it. If you stand out in the sun with your dog, you'll be hot. We perspire to cool down. Dogs have a few sweat glands on their feet but rely on panting to regulate

Above: *Waving his big, pink tongue in the wind will help your dog cool down on a hot summer's day.*

their body temperatures. It can be a pretty inefficient system especially for dogs that are overweight, have big double coats or short muzzles like Boxers. Don't let Silva overheat.

Find shade Keep Silva out of the direct sun as much as possible. Look for shade under the trees or behind a building. Make a tent out of reflective sheets where she can shelter.

Provide fresh water Keep Silva's water bowl full so she can cool down with a drink and avoid dehydrating. Add a few ice cubes. Freeze a bowl of water the night before to take with you to agility shows.

Wet, wet, wet Is there a clean stream near the show ground where you can let Silva have a quick swim? If you are going to be away for the weekend, consider packing a kiddie pool. Many show grounds have stand pipes that are perfect for doggy showers. What about a water pistol? Some dogs enjoy having their tongue, toes and tummy misted, but not those who have been squirted in the past for being naughty!

Summer accessories
You can buy hats, bandanas and sun glasses. Would Silva shake her head in disgust until they came off? Try keeping her body temperature down by dressing her in a reflective coat or wet toweling jacket (these dry quickly, but the wet dog smell lingers on). For Silva's traveling crate you can buy a cool bed and pillow to keep her chilled as well as a battery-operated fan. Don't forget the sun block for areas of exposed skin.

A hair cut There are a number of agility dogs sporting summer hair cuts. Who needs a furry coat on a July day? Be aware that Silva may look hot, but her fur is there to insulate her (keeping her cooler) and to protect her skin. And, remember that although Silva's coat can be taken off in minutes, it will take months to grow back. She'll stay pretty with a simple tidy up and trim. Avoid shaving to the skin.

I keep my cool on hot days by lowering my expectations. I know my dogs will perform a bit slower. I do, too. We run slower, think slower and pant more. I try and arrange my runs for early morning or evening. And if it's unbearably hot, I forego the runs and join my dogs in the kiddie pool.

Warming Up

Q *I have started entering my collie Storm at agility shows. I'm an athletic type, in good physical condition and use my gym membership! How can I warm up inconspicuously at an agility show? I don't want to cut my competition season short with a sprained muscle, but I don't want to draw attention to myself either.*

A Never fear, if you have to spend the rest of the season with your leg in plaster, your agility club will find some work for you to do in the score tent at shows!

The majority of the injuries in agility happen through a single accident, like tripping over the dog walk, or they are the result of an inefficient action over time, like repeatedly bending to pull a dog down the contacts. You can avoid injury by making sure that you are in good physical condition, but you need a warm-up routine too. It will not only reduce the risk of injury but it will help you give Storm 100 per cent on the course. You'll perform better and so will he. Develop a warm-up routine that will start your heart pumping. All your body's systems should be warm and ticking over, ready for ignition. It will only take five minutes or so.

Make warming up a joint enterprise If you tend to feel self-conscious when you do exercises in public, try warming up with your dog for company. Can you beat Storm to his ball? If you run away, can Storm catch you? Don't do heelwork – do runwork. Who can jump up in the air higher? You'll both end up out of breath.

Above: *A little jogging on the spot and few simple muscle stretches may be enough to protect you from injury when you are running in the ring.*

Disguise your warm-up exercises so you can do them in the line

- Touch your toes, but pretend you are bending down to tie your shoe laces. Remember to keep your legs straight and exhale as you bend.
- Reach to the sky. Stretch your arms as high in the air as you can till you are pulled onto tiptoes. Then give a big yawn. It will make your work-out look like you are merely stretching after a mid-morning nap.
- Place your hands on your hips. Keep your hips facing forward but twist to your left and chat to your neighbor in the line. Now, don't be rude. Twist to the right and chat to your other neighbor.
- Take off your hat and do a few head or shoulder rolls. It will look like you are flicking the sweat off your forehead.

Look cool and you'll get away with it No one will ever know. Tighten and relax your tummy muscles. How about some pelvic floor exercises? And flexing your leg muscles. All while standing still in the line.

Take a look at your fellow competitors. They'll be warming up, too. Completely oblivious to anyone that may be watching. Over time, you'll lose your shyness and be just as bold. You'll feel as comfortable stretching your quadriceps with your agility buddies as you do with the guys at the gym and you'll be able to warm up less covertly.

Casting Doubt

Q *You will probably think this is a really stupid question. I fell off the curb and broke my arm. I'm absolutely fine but the cast will have to stay on for at least four weeks. My dog Otley has been doing really well and I don't want to miss any training sessions or shows. Will the cast be a problem?*

A There are many that would argue that if the cast is too much of a hindrance for ordinary household chores like the laundry, it's bound to stop you from agility training. But the bottom line is do whatever you can manage without hurting yourself or confusing your dog. Remember that the cast is there to stabilize and protect your arm so that the bones will knit satisfactorily. Don't let your zeal for agility jeopardize the healing process.

Above: *You can run with a cast on your arm, but can you do agility? You won't know till you try, but, if it hurts, stop before you do yourself more damage.*

Balance You will find it more difficult to balance with only one working arm. Walking is easy, but running and pivoting over rough ground will give you a few problems. If you fall over, please don't break the other arm or a leg!

Cues You will not be able to give Otley the visual cues that he has learned. If your arm is tender and your cast is heavy, you will probably be clutching it close to your chest to stop it jiggling up and down. Vibration can be painful. Now you know why your doctor told you to take it easy. Otley wonders what he is supposed to do when you clasp your arm to yourself. In fact the lop-sided way that you are running is a mystery to him. No wonder he looks confused.

Training aid It might seems like good idea, but do refrain from teaching Otley that your cast is a tug toy. Think how embarrassing it will be at the doctor's explaining all those teeth marks. As for competitions, I don't think a judge would eliminate you for competing with a cast – it's not a training

aid and it's not something you can remove at a moment's notice.

The cast could be a big problem initially. However, the longer you wear it, the more comfortable it will become and Otley will find it less distracting as the days go by. You will both adapt. Be honest with your doctor and follow his advice. If he thinks that agility is a gentle stroll with your pet, he will give you the OK to continue. But he would be horrified if he saw you tear around the course and fall over the finish line in an exhausted heap!

Agility Bump

Q *I have just had it confirmed by my doctor – I'm pregnant! My husband and I are delighted and our families and friends are helping us celebrate our good news. The only one who seems a bit down is our agility dog, Kimmy. I've reassured her that she and I will still go to agility classes and competitions. I won't have to quit agility because I'm pregnant, will I?*

A Congratulations! You will be able to continue training and competing with Kimmy as long as you feel able to do so. But don't be surprised if your child's first word is "dog." When you decide to halt is up to you.

Above: *Pregnancy is a very special time for your family and pet. Let caution be your watchword. Don't risk it by falling on the agility field and harming your baby.*

You may suspend training immediately
I have friends who gave up agility in their third month and passed their dogs to their husbands to take to training and competitions. This meant that life didn't change very much. Although taking a back seat, they were still involved in the social whirl of agility. At shows they could help in the score tent when they weren't grooming for their other halves. Just make sure that if you decide to sit on the side lines, you make your coaching positive and don't sound like a nag. Do not wail, "Why did you let Kimmy take the tunnel instead of jump number ten?" Instead, say "let's work together on why Kimmy was eliminated so we can avoid traps like that in the future."

You may continue to the bitter end of your pregnancy
I have watched a lady who was in her ninth month work her dog at an agility show. She had the judge and spectators in the palm of her hand because we all thought the baby would be born at any moment. She waddled a few steps here and there and managed a top ten place. The dog was superbly trained and worked at a distance while responding quickly to directional commands. She gave birth the following week. The woman is exceptional. She is amazing and so are her dogs.

Comfort and safety should be your prime considerations
As you grow larger and your shape changes, you probably won't be able to move around the agility course so easily and you will tire more quickly. And remember that if you slip on wet grass, you could hurt not only yourself but your growing baby.

Listen to your instructor
If your instructor thinks that the continued training of your dog during your pregnancy is doing you no favors, he will say so. During pregnancy your timing will be off and your body language will be heavy. Kimmy will wonder what's up. You will start making errors on the course that you normally would not make and become frustrated. Kimmy won't thank you. And neither will your instructor if you give birth or fall over in his class. When he starts keeping a first aid box by his side and covering his eyes when it is your turn, it's time to stop.

More Women's Troubles

Q *I am a lady agility handler and I'm a slave to my hormones. I suffer painful period cramps and really don't feel like running my dog, Luger. If I go to training, I can't remember the course and I blame Luger for taking the wrong turn. PMS is a nightmare! Can you help?*

A It's all too easy to blame five faults or an elimination on raging hormones. Without a doubt, many of us ladies do not feel ourselves when we are premenstrual. We become short-tempered and moody. Our bodies seem to have a life of their own. No wonder our friends, family and dogs try to stay out of our way! Try and remember that although your body, mind and emotions may change when you are premenstrual, your dog remains constant in his affection and loyalty.

Damage control Preventative measures go a long way towards reducing the symptoms of PMS. Make sure your diet is healthy and you eat regular meals.

Below: *Try yoga to relax. Your dog will want to go with you to the spot in your mind where you find inner peace.*

Get a good night's sleep. Avoid stress and learn to relax. Yoga teaches you how to breathe as well as how to relieve tension. I have a friend who swears by it ... And so does her dog.

Change your expectations If it is that time of the month, work on something light and fun rather than training exercises that require concentration and precision. Leave refining your contacts to another time. Forget about weave entries. Concentrate on motivation exercises or general conditioning. This is not the time to try and teach Luger something new. If you are not totally with it, he's bound to make mistakes.

Have a break Practice does make perfect, but give yourself a break for holidays, vacations – and PMS days. If you think you will not be able to accomplish anything positive, have a rest. Give agility a pass. You and Luger will return to the training ground refreshed and eager to get stuck in.

Grin and bear it Sometimes working your dog is unavoidable. Show organizers are not going to rearrange the competition calendar just because you are premenstrual. So get on with it. There are plenty of other ladies out there who feel bloated and irritable. For the few minutes that you are running in the ring, try to be a human being and agility handler. Remind yourself that a little exercise is good for cramps!

Dogs are wonderful, forgiving creatures. They love us even when we haven't brushed our teeth or combed our hair. And they still think we are the best person in the whole world despite PMS.

Agility Wheels

Q *I am a wheelchair user and bought my Golden Retriever, Reekie, as a companion. She has opened the doors to a whole new world. I take her to obedience classes and have met a group of fellow dog lovers who are now my best friends. We now enter heelwork to music competitions and have done very well. If we try agility, do you think we will be biting off more than we can chew?*

A I think you are already a very able dog trainer who will be able to go far in whatever canine sport you choose. If you want to do something, try it. Adapt the task to your abilities. You won't be alone and you're ahead of the game. Reekie is already competent with obedience basics and is clicker trained.

Growing number There are a growing number of agility competitors who work their dogs from a wheelchair with excellent results. Choose an instructor who shares your ambitions and has an accessible venue.

Training strategies The strategies you use to train Reekie may be a little different from those used by the rest of the class. You will have to develop your own ideas for teaching agility basics like the contacts or the weaves. Don't be afraid to double handle the initial stages. And your training focus may be a little different, too. Wheelchair handlers need their dogs to work independently from their position on the course. Your instructor will help you find a way to teach Reekie distance control and obstacle discrimination as these skills will be especially useful to you.

Wheelchair power Start training Reekie with what you've got. You will be accustomed to its operation and there will be enough new things to learn in class. Later on, you may decide to upgrade to something more powerful and maneuverable. Look at chairs that respond quickly and can cope with different terrain, especially muddy, bumpy fields.

Invaluable resource In the UK, The Disabled Handlers Association is an invaluable resource and will help you find out how other people have met training and mobility challenges on the agility field.

If you do decide to try agility, you will make even more friends who are dog lovers. Make agility a game that's fun to play and Reekie will love learning how to jump hurdles and climb the A-frame with you. If you live in Britain, you can register with the Disabled Handlers League and submit your places for the points table. And why stop there? If you are feeling adventurous, consider entering the Para-Agility World Cup (PAWC).

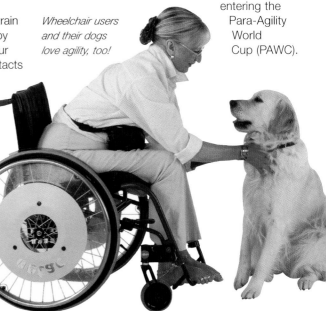

Wheelchair users and their dogs love agility, too!

RESOURCES
& INDEX

Don't you hate it when someone gives you advice but not the resources to act on it. "Go find your local agility club," they tell you. Where do you start looking? Do they expect you to drive around looking for a field of hurdles? If you are lucky enough to find a field full of agility equipment, do you have to camp by the gate waiting to meet someone to ask about memberships and classes? There has to be an easier way! There is. The Resource section is intended to give you a starting point in your hunt for further agility information. The more answers you find, the more questions you'll want to ask. And the more resources you'll discover. Good luck and have fun learning new things!

Resources

Entering a show

There will be more than one organization sanctioning agility shows in your country of residence. Each is governed by its own set of rules and regulations regarding registration, competition and progression through classes. Some organizations are large national bodies covering a number of canine disciplines in addition to agility and others are regional groups that are purely focused on agility. Any additional services that they offer will vary but may include newsletters, lists of training clubs, or discussion forums.

Agility Association of Canada (AAC)
Secretary: Donna Kloc
E-mail: maplelass@yahoo.ca
www.aac.ca

American Kennel Club (AKC)
260 Madison Ave
New York, NY 100
Telephone: (212) 696-8200
www.akc.org

Australian Shepherd Club of America (ASCA)
Secretary: Ann DeChant
E-mail: ann@sundewfarm.com
www.asca.org

Canadian Kennel Club (CKC)
89 Skyway Avenue, Suite 100
Etobicoke, Ontario
M9W 6R4
Telephone: (416) 675-5511
E-mail: information@ckc.ca
www.ckc.ca

Canine Performance Events, Inc. (CPE)
E-mail: cpe@charter.net
www.k9cpe.com

Dogs on Course in North America (DOCNA)
E-mail: info@docna.com
www.docna.com

The Kennel Club
1 Clarges Street
London
W1J 8AB
Telephone: 0870 606 6750
Fax: 020 7518 1058
www.the-kennel-club.org.uk

Northern American Dog Agility Council (NADAC)
E-mail: info@nadac.com
www.nadac.com

United Kennel Club (UKC)
100 E Kilgore Road
Kalamazoo MI 49002-5584
Telephone: (269) 343-9020
Fax: (269) 343-7037
E-mail: dvavla@ukcdogs.com or
mmorgan@ukcdogs.com
www.ukcdogs.com

United Kingdom Agility

Langdale
Church Street
Offenham Evesham
Worcestershire
WR11 8RW
Telephone: 01386 424218
E-mail: info@ukagility.com
www.UKAgility.com

United States Dog Agility Association (USDAA)

P.O. Box 850955
Richardson, TX 75085
Telephone: (972) 487-2200
Fax: (972) 272-4404
www.usdaa.com

International

International competition is growing and there are a number of organizations, each with its own rules and regulations, hosting world championship competitions. The **FCI** (Fédération Cynologique Internationale) is the oldest and best known. To participate, your Kennel Club must be a member or associate of the FCI and your dog must be a pure breed recognized by your home Kennel Club. By contrast, the **IMCA** (International Mix and Breed Championship Agility) is open to both pedigree and mixed breed dogs. This competition is held in conjunction with **PAWC** (ParAgility World Cup) for disabled handlers. The **IFCS** (International Federation of Cynological Sports) also welcomes pedigrees and their crosses. It holds a biennial event and countries must be IFCS members or associate organizations in order to be represented. And, not to be overlooked, the **European Open** has a growing number of competitors of both pedigrees and crosses each year. The introduction of pet passports has meant that many people are combining a holiday abroad with agility competition.

Are you a disabled handler looking for help and support?

The Disabled Handlers Association was set up in 2005 and is run by disabled handlers for disabled handlers. There's a league table too!

The Disabled Handlers Association

Co-founded by Anne Gill
63 Fairfax Road, Farnborough, Hants, GU14 8JR
Telephone: 01252 661442
Email: annegill48@hotmail.com
and
Philippa Armstrong
Telephone: 01803 867074
Email: philippa.armstrong@lineone.net
www.disabledhandlersassociation.co.uk

Becoming an instructor

Put something back into agility and teach.
There are a number of routes you can take. Each organization will have specific criteria for certifying trainers and courses will vary in length and assessment methods.

Association of Pet Dog Trainers (APDT)

150 Executive Center Drive
Box 35
Greenville, SC 29615
Telephone: (800) PET-DOGS
Fax: (864) 331-0767
E-mail: information@apdt.com
www.apdt.com

Something to read in bed

Clean Run Magazine
35 North Chicopee Street
Chicopee, MA 01020
Tollfree: (800) 311-6503
www.cleanrun.com

Leach, Laurie, *The Beginner's Guide to Dog Agility*, TFH Publications, Neptune City, 2006.

Getting the latest news
If you are hungry for agility news with your morning coffee, check out the Dog Agility Page for links to just about everything agility-related on the internet! It's got information about clubs and events, forums to connect with other agility lovers, articles to read, and much more.

DOGSport Magazine
735 Delaware Road #111
Buffalo, NY 14223-1231
Toll-free: 1-866-364-7778
www.dogsportmagazine.com

The Dog Agility Page
www.dogpatch.org/agility

See you and your dog in lights!
You may already be on film – your best and your worst runs! Check out this website to find out if you or your friends have been caught on video.

Agility Movies
Contact: Amanda Brophy
Email: amanda@agilitymovies.com
www.agilitymovies.com

How to find the perfect present for you and your dog

Not everyone wants flowers and chocolate. And not everyone wants to pound the pavement looking for the perfect present. Explore these online shopping sites instead. You will find everything you will ever need to compete, train and love your dog. There is camping equipment, clothes, toys and hundreds of other things you have never even thought of... Why not treat yourself to an A-frame!

Clean Run
www.cleanrun.com
Everything for the dog agility enthusiast.

Agility Trial Genie Trial Secretary Software
www.trialgenie.com

Canine Shenanigans Agility Dog Superstore
www.agilitydogs.com
Assortment of products and accessories to aid in the performance of your agility dog.

If you'd like to rescue or adopt a dog

American Humane Association (AHA)
63 Inverness Drive East
Englewood, CO 80112
Telephone: (303) 792-9900
Fax: 792-5333
www.americanhumane.org

American Society for the Prevention of Cruelty to Animals (ASPCA)
424 E. 92nd Street
New York, NY 10128-6804
Telephone: (212) 876-7700
www.aspca.org

Royal Society for the Prevention of Cruelty to Animals (RSPCA)
Telephone: 0870 3335 999
Fax: 0870 7530 284
www.rspca.org.uk

The Humane Society of the United States (HSUS)
2100 L Street, NW
Washington DC 20037
Telephone: (202) 452-1100
www.hsus.org

If you are looking for health and veterinary advice

Academy of Veterinary Homeopathy (AVH)
P.O. Box 9280
Wilmington, DE 19809
Telephone: (866) 652-1590
Fax: (866) 652-1590
E-mail: office@TheAVH.org
www.theavh.org

American Academy of Veterinary Acupuncture (AAVA)
100 Roscommon Drive, Suite 320
Middletown, CT 06457
Telephone: (860) 635-6300
Fax: (860) 635-6400
E-mail: office@aava.org
www.aava.org

American Animal Hospital Association (AAHA)
P.O. Box 150899
Denver, CO 80215-0899
Telephone: (303) 986-2800
Fax: (303) 986-1700
E-mail: info@aahanet.org
www.aahanet.org/index.cfm

American College of Veterinary Internal Medicine (ACVIM)
1997 Wadsworth Blvd., Suite A
Lakewood, CO 80214-5293
Telephone: (800) 245-9081
Fax: (303) 231-0880
Email: ACVIM@ACVIM.org
www.acvim.org

American College of Veterinary Ophthalmologists (ACVO)
P.O. Box 1311
Meridian, Idaho 83860
Telephone: (208) 466-7624
Fax: (208) 466-7693
E-mail: office@acvo.com
www.acvo.com

American Holistic Veterinary Medical Association (AHVMA)
2218 Old Emmorton Road
Bel Air, MD 21015
Telephone: (410) 569-0795
Fax: (410) 569-2346
E-mail: office@ahvma.org
www.ahvma.org

Thanks For Their Help

Acknowledgments

This book must mention my ninth grade teacher, Mrs. Lucas, who told me, "You must write!". Mrs. Lucas tried to commit suicide under a train a week later and was subsequently committed so I never really took her threat seriously. That is until Ellen Rocco of www.agilitynet.co.uk asked me to write a book review for her internet magazine. Ellen has encouraged me to put fingers to keyboard and supported me for many years. She gave me the job of "Agility Auntie" for Agilitynet and it is that body of work that forms the foundations of this book. I would also like to thank my friend Melanie Raymond who not only shared my excitement for the project but has continued to be enthusiastic to the very last page, all my colleagues at VetsNow Emergency Service (Northampton) who held my hand when I was flagging and Anthony Medcalfe who loaned me Ridducks Agility School to help in the book's production and photoshoot. Thanks also to Philippa Armstrong for her input on "agility wheels". Moreover, it is impossible to forget the many people who have helped me problem-solve in my own agility career. Thank you Mary Ray for showing me how to "smush" cheese! And where would I be without my Mom who allowed me to have a variety of pets eventually leading to my first agility dog, Aslan? Aslan got me hooked on agility and I've been an addict ever since.

My thanks also to everyone who agreed to take part in the photoshoot (and their dogs). What naturals you all are in front of the camera – true agility stars! Step forward each of you and take a bow...

Peter Alliot and Ember and Sunny

Harriet Anthony and Bella

Sarah Arnold and Toody

Maureen Goodchild and Woody and Lou

James Greenhow and Marley

Lisa Greenhow and Tyler and Bailey

Amy Lightfoot and Basil

Lynn Marlow and Shandy

Jill Pipe and Marco

Toni Slater and Peggy

Lynet Smith and Sara

Marion Watkinson and Jenny

Jo Bidgood and Henry

Lorraine Chappell and Meg and Deefa

Maggie Cheek and Rupert and Pascal

Christine Cowling and Conker

Carolyn Errington and Murphy

Jo-Ann Essex and Sumi-e, Suggs and Bacon

Gillian Griffiths and Bryn

Clare Griffiths and Lucy

Tim Griffiths and Travis

Bridget Hardy and Archie

Bridget Jamieson and Rupert, Brodie and Bailey

Ken Jeffery and Suki III

David Piper and Barclay and Jack

Soraya Porter and Ernie

Maxine Pymer and Bob

Christine Ripley and Rufus and Robbie

Alma Ryman and Tilly and Starr

Tony Ryman and Bluey

Lesley Wells and Barney and Bonnie

Index

Note: Page numbers set in *italics* refer to captions to illustrations

A

ABC (Anything But Collies) classes 8
A-frame 6, 8, *8*, 18-19, 24, *24*, 28, *31*, 38-9, 41, *41*, 56, 70-1, *73*, 77, 85, 91, 99, 101, 102, *102*, 108, 110, 115, 116, *116-7*, 120-1, 134, 151, *151*, 154, 158
A-ramp *see* A-frame
age of dog for beginning agility 28
age of dog for retiring 176-7, *177*
ages of handlers for agility 56-7, *56-7*
aggression towards other dogs 71
agility course defined and explained 8, 18-19
agility defined as a sport 25
agility instruction classes 21, *21*, 24, 27, 32, 34-5, 40, 42-3, 46-7, 75, 94, 96, *96*, 108
agility terms, A-Z of 8-15, *8-15*
agility trainer, characteristics of expert 48
astro-turf 152
attention exercises 68
"away" command 135

B

back chaining 8, 116-7
back cross *see* rear cross
back jumping 8
back weaving 8
ball, obsession with 99
banking 8
barking problems 7, 62, *62*
barrier shaping 41
baton 8
Beagle *31*

Bearded Collie 33
Belgian Shepherd Dog 30, 71, *71*, 75, 176-7, *177*
Bernese Mountain Dog 46, 147
best dogs for agility 30-1
Bichon Frise 45
bitch in season 169, *169*
biting handler's feet 65
biting poles 64, *64*
blind cross 8, 96, 136, *137*
blocking 8
body language of handler 134, *134*, 150, 172-3, *172-3*, 175, 177, 188
bonding with dog 74
boots 181
Border Collie 22, *22-3*, 34, 45, 58, *58-9*, 72-3, *72-3*, 171, *171*, 174
Border Terrier 42
bounce jumps 179
box 8, 18, *168*, *168*
Boxer 112, *112*, 185
breeding 171
briefing 8
Brittany 120, 133
brush jump 8-9, *9*

C

cage fan 146, 185
Cairn Terrier 153, *153*
call off 9
caller 9, 148
carousel 9
carpet surface 152
castration 100, 174
Cavalier King Charles Spaniel 18, 30, 123, *123*
channel weaves 9, 84, 124-5, *125*
characteristics of ideal agility dog 44
Chihuahua *47*, 147

children and agility 57
chiropractic 167
chute tunnel *see* collapsible tunnel
classes (in agility competitions) 18-19
clear round 9
clicker training 9, 41, 43, 50, 68, 84, 106, 114-6, 124-5, 130, 146, 173
clipping 185
cloth tunnel *see* collapsible tunnel
clothing for agility handler 21, 37, *37*
Cocker Spaniel 38, 57, 149, 155
cocking the leg 100, *100*, 174, *174*
collapsible tunnel 9, *9*, 18-19, 46, 53, 56, 72, *73*, 82, 85, 100, 106, *106*, 108, *112*, 128, 132-4, *133*, 135, *135*, *137*, 140, *140*, 175
    fear of tunnel 133, *133*
collar and lead 50, 72, 97-8, *97-8*
    difficulty in releasing 98
collie 27, 30-2, *31-2*, 41, *51*, 63, 69-70, *70*, 84, *84*, 88-9, *88*, *92-3*, 93, 99, 129-30, *129*, 134, *134*, 162, *162*, 176, *176*, 186
"come" command 9, 41, *173*
competition, judging readiness for 145, *145*
concentration exercises 71
"contact" command 116
contacts and contact training 9, 38, 40-1, *41*, 69, 70, 91, 114-22, *115-20*, 153, 158, *158*
coprophagia *see* eating feces
correction *see* punishment
cost of starting agility 21
course, handler getting lost on 106

course builders 9
course time 9
cross-bred dogs and agility 33-4
Crufts 152

D

Dalmatian 30, 126, *126-7*
deaf dog, training 172-3, *172-3*, 177
defensive jumping 179
dietary needs 168, *168*, 183
directional commands 9, 43, 106, *106*
dirt arena 152
Disabled Handlers Association 190
Disabled Handlers League 190
distracted by family of handler 81
dog running loose in the ring 156, *156*
dog towel 146
dog walk 9-10, *10*, 18-19, 28, *38*, 39, 46, 70, *86*, 117, 120-1
double handling 10, 161, 190
"down" command and position 32, 40-2, 65, 113, *173*
"drop" command 97
dummy turn 140-1

E

E (Elimination) 10, 19
eating feces 183, *183*
eating grass 80, *80*
electronic timing 10
elimination and out 10
equipment for agility classes 50-1, *50-1*
equipment for shows 146, *146*, 157
exercises and fitness routines 166-7, *166-7*, 180, *180*
eye infections 175, *175*

F

false turn *see* dummy turn
faults 10
fence *see* hurdle
fighting 156
flat work 42
fleas 182
flick flack *see* snake
flyball 22
frisbee 99, *99*
foundation classes *see* pre-agility classes
front cross 10, 132, 136, *137*, 141
fundamentals for agility *see* pre-agility classes
fungal infection 182

G

gamblers 19
Gentle Leader head halter 66
German Shepherd 33, 51, 86, *86*, *120*, 128, *128*, 132, *132*, 161, *161*
Golden Retriever 30, 81, 85, 170, *170*, 172, 190, *190-1*
"go on" command 10, 93, 135
"go to sleep" 114, *114*
Great Dane 46, *47*
Greyhound *120*, 131, 141
grooming 162, *162*

H

Halti head halter 66
handler falls in the ring 157, *157*
handler focus 10
hand-shy dog 35
hands-on shaping 41
hats, distracted by 86, *86*
head collar 68, 70
head harness 66, *67*
heel position 10

heelwork 40-1, 66, *67*
heelwork to music 22, 85
heights, fear of 102, *103*
helping at show 148
herbal remedies for over-excitement 69
herding instinct (Border Collie) 72-3, *72-3*
hoop *see* tire
Hungarian Vizsla 152
hurdle (fence or jump) 10, *10-11*, 18-19, *18*, 24, 28, *30-1*, 38-9, 41-2, 53, *56*, 64, 69, 72, 78, 85, 90-1, *91*, 99, 108, 112, 132, 138-9, *138-9*, 160, *160*
husband-and wife teams 58-9, *58-9*, 162-3, *162-3*, 188
hydro-therapy pool 166, *166*

I

instructor working own dog 96
Irish Setter 121
Irish Wolfhound 40, 46
Italian Greyhound *83*
Italian Spinone 33
itching and scratching by dog 182, *182*

J

Jack Russell terrier 33, 77, *77*, 154, *154*, 157, *157*
Japanese Spitz 33
judge 11, 18-19, 44, 110, 148-9, 156, 187
   disputing judge's decision 151, *151*
   hand signals by 149, *149*
jump *see* hurdle
"jump" command 91
jump heights 45, 88-9, *88-9*
jumping classes 19
jumping out of the ring 160
jumping vertically 178-9

jumps and jumping course 11, *74*, *76-7*, 82-3, *83*, 88-93, *88-9*, *91-3*, *95*, 106, 126, 128, *134*, 135, 140-1, *141*, 160, *160*, 177-9, *177*, *179*

K

King Charles Spaniel 87, *87*
knocking down poles 92, 136
knock-outs 19

L

Labrador 62, *62*, 78, 110, *110-11*, 117, 154, *154*
lack of confidence 85
ladder for training 43, *43*

large dogs 11, 45, 46-7, *47*, 147
  special training needs 178
lead, obsession with 97, *97*
"lead off" command 98
lead-out 11
leash runner 11, 148
"leave" command 77, 79, 97, 183
"limbo dancing" at jumps 90-1, *91*
limping dog 180
lining up 68, 162
long jump 11, *11*, 18, 108
lurcher 6, 32, 36, *36*
luring 41, 106, 115, 121

M

manic behavior 69
manual timing 11
measuring at show 147, *147*
medium dogs and agility 11, 18, 45, 147
miniaturized training equipment 39
movement and speed exercises 71
multi-dog handling 154
muzzle 183, *183*

N

naming a potential agility dog 49, *49*
neutering *see* castration
NFC (Not For Competition) 11
nipping the handler 63
nonstandard class 11-12

O

obedience competitions 22
obedience training 27-8, 36, 38, *40-1*, 40-2, 72, 85
obstacle discrimination 12
obstacle focus 12
off-course 12
off side 12
"on it" command 116
origins of agility 20
"over" command 108
over-excitement 70
over-heating 185, *185*
over-sensitivity 82
over-socializing with other dogs 78

P

pad runner 12, 148
paddling 12
paddling pool 185
pairs competitions 19

Papillon 30, 44, 51, 122
Para-Agility World Cup (PAWC) 190
partially sighted dog 175
Patterdale Terrier 40, *40*
"peck and go" 114
peeing in the ring 160
"pee posts" 100
perfectionist dog 74
persistent sniffing 77
Petit Basset 140
physiotherapy 167
pinwheel *see* star
pivot 12

plank for training 43, *43*
poodle 30, 33, 39, 124, *124*, 158, *158*, 175, *175*
pole 12, 43, 64, *64*, 69, 85, 136
pole picker 12, 64, 92, 148
poop bag 50, 146, 153
practicing agility in limited space 38-9, *38-9*
practicing agility with improvised equipment 43, *43*
pre-agility classes 42-3
pregnancy (dog) 171, *171*
pregnancy (handler) 188, *188*
premenstrual syndrome (PMS) 189

pulling on lead 66-7, *66-7*
pull-off 12
pull-through 12, 14. 138-9, *138-9*
punishment, methods of 110, 183
 ignoring as punishment 66, *66, 81, 81*, 110, *110*
puppies
 choosing a puppy 29
 general 57, *57*, 169, *169*, 183-4
 pregnancy and 171
 socializing 28, 42
 training 28, *28, 42, 55*, 77
Pyrenean Sheepdog *33*

Q

quick-release collar 98

R

rear cross (back cross) 12, 132, 136, *137*
recall and recall training 36, 40, 77, *78*, 91, 113, 131, 135
reflective coat 146, 185
refusal 12, 19, *74*
refusal at last fence 93, *93*
refusal to toilet 87
release commands 116
reliance on companion dog 95
reluctance to leave handler 132
reluctance to line up 68, *68*
remote spray collar 110
rescue dogs 32, 34-5, *34*, 84, 128, 172
reverse flow pivot *see* dummy turn
rewards *see* treats and toys
rigid tunnel 12, *12*, 18-19
ring 12
ring manager 148-9
ring number 13
ring party 12-13
Rottweiler 178, *178*
run 13
run by 13
running a friend's dog 155, *155*
running away from handler 79, 144, *144*
running contact 119, *119*
running order 13
running surfaces 152, *152*
running two dogs in different classes 154, *154*
running two dogs in same class 94, *94*
running when in wheelchair 190, *190*
running with arm in cast 187, *187*

S

Samoyed *47*
scent-marking 100, 169, 174, *174*
schedule 13
Schnauzer 114, *114*
score keeper 13, 148
scratching *see* itching and scratching
scribe 13, 148-9
scrimer 13, 148-9
season *see* bitch in season
seesaw 13, *13*, 18-19, *34*, 43, 46, 70, 82, 108, 121, 122, *121*, *122*, 144, 159, *159*
send away *see* "go on"
sequencing 18
Sheltie 44, *89*, 130, 184
shaping 120
show manager 13
shutting down 74
"sit" command 32, 40-2, 98, 110, 131, *172*
sit-stay position 112-3, *112*
small dogs 13, 18, 45, *45*, 147
snake (flick flack) 13, 141, *141*
socialization 42
soft tunnel *see* collapsible tunnel
sore and tender feet 84, *84*, 130, 181, *181*
spaniel 30, *30*
spaying 169-70, *170*
split personality/eccentric behavior 76
spread 13, *13*, 18
Springer Spaniel 28, *28*, 31, 118, 136, 144
Staffordshire Terrier 21, 90, *90*, 106, *106*, 119*, 119*, 135
stage fright 74-5
Standard Poodle 24, *24*
standard classification 13
standard marking 13

star (pinwheel) 14, 18
starting positions 113, *113*
"stay" command and position 40, 42, 112, *112*, *172*
"steady" command 120
surfaces *see* running surfaces

T

table 14, *14*
target and target training 14, 38, 50, 93, 114-5, 119, 120, 135, 146
threadle 14, 138, 140-1, *141*
three-legged dog 176
Tibetan Terrier 115
time faults 19
time keeper 14
tire 14, *14*, 18, *25*, *59*, *126*, 134, *170*
"touch" command 106, 114-5
toweling jacket 185
toys *see* treats and toys
training bag 50, 146
training diary 50, 146
training discs 81
trap 14
traveling kennel 185
travel sickness 184
treats and toys 7, 27, *34*, 41-3, *41*, 43, 45, 49, 50-6, *50-1*, *53-5*, 62, *62*, 65, 68, 71-2, *73*, 74-6, 78-80, *78*, *81*, 84-6, 93, 97-9, *99*, 102, 106, 110, *110*, 112-5, *112*, 116-9, 121-3, *122-3*, 125, 126, *126*, 128, 131-3, 135, 144, *144*, 146, 153, *153*, *161*, 173, 183, 184
trick training 42, *42*, 72

U

"undress" command 98

71, 77, 79
water bowl 146, 185
water pistols and sprays 62, 65,
   81, 110, 183, 185
weaves and weave poles 14, *14-
   15*, 18-19, *20*, 44, 46, *47*, *49*,
   56, 75, 76, 82-4, *84*, 96, 101,
   101, 106, *109*, 110, 123-6,
   123-8, 128-31, *130*, 175
wheelchair, handler in 190, *190*
Whippet 82-3, *82-3*, 131, *131*
wings 14-15, 43, *43*, 138-40,
   138
wishing well 15, *15*
wobble board for training 43, *43*,
   121
working sheepdog 91, *91*, 115,
   115, 116
World Agility Championships 180
worming 182

Y

yoga 189, *189*
Yorkshire Terrier 52

Z

zoomies 15, 132

"up" command 108

V

V-weaves 14, 128
verbal commands, use of 108,
   108, 158, 172, 175, 177
veteran classes 19, 175, 177
veterinary advice 69, 75, 85, 100,
   166, 168, *168*, 170-1, 175,
   175, 177, 180-4, *181*
video camera, use of 101, *101*,

151, *151*
vomiting 184, *184*

W

"wait" command 40, *40*
walking the course 14, 106, 150,
   150, 157, 160
wall 14, *14*, 18
warming-up exercises for handler
   186, *186*
"watch" command and exercise

Editor: Philip de Ste. Croix
Designer: Philip Clucas MCDS
Photographer: Mark Burch
Cartoons: Kim Blundell
Diagram artwork: Martin Reed
Index: Richard O'Neill
Production management: Consortium, Suffolk
Print production: tbc

Picture Credits

Unless otherwise credited below, all the photographs that appear in this book were taken by **Mark Burch** especially for Interpet Publishing. The credits for the inset pictures on pages 1-3 number the images from left to right on their appropriate pages.

Jane Burton, Warren Photographic: 95 bottom, 114, 160, 170 bottom, 174 bottom.

Interpet Archive (Neil Sutherland): 50, 51, 54 both, 57 bottom, 58, 62 bottom, 64 top, 66, 67, 68 top, 69, 72 top, 78, 79 bottom, 81 bottom, 97, 98, 110 both, 112, 146 left, 149, 153 left, 161, 168 top, 183 top left, 190.

iStockphoto.com:
Ana Abejon: 165.
Scott Anderson: 189.
Galina Barskaya: 57 top left.
Tamara Bauer: 131.
Dagmar Bensberg: 70 top.
Hagit Berkovich: 188.
David Brimm: 64 bottom.
Captured Nuance: 184.
Andraz Cerar: 22 top, 22 bottom, 71, 75.
Robert Churchill: 72 bottom.
Anne Clark: 96.
James Cote: 1 (inset 2 and inset 4).
Barry Crossley: 174 top.
Jaimie Duplass: 175 top, 175 bottom.
Lee Feldstein: 76, 83 top, 171.
Joy Fera: 81 top.
Peter Finnie: 1 (inset 3).
Bill Hanson: 163.
Mandy Hartfree-bright: 183 right.
Andrew Hill: 36.
Rick Hyman: 99 bottom.
Eric Isselée: 1 (inset 5), 2-3 (inset 3), 47 top right, 178.
Suzann Julien: 185.
Renee Lee: 99 top.
Sue McDonald: 34, 74, 84 bottom.
Dennis Minix: 182.
Peter Mlekuz: 123.
Iztok Nok: 15 top, 17, 23, 24 top, 31 top right, 47 bottom, 77, 109.
Leif Norman: 146 right.

Photopix: 2-3 (inset 9).
Thomas Polen: 83 bottom.
Glenda Powers: 186.
Tina Rencelj: 80.
Ashok Rodrigues: 187 right.
David Scheuber: 28 top.
Leigh Schindler: 169.
Tomislav Stajduhar: 111 bottom.
Jolanta Stozek: 152.
Willie B Thomas: 166 left, 168 bottom left, 181.
Jan Tyler: 25, 59 bottom, 166 top right.
Craig Veltri: 153 right.
André Weyer: 32.
Roger Whiteway: 154 left.
Annette Wiechmann: 27, 59 top, 167.

Shutterstock Inc:
Laura Aqui: 61.
Andraz Cerar: 8, 26-7, 33, 192-3.
J Crihfield: 42.
Waldemar Dabrowski: 87 top left.
Slobodan Djajic: 38.
Dewayne Flowers: 85.
Sergey Ivanov: 204.
JD: 40 top.
JoLin: 30, 89.
Erik Lam: 47 top left.
Michael Ledray: 53 top.
George Lee: 2-3 (inset 10), 200.
Litwin Photography: 73 top.
Cristi Matei: 62 centre.
Tammy McAllister: 39.
Iztok Nok: 1 (inset 1), 2-3 (inset 1, inset 2, inset 4, inset 5, inset 7, inset 11, inset 12), 20, 44, 45, 60-1, 73 bottom, 87 right, 88, 90, 104-5, 105, 115, 124, 126, 127, 164-5, 128, 129, 136, 139, 141, 142-3, 154 top right, 158, 162 left, 176, 177 top, 177 bottom, 179, 193, 195, 196, 203, 206, 207.
Jason X Pacheco: 100.
SI: 84 top, 95 top, 143, 170 top, 191.
Fernando Jose Vasconcelos Soares: 55.
Claudia Steininger: 53 bottom.
Magdalena Szachowska: 82.
Jeffrey Van Daele: 37.